The
Truth
About
Lisa
Jewell

The Truth About Lisa Jewell

A Year in the Life of a Bestselling Novelist

Will Brooker

CENTURY

1 3 5 7 9 10 8 6 4 2

Century
20 Vauxhall Bridge Road
London SW1V 2SA

Century is part of the Penguin Random House group of companies
whose addresses can be found at global.penguinrandomhouse.com.

Penguin
Random House
UK

First published in the UK by Century in 2022

www.penguin.co.uk

A CIP catalogue record for this book is available from the British Library.

ISBN 978-1-529-13602-9

Typeset in 12/14.75pt Bembo Book MT Pro by Jouve (UK), Milton Keynes.
Printed and bound in Great Britain by Clays Ltd, Elcograf S.p.A.

The authorised representative in the EEA is Penguin Random House Ireland,
Morrison Chambers, 32 Nassau Street, Dublin D02 YH68

Penguin Random House is committed to a sustainable future for
our business, our readers and our planet. This book is made
from Forest Stewardship Council® certified paper.

Dedicated to Ethan Brooker, as he learns to read

Contents

Preface

I probably *am* more interesting than I would like people to believe I am. But then again, not much.

Lisa Jewell, personal email (27 May 2021)

When I started this project, I'd met Lisa Jewell once in person, between the summer and autumn lockdowns of 2020. I'd read four of her recent books by that point, and I was captivated by them, not just intellectually as a scholar of popular literature, but emotionally, even physically. Their revelations – the dramas she inflicts on her characters, the traumas she puts them through – grabbed me deep inside, making me gasp for breath: these weren't just effectively plotted thrillers, but stories about people at their most vulnerable and raw, told with startling insight and compassion.

In January 2021, with London still in lockdown, Lisa and I started talking on email and Zoom. She'd just committed to writing a sequel to her most successful novel so far, *The Family Upstairs*, and had no ideas for it beyond a single character arc. She told me she was terrified. I wasn't sure if I believed her. What could she possibly be scared of, at the height of her success?

This is the story of how she wrote that novel – which at that point was simply titled 'Book 20' – her second-ever sequel, and what felt like the biggest risk of her career. It's the story of how she inched slowly forward with her draft manuscript as I read steadily backwards through her novels to date, from the thrillers

(*Watching You, I Found You*) and family dramas (*The House We Grew Up In, The Truth About Melody Browne*) to the romantic comedies and her 1999 debut, *Ralph's Party* — written after she lost her job as a secretary — which earned her a £120,000 advance.

This is the story of a bestselling novelist who left school at sixteen and now sells 500,000 copies of her books, and a professor of cultural studies, a career academic, who's lucky to sell 10,000; two very different writers getting to know each other gradually through words, finding common ground at a distance before meeting again and forming a unique relationship.

The Truth About Lisa Jewell is the story of how a novel is written, from before the start to after the finish; it's an in-depth analysis of how that novel fits into Lisa's career and her previous work, and what her style shares, surprisingly, with authors from James Joyce to Martin Amis. Following her as a public figure, it explores how that book is promoted, how she is branded, and how she interacts with fans. And like all her novels, it's also the story of a relationship, evolving slowly as the world comes gradually out of Covid — two complete strangers becoming something more like friends.

This book takes us from one January to the next, through the gradual build of spring to the slow stretch of summer, via the flurry of activity to promote the last book, and into the serious, buckled-down writing of autumn and winter. Its chapters, in turn, alternate between Lisa's writing — first her back catalogue, then her novel-in-progress — and Lisa as a writer. Often, inevitably, these two subjects overlap and blur, because to an extent, Lisa *is* her writing. And inevitably — although some of the dialogue, subplots and scenes I discuss in this book didn't make it to the final edit — there are spoilers here, not just for all Lisa's previous work, but for the story that, during this year, evolved into *The Family Remains*.

PART ONE

The Houses I Want to Live In

28 January 2021

Lisa Jewell is terrified, she tells me. I'm not sure whether to believe her.

She's sitting in what she describes as an office across the road from her family home in North London. I can see it on Zoom: beige walls, buff curtains. It looks boring, I tell her. 'Hold on,' she says, and turns the phone to show me the balcony with its view of Finchley Road on one side, and the spacious suite, complete with double bed, on the other. It's not an office, in fact: it's a studio flat in 'a four-, maybe five-star hotel', designed for international students with rich parents. She saw the building from her house and thought, I bet they're nice, and rented a unit for herself during the first lockdown.

Lisa is very successful. She has published eighteen novels at this point, in January 2021; the seventeenth, *The Family Upstairs*, was a number-one bestseller and Richard & Judy Book Club pick. She's just bought a 'huge white house on a cliff overlooking the sea on the south coast. It's every inch the successful lady novelist's seaside home.' Now finally she's going to live in a tall house, like so many of the people in her stories: there's a cluttered home full of family secrets in *The House We Grew Up In*, one towering manor on a cliff by the sea in *I Found You* and another in *Before I Met You*, a Chelsea mansion at the heart of *The Family Upstairs*, a row of pastel-coloured houses on the peak of a hill in *Watching You*, and another dark mansion crouching at the centre of her latest, the nineteenth and as-yet-unpublished novel, *The Night She Disappeared*.

'As soon as I saw a picture of it, I thought *that's my house*.' She used to walk around Hampstead, she tells me, feeling genuine sadness that she couldn't live in all these beautiful old houses with their rich histories; she began writing about them as a way of inhabiting them.

Lisa's success story began just over twenty years ago. Her debut novel, *Ralph's Party*, became one of the biggest sellers of 1999. On the night of its launch, it was praised by Tom Paulin, Bonnie Greer and Tony Parsons on *Late Review*. She'd just turned thirty. It was an impossible dream come true, at the start of a new millennium. She told the *Daily Express* in 2017 that 'it was just the most extraordinary moment of being in a room with all the people closest to me and these three great journalists all loved it.' She went on:

> Everything was going right and it was just one of those times that I look back on and it feels like an enchanted time, like a fairy tale . . . That night was the time that I stopped waiting for everything to go wrong.

So, eighteen bestselling novels later, what does Lisa Jewell have to be worried about?

'It's . . . I dunno, it's just been quite an interesting . . . *arc*,' Lisa begins, sketching an arc in the air with one finger. 'Starting off with a really successful novel, and being the, you know, one of the Hot New Novelists, they wheel them out every year and everyone gets super-excited . . . and to have that moment in the white heat of *respect*, and publishers falling over backwards to make you comfortable and happy, and make you feel special . . . and then for that to just . . .'

She leans back and takes a breath, considering. 'I never felt my career was running away from me, but there were certainly points where I thought: Am I ever going to have another really successful novel? And then for it to happen again . . . it just feels super-important that I can hold on to it, this time. The first time round, I was caught up in the energy of the whole thing, and the *unlikeliness* of the whole thing, as well. The first time it happened, it felt so unlikely that this could have been happening to me, a secretary who never even went to university, and didn't do A Levels . . . I was in this fairy tale, and it was all magic, and now it feels *real*. It feels solid. And I feel I need to be sure I don't put a foot wrong.'

Lisa has just completed the last draft of *The Night She Disappeared*. Her most recent edit, she tells me, fixed its final issues. She's comfortable now for it to go out into the world, or off to the copy-editor at least. It's already available for pre-order on Amazon, even though it's not scheduled for publication until July, and there's a flashy, animated image of the cover pinned to her Twitter feed. Thousands of readers are waiting for it.

'Everything feels super-important, which is why I've had such a great week editing this book, because I was so worried that to get to this point of having written four or five books in a row that everybody really liked, that I might write a book that didn't quite *cut it*. And I've done some things to it this week that have put it up at the same level as the other ones. I don't know, it just feels massively important to me that this isn't just another phase of my career.'

So what's her aim, after nineteen books? Surprisingly safe and small-scale. She isn't asking for much. She doesn't want to break through to a new level of fame or success. She's comfortable. She just wants to carry on as she is. What matters to her now is that 'this slightly roller-coastery thing that I've been on' – her palm swoops up and down, helpfully illustrating – 'just plateaus now, and that I can just be an author that my publishers can depend on, every year, to write a really good book, to put it out there, to sell enough copies to keep the guys on the top floor happy, and just to keep doing this.'

Lisa moves a lot while she talks, her gestures too fast for the webcam to capture clearly: she blurs, and then stills in a new pose. She adjusts her glasses, clasps her hands, cups her face, fiddles with her necklace, stares off into space. She looks as though she's really thinking about it, feeling for the truth of each sentence rather than reeling off a rehearsed speech. She is instantly plausible, endearing, likeable. She's like someone who's come into an annual appraisal at work and told you earnestly that they absolutely love their job as it is, have no ambitions of promotion but really, really don't want to be fired.

I believe she's entirely genuine, that she means what she's saying, and isn't just delivering a mock-humble spiel, a convenient story to fob me off so she can focus on her work. But I keep questioning, not quite getting or accepting it. I think it's because Lisa Jewell isn't fitting my idea of a bestselling author. She still sounds unabashedly working-class: self-effacing, unpretentious and down-to-earth. Her accent isn't far from the one I grew up with at Charlton comprehensive schools, Lewisham shopping centres and Woolwich street markets.

It's something to do with genre, perhaps – she was pigeonholed as chick lit for a while, and now fits into psychological thriller, though she describes it as 'domestic drama' – and partly to do with gender. I can't imagine Ian McEwan, for instance, or Martin Amis (we will come back to Martin Amis) or even a humbler chronicler of contemporary culture like Jonathan Coe saying openly that they want their careers to plateau now, rather than fail.

I put this to her: that it sounds very modest, and that if we heard a male author saying that his only ambition was *not to go wrong*, we'd be surprised.

'Yeah. Yeah, no, you're right,' she concedes. 'It is, I think, about where the line between commercial and literary sits.'

But I can't imagine a male author of light, nostalgic romantic and family drama like David Nicholls saying it either, or a fantasy writer like Phillip Pullman, or a machine for producing page-turners like Lee Child. So I keep prodding and pursuing, interrogating her account, double-checking that I've heard it right.

'You're not saying you want this book to transcend, or be, like, *better*.' I'm squinting, trying to process it. 'You're just saying you don't wanna go *wrong*.'

'I don't wanna go *wrong*,' she confirms. 'Exactly, yes. I want to be consistent. That's exactly what I want to be. I don't want to go wrong.'

'But you don't want a huge, bigger hit.'

'No!' she protests, clasping her hands together as if she's at the appraisal again, and has just been offered that promotion. 'No. No. No. No.' It takes her a moment to settle. 'I write what I write, and while I can't feel that it's anything special while I'm sitting writing the words, the magic happens afterwards when people tell me how much they enjoyed it. And that's what I want to maintain. I don't want to lose anybody . . . ?' It's a trailing, plaintive question; she seems genuinely pained at the thought of disappointing even one fan. Her hands clutch the air, grasping abstract ideas, making them solid. 'I don't want to lose readers because I've started doing things that don't fit in with the feeling that they expected to get when reading one of my books. That's what I want to focus on. Just *maintaining standards*.'

And she laughs, maybe because she really does sound like a

manager now rather than an author. Lisa's laughter, like everything else about her, is utterly honest, instantly winning. 'I'm not trying to break through to another literary plane, or win awards, or get the broadsheets frothing at the mouth, or anything like that.'

Perhaps she doesn't sound like a bestselling novelist, to me, because I was imagining the wrong kind of novelist. Who does she admire, and what does she aspire to?

'If I look at an author whose career I'd want to emulate . . . probably that Barbara Vine, Ruth Rendell type place. She didn't win any awards. But she just wrote consistently good books.'

Doesn't it get boring, I venture, just trying to be consistent?

No, she tells me again, forcefully. What keeps her going are the characters, who are new and shiny each time. 'It's the people. The people in the houses. It's the people that I want to be and the houses that I want to live in, and then it's just a question of fixing everything around them. So if I get the right people, and the right house . . .'

'There's probably a book title in there,' I suggest. '*The Houses I Want to Live In*. It sounds like one of your novels.'

'It does, it does,' Lisa agrees, obligingly, and we both laugh, and it feels reassuringly as if we're both on the same page now, even if it's the same empty page, at the start of something new.

We are about to start an entirely unfamiliar project together. Lisa is about to write a book, and I've asked her if I can write a book about the process. It's her twentieth novel, and only her second attempt at a sequel. The first, *After the Party*, was not an experience she remembers fondly; it was an unhappy, unsuccessful effort at rekindling the spark of her breakthrough debut. This twentieth book will be a follow-up to *The Family Upstairs*, one of her biggest hits to date. She's already told her fans on Twitter, Facebook and Instagram. She's committed to it.

And she's got nothing. 'Not one iota. I know what three characters' points of view I want to write from, and that's it.' So she's terrified, because after everything she's said about consistency, she's trying something new; but it's only January, and she doesn't usually start a new project until March, so she has three months to move on from the just-finished *The Night She Disappeared* to this untitled novel.

That was the plan, anyway. As it happens, she emails me a few days later and tells me she's got a character, and 'crazily, a kind of narrative arc for her too'. Soon after that, she starts writing, and sends me the first paragraphs of her next novel. I'm the first and only person to see them. She describes this early draft as the rawest incarnation of her work – 'so tiny, like a premature baby' – and yet she's trusting me with it.

Lisa and I barely know each other at this point. We've met once in real life, and once on Zoom. We've exchanged perhaps a dozen brief and businesslike emails. She has no reason to trust me, but she seems to. 'I like to think I have a pretty good instinct for these things,' she tells me: that is, she trusts herself and her own judgement. She doesn't know me, but she knows herself. That's another key trait about Lisa Jewell that comes across instantly. She's *comfortable*, and while that word may on a superficial level sound modest and unadventurous, with connotations of woolly safety – she describes her brand as 'a nice woman in a jumper' – it's actually a rare strength. She knows what she's good at, and she wants to keep doing it.

So we agreed to meet again at the same time on Zoom the following Thursday, to continue our unique project; and that's how both books began, in tandem, at the end of January 2021.

The Support Act

How did we get here? It started pre-Covid. I was booked as a support act to Lisa in December 2019, at a literary salon run by author and journalist Paul Burston, on the top floor of the Southbank Centre, overlooking the Thames. Nobody realised at the time that this would be one of the last galas before lockdown, and with hindsight it seems like a cabaret suitable for the end of an era: one last blast of camp sophistication in the neon light of the London Eye, shortly before we succumbed to the new age of online meetings, home-schooling, Joe Wicks workouts and quarantine hairstyles. Paul was wearing one of his loud, dandy-ish designer shirts decorated with pirates, skulls and bees; I wore a yellow suit modelled faithfully after a 1974 Bowie photoshoot; and the cartoonist Stephen Appleby, reliably, arrived in elegant drag. Lisa was the main event – in a black lace mini-dress with gold brocade – and I was one of the warm-ups, talking about my own recent book *Why Bowie Matters*. I didn't know Lisa or her work at the time: I'd read *Ralph's Party* in 1999 because it was what you did, like listening to U2's *Achtung Baby* in 1991 or watching *Trainspotting* in 1996. I didn't recognise her until she took the stage.

Before reading from *The Family Upstairs*, Lisa told a story about cupcakes. At one point around the middle of her career, she explained, her sales had stalled, and her agent, Jonny Geller, had taken her out to lunch for a serious discussion.

'This was during the lull, when I was writing the family dramas which my publishers didn't really know how to publish because they were non-genre. I still had my original readership of 100K or so, but try as they might, they couldn't grow it. And during this lunch Jonny suggested (*a*) maybe I could change my name – that really is a rock-bottom suggestion to make to any author, particularly one selling 100K copies of each book! – and (*b*) that I might consider sending cupcakes to my publishers on occasion.

'I actually felt genuinely aggrieved by the cupcakes suggestion. I'd spent ten years being a wonderfully polite, easy-going, kind, grateful and hard-working author, delivering good book after good book, which I thought was my half of the contract, and I could not understand why I should be expected to do any more than that. I remember ranting in my writers' chatroom about it and couldn't help noticing that it was the more successful writers who were saying that they'd sent gifts and cakes to their publishers in the past.

'So the next time there was some good news – I think it was when I cracked the top ten with *The Making of Us* – I thought: This feels like a cupcake moment. So I ordered twenty-four to be delivered to my publishers and they were delighted and I liked the feeling so next I sent my foreign rights agent a gift voucher because I was basically living off foreign money at that time and I wanted to let her know how much I appreciated her.

'And then there was some good news in the US so I sent them some cake pops and after a year or so I could see a *definite* correlation between the amount of nice things I sent, as a result of focusing on what *was* happening for me rather than on what wasn't, and my book sales and successes. So I think maybe it was less the cupcakes themselves – although, if publishers are used to getting cakes and gifts from their more successful authors, it probably does help shift their perceptions of your status – than the fact that I was actively looking out for moments to give thanks and show appreciation. Which is clearly a very positive mindset to have. Anyway, I call it Cupcake Karma and stand by it as a hugely formative strand of my recent successes.'

It was a well-formed, perfectly finished, charming anecdote, a little gift for the audience. She had probably told it before, perhaps more than once. But I was struck by this discussion of failure from someone who'd been invited as a glittering example of literary success; and looking back, I can see the intriguing balance the cupcake story strikes between two apparently incompatible approaches: an open-hearted, almost naïve *niceness* and a canny, pragmatic talent for marketing and branding. There are two versions of Lisa in this short tale: that they co-exist, blending easily into a genuine, honest charm, is part of her complexity as an author.

I liked the chapter she read from *The Family Upstairs*, with its child's-eye apprehension of the shifting power dynamics between Henry's dad and the newcomer, David Thomsen, but I didn't buy the book at the time, because everyone else was buying it. I bought it later, during lockdown. I liked that book enough to buy another, *Watching You*, and I enjoyed that, too. It wasn't my usual genre but I admired the craft involved in the structure, the precise details of clothes and brands to reveal character, the keep-you-guessing ambiguity that denied any clear distinction between heroes and villains.

And then I read a passage that surprised me so much, I had to put the book down and stare into space, re-evaluating it. Freddie, a teenage boy, has been spying on his neighbours from an upstairs window, and is becoming obsessed with one of the schoolgirls he regularly watches. Stalking her through town, he fantasises about . . .

. . . walking into Ryman's and deliberately pushing himself up against Romola Brook, wordlessly pressing her into the filing display; he imagined the sweet sugar of her shocked breath against his cheek, the slight tremor in her skinny legs. He wanted to do it; he wanted to do it really badly.

Locked in his bedroom, Freddie takes a picture of Romola and photoshops it on to the image of a naked woman. But as he prepares to subject her to his fantasies, 'he saw something . . . that took his breath away':

> He saw a human being looking at him. He saw a skinny girl in a new town and a new school. A girl who loved a stupid tiny dog and wanted things from Forever 21 that she couldn't afford. A girl who went into Ryman's for folders oblivious to the strange boy loitering outside.

Freddie feels 'the shockwaves of something new and extraordinary ricochet around his head.' As I put the book down, I felt the same. The novel had pushed through a wall of its character's perception that, as a thriller, it could legitimately have ignored in order to carry on with the practical business of plot.

This startling shift of perspective, which hurtles Freddie from his voyeuristic distance – seeing Romola as a convenient object – to a position inside her consciousness, inhabiting her briefly as a person, seems as remarkable to me in its way as the more celebrated paragraphs in Ian McEwan's *Atonement*, where thirteen-year-old aspiring writer Briony Tallis – who also likes to spy from an upstairs window – makes a similar discovery. Witnessing an unsettling encounter between her sister and the cleaner's son Robbie, she knows that what she has seen is beyond her current comprehension, and as she struggles to make sense of it, she realises that her childish conventions of storytelling are too simple to contain or explain the complexities of adult relationships. The world is not, she suddenly realises, about 'good and bad, heroes and villains': as a writer, she need only 'show separate minds, as alive as her own, [and] grasp the simple truth that other people are as real as you . . . only in a story could you enter these different minds.'

What both passages have in common is that they both shock me out of my immersion: they are both points where the novel leaps briefly beyond its boundaries, doing more than simply telling a story and revealing something about storytelling – beyond that, about human beings and the way we construct the world – and other people, as characters, in our own lives. Rather than a distant intellectual admiration, I felt that paragraph in *Watching You* as a hard push to the chest, stealing my breath. It transcends genre.

There was more to come; more sentences that made me sit back and need a moment to recover. Jenna, one of the schoolgirls, lives with her mother, who suffers from paranoia. At one point, half believing the conspiracy theories that circulate around her community, she investigates online and finds nothing, but can't settle her unease. 'Was she, Jenna, perhaps mad too?' She picks up her phone, which usually links her instantly to her best friend Bess, but Bess isn't there. Jenna is stranded.

> She felt a terrible hollowness open up inside her, a sense that she was all alone, that she had in fact always been all alone, that the corners of her life were folding in and folding in and that there was nothing she could do about it.

Again, this last sentence does so much more than the story actually requires at this point; rather than wrapping up the scene efficiently, it chooses to push further at Jenna until it taps into something startling, dark and deep, and then lets that emotion flow, filling the end of the chapter with blackness, with unapologetic bleakness. Its painful revelations remind me of this passage:

> . . . she was going to die, in truth, without having been liberated . . . she was stifling under a huge weight that . . . she had been dragging around for twenty years.

Those lines are not from a thriller, but from a short story, 'La femme adultère', ('The Adulterous Wife') written in 1957 by the existential philosopher Albert Camus. And the end of Lisa's chapter also shares its rhythm with the final words in Joyce's story 'The Dead':

> His soul swooned slowly as he heard the snow falling faintly through the universe and faintly falling, like the descent of their last end, upon all the living and the dead.

Folding in and folding in, and falling faintly, faintly falling. A funeral litany. I don't feel we have to put Jewell next to Joyce to justify her work: those passages simply have the same emotional force for me, and I can't read either of them without sitting back for a moment and simply staring.

A final example. Jenna and Bess are on a school trip, and their headteacher, the charismatic Mr Fitzwilliam, comes to their shared bedroom late at night to scold them gently about their behaviour. 'And there followed a strange moment, brief but loaded.' Jenna is in pyjamas, 'fresh-faced and scrubbed,' and Bess 'still in her party clothes, her hair awry and her heeled boots clutched in her hand' . . .

> . . . and there, stationed between them, a tall, broad-shouldered man who was neither their father nor their friend. In the background of the vignette lurked the double bed spread with the ephemera of teenage girls: a red bra hooked over the bedpost, a

crumpled, lipstick-stained tissue on the bedside table. The room held the sugary smell of the Superdrug beauty aisle, the medicinal tang of Clearasil. The scene seemed like a portrait, captured in minute detail with tiny touches of a tiny brush, before suddenly vaporising into nothing as Mr Fitzwilliam straightened and smiled and said, 'Well, goodnight, ladies . . .'

Compare this with the moment in Henry James's *The Ambassadors* where the protagonist, Strether, is leaning against a post by the side of a river, when 'he saw something that gave him a sharper arrest':

What he saw was exactly the right thing – a boat advancing round the bend and containing a man who held the paddles and a lady, at the stern, with a pink parasol. It was suddenly as if these figures, or something like them, had been wanted in the picture, had been wanted more or less all day, and had now drifted into sight, with the slow current, on purpose to fill up the measure . . . The air quite thickened, at their approach, with further intimations; the intimation that they were expert, familiar, frequent – that this wouldn't at all events be the first time. They knew how to do it, he vaguely felt . . .

And then Strether realises that the lady in the boat has spotted him and recognised him, but that the gentleman is keeping his back turned; and long seconds seem to stretch, because he recognises them too, and knows instantly because of their familiarity that they are having an affair; and knows in turn that they know he has seen everything. 'The air quite thickened . . . with further intimations', echoing another precisely weighted line in *Watching You*, where 'for a moment the already charged air filled with small particles of yet another substance.'

If the lady and gentleman continue to ignore Strether and pass him by, pretending not to see him, the situation will become even more awkward, more painful – a social 'cut' would be experienced like violence in this genteel setting – but Strether has only an instant to rescue the scene by hailing them as if it's a happy accident, and pretending, with them, that he believes the couple are innocent friends.

James's novel is taut with the morals and manners of polite society in 1903, but the scene in *Watching You* captures the same, almost imperceptible tension, the same almost-unnameable sense of something terribly wrong, of a tableau frozen for a second and then released so its characters can move and breathe again, pretending they didn't notice. *Watching You* creates a 'vignette', a 'portrait', its painstaking definition juxtaposing the big man who suddenly doesn't belong with the small, intimate and awkward details of the teenage girls' shared sleeping space. Strether, in *The Ambassadors*, also appreciates his view as a 'picture', just needing human figures as features in its empty landscape, and it is when the boating couple completes its composition, filling the gap, that his realisation clicks into place. James's image of the air thickening gives the same sense as Jewell's 'captured'; a slowing and stopping, allowing the awful but subtle revelation to build; and then there is movement, and time accelerates and the frozen moment 'vaporises', but the knowledge of what has been seen remains.

One word for this sensation, again associated with James Joyce, is 'epiphany': a shock, a showing, a sudden *seeing*, a shining of new light. I had to stop at those moments of *Watching You*, as I did with the novels of Joyce, James and McEwan, because of the force with which they made me realise a new truth through their characters.

After *Watching You*, of course I couldn't stop, and tore through *I Found You* and *Then She Was Gone*, both of which also grabbed me round the neck and punched me in the heart and left me battered and exhausted. I often had to stop reading between chapters to recover from the emotional onslaught and settle from the unbearable tension. I tried to connect the sometimes sadistic force of those books with the endearingly modest woman I'd seen reading at the Polari salon. I hadn't spoken to Lisa then, but now I was desperate to sit opposite her and ask her how she did this: to try to see what it was in her that enabled her to torture her characters so effectively and unrelentingly, but also to embrace them at their lowest, to find sympathy for their faults, to cradle them with words as they died. I couldn't match up the Lisa Jewell of the cute cupcakes story with the Lisa Jewell who had allowed teenage Kirsty to be violated in front of her brother in *I Found You* or left little Ellie Mack alone to starve in a basement in *Then She Was Gone*. I realised I wanted to write about Lisa Jewell. It was, if you like, an epiphany of its own.

I contacted Lisa through Paul Burston, and as a guide and consultant, I reached out to author Andy Martin, who single-handedly invented a new genre with his book about Lee Child and *Make Me*. Lisa agreed to meet. She suggested the Groucho. I said nothing, hoping I could pretend I hung out regularly at the Groucho. I was relieved when we opted instead for a modest café in a shopping centre.

It was the end of summer, and London hovered in a brief, hazy window of freedom between lockdowns. I waited with Andy Martin for Lisa Jewell. When she arrived, I suggested we should bump elbows to say hello.

'That's very March 2020,' she said dismissively, which I thought was both rude and clever.

Then I sat between Lisa Jewell and Andy Martin, and she talked to him about her WhatsApp group with Sophie Kinsella and Jojo Moyes, and he talked to her about being pals with Lee

Child, and I felt out of my depth. But there came a gap in the conversation, and I thought about Ellie Mack in a cellar on her own, and Kirsty floating out to sea, and Jenna's deep, dark loneliness, and Freddie being catapulted into Romola's consciousness, and I channelled my feelings about those characters in a rush towards the one person who I knew would understand. It was enough: enough to convince Lisa that there was a possibility there – or at least not to rule it out completely. It was enough, I think, to show her that I hadn't approached her out of academic curiosity, but from a deep, gut-level connection with what she'd created.

Months passed; autumn passed, and we retreated back into lockdown for winter, and every couple of weeks I sent a polite enquiry or a gentle nudge, and Lisa assured me she was still considering it, and checking with her people. 'She won't do it,' Andy told me regularly. 'It's too much of a risk. Even if she wants to do it, her publisher won't let her.' He was right in a way: Lisa talked to a lot of people and did her due diligence. But ultimately, fortunately, his misgivings were proved wrong. Lisa wrote again in early January 2021 to say she was looking forward to giving it a try. We set a date for our first Zoom, and while she put the finishing touches to *The Night She Disappeared*, I continued to read her work in reverse order, working through her back catalogue.

Rachel and Revisions

4 February 2021

Lisa's new novel is, at this point, 344 words long, and called 'Book 20'. She hasn't even got a working title yet, 'though I don't want to call it something like *The Family Downstairs*'. It starts with an early-morning 'phone-call from a French number', and a woman peering groggily at the screen, deciding not to answer.

'I knew I wanted to come back to this idea of Lucy's ex-husband, who she murders in the kitchen, because that's a loose end that didn't get tied up. And I thought the best place to come back to it from would be his wife, because he's actually married, to this woman called Rachel. So I knew that I wanted to use Rachel as one of my three characters this time round. And she's just been told that her husband's been murdered by gangsters.'

'By business associates,' I pointlessly interrupt.

'Yes. But she knows that's not right. So maybe she speaks to the housekeeper and maybe she mentions that his ex-wife hap-pened to visit a couple of times before he died.'

Until last week, those vague speculations were the extent of Lisa's plans for her twentieth novel. Then, lying in bed one night, 'I suddenly had a name for her. I suddenly thought she's Jewish. Her name is Rachel, so that lent itself very easily to her being a Jewish character. So her name is Rachel Gold. And I had an arc for her, which I can't share with you because it would give away where I feel she's going to go with her exploration of what really happened to her husband. And obviously it's going to be a really good opportunity to revisit those themes of domestic abuse and see how that impacted on her.'

I don't press for more information. As well as respecting her authorial right to secrecy, I don't want the rest of the story spoiled for me. Despite this unique situation, with me joining her at the very start of the book, we're still occupying the power dynamic of writer and reader. She holds the cards, and she's dealing them out to me as she chooses.

What surprises me is how few cards she's holding at this stage, and how their shapes and suits are changing in front of her eyes.

'I'd always had this idea that I might have to go on a safari holiday, for research. Because Henry and Miller and Libby are all going to go off to . . . can you remember what country?'

I check the text. 'Botswana. The Chobe Game Lodge.'

'Yes! Which exists! I just googled game lodges in Botswana, and that one came up as a deluxe one. And then someone wrote to me and pointed out that it's the only game lodge in Africa where they only employ local people. Which is a bit of a disaster in terms of Phin being there. Maybe he could be a trainer.'

It's funny, I say, that she felt Rachel was a loose end. 'Because when you told me you were writing a sequel, I assumed immediately it was going to be about Henry and Phin.'

'Yes,' Lisa says again, politely. I appreciate the way she says 'Yes' even when I'm annoying or wrong – *Yes, that is certainly what you think* – before moving on to a gentle correction. 'Well, it just seemed to make sense. I wanted it to be a stand-alone. So I didn't want it to just be revisiting the same characters and continuing the same story. I wanted it to be fresh and new, and something you could read on its own.'

'So does coming up with Rachel's new character arc give you that sense of novelty and shininess, again?'

'Yes. Yeah. Exactly. Exactly. I just suddenly thought: Oh,

this is a fresh beginning, this is a whole world I haven't explored yet, a whole person I haven't thought about yet, and I could make her really interesting. And I like that idea of her just being mentioned in passing, in the first story. Nobody thinks about her. Nobody cares that he's died and left his wife alone, with all these unanswered questions.'

I stick stubbornly to my own interpretation of her work. 'But was it not the Phin and Henry story that inclined you to write a sequel?'

'Yes. Yes. It was writing that last chapter, that unexpected last chapter, and particularly that last line of that last chapter. I suddenly thought, I really want to go to Botswana with them and see what happens, and see how Phin reacts to meeting his daughter, and find out what Henry really wanted from Phin, and how twisted Henry really is. So I guess I'll be sticking with Henry . . . but I don't even know if I am going to be sticking with Henry! I don't know. I don't know. It's absolutely a blank canvas at the moment, apart from this Rachel Gold character.'

It could be something looser than a sequel, I suggest, more of a paired book, a sister to the first.

'Correct,' she declares. 'I'm going to leave myself that option open. I think what's important for readers is that they find out what's happened in Botswana, and that they find out what's happened with Henry and Phin, but that doesn't have to form the backbone. It will exist very much in the little universe that I created for *The Family Upstairs*, but it may not necessarily focus on the same characters to the same degree. I'm certainly not designing it to follow up every little avenue from the original book.'

I'd seen Lisa talking in a 2019 interview about the origin of *The Family Upstairs*: a chance sighting of a woman – who developed into Lucy – sneaking her children into the showers of a beach club in the south of France. 'I felt very strongly that I wanted to write a book about her,' Lisa explains in that interview, 'and write a story about her.' Character, I'm learning, is the seed at the centre of it all: the plot grows from them and around them, following where they lead.

'It's all emerging out of character, again, isn't it?'

'Yes. That's why I'm not one hundred per cent convinced that I'm going to go back to Henry, because Henry gave me so much when I was writing him that I felt that I was sated? So it was more about wanting to know what happens next, rather than wanting to spend more time with him, seeing the world from his perspective.'

Meanwhile, Lisa sends me the entire manuscript for *The Night She Disappeared*, which I consume in two days. The story I receive, though, is very different from the one that existed just a couple of weeks before. Lisa doesn't tell me what she changed in that final rewrite until I've finished reading. I assume it must be a matter of minor tweaks, and I'm astonished when she reveals that it's a huge shift, like tectonic plates moving under the little world that contains Tallulah's cul-de-sac, and Scarlett's mansion, and Sophie's cottage.

'In the thriller genre, everything needs to mean something,' she explains. 'Everything needs to happen for a reason, and you can't introduce a character, an object or a location unless it has something to do with the dénouement. Those last few chapters have got to make sense of every little thing that happened before. When I used to write out of this genre, in romantic comedy, you could be a little bit self-indulgent, you could write a set piece just because you fancied writing a set piece, because it would be fun, and it wouldn't have to feed back into the narrative once you got to the end.

'But what I think people like about my novels is that there aren't any loose ends, or if there is a loose end, it's there on purpose. And that's what I fixed last week. I'd introduced this female character, and felt very strongly that she was the wrong character? Because although she was doing the detective work, equivalent to what Libby did in *The Family Upstairs*, she didn't have her own arc. She had no other function in this story except for asking people questions and being a bit nosey. And that was what I did. I found a function for her. And the clever thing about it . . .' She hesitates for a fraction of a second, then seems to decide that yes, it was clever. '. . . was that the function I gave her was so profound, yet simple enough to be fed into the book with about six extra paragraphs, just sprinkled throughout.'

She's talking about Sophie Beck, detective author and the girlfriend of Maypole school's new headmaster, Shaun Gray. In the previous version, Sophie began investigating the central mystery simply because she was there and available; in the final version, the intrigue interlocks closely with her own books, and the clues are planted by other characters specifically to draw her in. The signs inviting her to 'Dig Here' are not random, as they were until this final draft, but deliberate references to her previous published work.

'The thing about the "Dig Here" sign being in her book . . . that was what I added afterwards, at the last minute, to make sense of Sophie's role in the book, because she didn't really have one. So that was not in there organically. It was very much inserted after the event, and I had to stick it in without it having repercussions. I kept thinking that this whole story could be happening without Sophie in it.'

'Whereas this way, the whole story is happening because of her.'

'Exactly. I mean, people might have read the book and thought it was fine, but I felt really uncomfortable about it. In a thriller, everything has to work hard. You can't have anything extraneous. And I was just really haunted by the fact that the book would have worked perfectly well without her.'

As Lisa noted herself, she has placed her protagonists in an amateur detective role before. We've had Libby in *The Family Upstairs*; Freddie in *Watching You* and Saffyre from *Invisible Girl* are both essentially teenage sleuths; and her third novel, *One-Hit Wonder* (2001), has Ana investigating the death of her pop star sister Bee. But this is the first time any of her characters have come quite so close to Lisa's own job as successful author, though many of them aspire to it. Minu, in *Before I Met You*, 'had been writing a novel for the past eighteen months'. Vince, from *Vince and Joy*, buys a book called *How To Write a Bestseller* and gets no further than the introduction; his rival George gives up his job to compose 'the Great British Novel', and enrols on creative writing courses. 'Publishing – it's all a matter of who you know,' he explains airily. Lucy's ex-husband Michael in *The Family Upstairs* tells her complacently that he's writing a 'book. Or, in fact, *a memoir*. Or possibly a blend of the two.' Elderly Gus Veldtman in *31 Dream Street* is still earning royalties (£5.26) from the book he published in 1930, and Sean, in *A Friend of the Family*, has a debut novel out, though he's worried that it, like Bee's solitary hit single, might prove to be a fluke. Robyn's boyfriend Jack, in *The Making of Us*, is the most established, currently working on his third book, but he's in literary rather than genre fiction: slim volumes with blurry cover images, one-word titles and modest sales. When Robyn's perfect life falls apart, she experiences it as a nightmarish shift from being a chick-lit heroine (in one of those books 'with shoes on the cover') to a hapless character in one of Jack's novels: the lurch from Sophie Kinsella to early Ian McEwan, perhaps. It's certainly easier to write about people in your own milieu, who share some of your own aspirations and experiences – look at David Lodge and the campus novel, for instance – and this tendency of Lisa's seems unconscious, a quick reach for familiar ideas that don't need research; the pattern only emerges when you join up details over several stories.

In *One-Hit Wonder*, bookshelves are a guide to other people's tastes, sometimes revealing hidden depths: Ana finds an unnamed John Updike novel in her sister's flat, chastises herself for only reading crime novels – 'Patricia Cornwell. Ruth Rendell. P. D. James. Agatha Christie' – and is pleasantly surprised when she sees that tough guy Flint owns *Midnight in the Garden of Good and Evil*, *The Prime of Miss Jean Brodie* and the screenplay of *Pulp Fiction*. 'She'd have put money on two Andy McNabs, one John Grisham and the Guinness Book of Records *circa* 1989.' Dig from *Thirtynothing*, by contrast, uses Alex Garland's *The Beach* as a coaster for his coffee – he 'wasn't one of life's great readers' – and Kim from *The Night She Disappeared* admits that she hasn't read a book 'since I was about nineteen'. In a neat irony, these two would never open the novels in which they appear.

This dalliance with literary references occasionally strays further into playfully meta territory. Jack promises he'll write the book of Robyn's encounter with her siblings, while in *After the Party*, Jem remembers her first kiss with boyfriend Ralph as 'like the last, breathy page of a novel', which of course it was: it was the last page of *Ralph's Party*, ten years earlier in real time. But *The Night She Disappeared* is the first time Lisa has included an author with an established brand: Sophie has published five books in The Hither Green Detective Agency series, under the pseudonym P. J. Fox.

I point out to Lisa that, having lived near Hither Green myself, the name doesn't carry connotations of the 'cosy crime' genre Sophie supposedly occupies; she assures me, having thought it all through at every level, that the agency is only based there, and investigates mysteries in bourgeois surrounding areas like Blackheath.

The layers deepen when Sophie Beck pretends to be her own detective protagonist, Susie Beets (just to make things even more confusing for the dedicated reader, there's a character in *After the Party* called Sarah Betts), and when Sophie turns to a paragraph from the first Hither Green to remind herself about the real-life crime she's now investigating, we enter a frame within a fictional frame.

All the boxes click together perfectly, and what could have been a pointless post-modern experiment pays off in narrative terms. But there must be a further risk in creating a character who so precisely mirrors your own situation as an author. Sophie finds herself at her laptop, firing off a few emails, looking up flights to Denmark and planning a haircut in town, which can double up as lunch with a friend – as a bonus, she can

see if her publishers would like her to visit. She feels herself get quite excited at the prospect.

After a while she switches screens to her latest manuscript. She hasn't looked at it for days . . . She hasn't been in the right headspace to get any work done. But now she has no excuse. The tail end of her last paragraph stares at her blankly . . .

And that's exactly where Lisa is now.

Origin Stories

Authors often come complete with origin stories: bite-sized hooks that give us a shorthand sense of where they came from and how they started writing. J. K. Rowling, famously, dreamed up Harry Potter while sitting on a train. Lee Child invented Jack Reacher after losing his job in television. Martin Amis was the son of Kingsley. And Lisa Jewell was a secretary who was made redundant and wrote the first three chapters of *Ralph's Party* as a bet with her friend. In their way, these stories are as simple as superhero origins – shy teen is bitten by radioactive spider; rich kid witnesses his parents' murder – and serve the same purpose.

Origin narratives become familiar through repetition until they can be condensed into a sentence, even a handful of words, as one recent comic book does with Superman's backstory: 'Doomed planet. Desperate scientists. Last hope. Kindly couple.' I read multiple versions of Lisa's origin story, in articles and interviews from the 1990s onwards. Some were simple and some more detailed, but all of them sounded like a fairy tale.

I was sceptical. I know that people who are asked the same question again and again develop neat, convenient answers, pre-packed responses for every occasion. (Fictional author Sophie does the same in *The Night She Disappeared*). I know that articles refer back to other articles rather than the source, smoothing and polishing previous versions until the story of 'How Lisa Jewell Got Her Big Break' becomes a shiny gem rather than the spiky rock that is real life.

I related her origin back to Lisa, in that Superman-style telegraphese – 'Redundant secretary. Holiday bet. Three chapters. Enthusiastic agent. Bidding war. Launch party. *Late Review*' – and asked her if it was true. Was it really the fairy tale presented by the *Daily Express* – 'Bestselling writer recalls a magical moment at her first book launch party when all her dreams come true' – above a photo of Lisa glowing in a pink dress? Was there no sense of doubt or struggle? Her reply was disappointing.

Whenever I think back to that period, all I can remember is feeling like I was in a dream or a fairy tale. A 'struggle' is the furthest thing from what my life felt like during those years. I'd been dating my husband for about six months when I started writing the book and I was desperate to move in with him but didn't want to ask as it seemed too early. So having the excuse of needing to be at his flat every day for a month to use his computer to write those first three chapters was perfect for me. Then I got the letter from the agent two months later asking to see the rest of the book and my boyfriend asked me to move in with him properly and I do remember feeling scared then, that at the precise moment in my life when I should be making decisions that would put me on track to a proper career, I was fannying about pretending to write a book. I was twenty-six and fresh out of a bad marriage and in a new relationship with a guy who had a proper job and was earning well and had loads of friends who formed 100 per cent of my social life at that time and he owned a property while I had nothing. I do remember thinking that if my boyfriend ended the relationship I'd be walking away with no money, no friends, nowhere to live and a stupid book that was never going to get published. I do remember having moments of feeling scared and vulnerable.

But no, writing the book was not a struggle. It was fun. I had no expectations of what I was doing, other than just getting it done. I didn't imagine a career as a writer for myself, I considered it a holiday from real life, not the beginning of a new life. I considered myself very lucky and privileged to have been given the opportunity to do something so self-indulgent. I was sending chapters every week to my friend in Australia who was cheerleading me through it. I had a hugely active social life and was madly in love and it was honestly one of the most joyful, magical periods of my life. The fact that it all ended with a £120,000 two-book deal with Penguin was just ludicrous, really. Beyond anyone's craziest dreams.

Obviously being wheeled out by a publisher as their 'big new thing' was quite overwhelming. I lost nearly a stone during publication month with all the nerves and adrenaline. But, no, not a struggle, just stupidly exciting and amazing and wonderful. All of it.

The only struggle, it seemed, was Lisa's honest effort to find any grittiness in the story. I came back to her on a Zoom chat, like Columbo, trying to catch her by surprise. *Just one more thing*.

'Your friend Yasmin Boland. The one who gave you the bet to write three chapters, while you were both on holiday. She was going to take you to a restaurant if you wrote those three chapters. What was the restaurant?'

'Ah!' says Lisa. 'OK . . . it was, and I hope it remains, Esarn Kheaw, which is a North-East Thai restaurant, on the Uxbridge Road. In Shepherd's Bush.'

It's an immediate and detailed answer. I look it up. It's entirely accurate. Unlikely as it seems, I have to conclude that Lisa really did live through her own Cinderella story, in 1990s North London. On the other hand, what about the cupcakes? Surely they speak to a struggle in the middle of her career.

If there was a low, she reflects, it struck in 2010, before *The Making of Us*, 'when I broke out of chick lit and my publishers didn't know what to do with me for quite some time.'

> The only time I've ever really felt concerned for my career was around halfway through when my publishers could not get me past the 60K sales mark (*Ralph's Party* had sold 250K) and the big advances dried up and while I was never even close to the scrapheap, I was aware of it lurking somewhere just below. I couldn't smell it but I knew it was there. So I did worry at times about my huge mortgage and if I'd ever be able to retire. But again, no, not a struggle. Just a niggling sense that things could go downhill. But probably wouldn't. And then I did the cupcakes, and then America started to happen, and then Richard & Judy happened, and then America properly happened, and the writing became easier because I knew what worked for me and my readers. And here I am.

Lisa's writing can be grouped roughly into three phases. First, there's what the papers called chick lit, and what she calls 'curry and flatmates', which took her from *Ralph's Party* through *Thirtynothing, One-Hit Wonder, A Friend of the Family* and *Vince and Joy* to *31 Dream Street* in 2007. Then followed the family dramas of the early 2010s – *The Truth About Melody Browne, The Making of Us, Before I Met You, The House We Grew Up In* and *The Third Wife* – before her more recent run of psychological thrillers, starting in 2015 (*The Girls, I Found You, Then She Was Gone*).

The novels that transition her out of one mode and into

another are obvious, with hindsight – *Melody Browne*, taking Lisa away from romantic comedy, is the first that introduces a heroine but allows her to solve the mystery alone, without a man's assistance, and *The Third Wife*, edging into thriller territory, is the first to include a possible murder. There are recognisable motifs, themes and patterns across the work as a whole – *One-Hit Wonder*, from 2001, is a detective story that starts with a death, and *Thirtynothing* introduces the 'themes of domestic abuse' that Lisa plans to explore in Book 20, twenty years later – but her back catalogue divides neatly into three, despite the fact that recent re-releases now present the earlier, brighter novels in a sinister light, with dark photographs and blaring neon capitals replacing both the cartoons and dainty drawings of the first editions and the tasteful pastels of the late 2000s. *Melody Browne* is currently available with three covers: the first is adorned with the curlicued font of chick lit above a whimsical pink cityscape and Tiffany-coloured park bench, while the second presents an Athena-style image of a girl's hands holding seashells, and the third is a moody mystery shot, designed to be sold alongside *The Family Upstairs* and *Invisible Girl*.

That career arc, with its near-effortless transition between genres, and bestsellers at the start and finish, still sounds like a fairy tale; but when I come back to it later, examining her more closely about its details, there are pockmarks in the surface: potholes and bumps that for someone else might have marred the smooth ride.

It's a matter of perspective. 'I am a person who considers themselves to be lucky', she tells me, 'even when I'm not. I don't think about negative things, I count my blessings, I focus on what's going right rather than what's going wrong, so maybe another writer would have found the same journey more of a struggle. I don't know.'

Melody Browne, she remembers now, was the 'watershed', the turning point and transition out of chick lit. But another, half-finished, ghost volume haunts that junction, and if she'd completed that story instead, her career would have followed another trajectory entirely.

'I was halfway through another book . . . these were the days when I thought I could be a different sort of writer, I suppose. And the working title was *The Wonderful World of Dave*. I just wanted to write about this guy who had a really shambolic, chaotic life, and lots of ex-wives and children all over the place . . . I guess maybe slightly, um . . .' She clicks her fingers in frustration. 'How can I not remember this writer's name? One of the most famous male writers of the nineteen seventies and eighties.'

'David Lodge?' I suggest.

'No . . .' Her head is in her hands. 'I keep thinking Will Self, but not Will Self. He was big in the seventies, and eighties, and early nineties . . . he wrote these big books about really ugly characters, behaving really badly . . . in London usually . . . he's such a famous writer.'

We leave it there, for now. But when she remembers, during our next meeting, it's a revelation: if *The Wonderful World of Dave* had been published in place of *The Truth About Melody Browne*, Lisa would be a very different author now, with a completely different brand. More on that later.

Phin and Gone

11 February 2021

This current novel, the as-yet-untitled Book 20, could have been very different, too. Lisa told me, before she'd written a word, that Rachel would be one of three central characters. This week, she sent me her second chapter, focused on Phin: the lost boy, the golden, glamorous mystery who was discovered working on a safari in Botswana at the end of *The Family Upstairs*: 'Phin hands his passport to the customs guy. He stifles a flinch as he always does whenever someone casts their eyes upon his passport. It's not a real passport. Nothing about Phin is real.'

'It's crap,' she says.

Is it? Phin emerges from the airport and sees a man waiting for him, the brittle sun catching his highlights, a pale shirt tucked into jeans. His name's Mac. The two men walk into each other's arms and kiss on the cheek. Mac has a dog, and Phin kisses the dog on the cheeks too, and Mac has a cool young mom and Phin loves Mac's mom too. And Phin 'casts his eyes upwards into the blue Chicago sky and he thanks God for finally giving him someone to love after so many years alone.'

It's a bit Armistead Maupin-lite, perhaps; *Tales of the City* updated and adapted into a wholesome daytime soap, or a progressive advert for American Airlines, launched in Pride Month.

'It's crap,' Lisa decides, 'but it's served its purpose. He's definitely gay and I could tell I was making him a bit of a stereotype, which makes me realise I don't have a handle on him at all. If he's gay, I need to know exactly who he is before I write him. I reread the last quarter of *The Family Upstairs* yesterday and remembered that the whole impetus behind me wanting to write a sequel lay in Henry's last lines, so I will start writing Henry now, from that moment onwards, in the first person, and try to launch into the story that way, rather than coming at it from a fresh angle. So right now I'm thinking just two points of view, Rachel and Henry. But we'll see.'

We leave Phin there, staring up at the pale Chicago sky, and as the sun hits his face he seems to fade like an old photograph. Phin is gone before he even took shape and solid form. This Phin is not real.

But the book is already taking shape in public space, in people's expectations. *The Family Upstairs 2* now has a provisional cover on Amazon. It's scheduled for summer 2022. And Lisa has just deleted her second chapter.

Author Theories

You can't tell academics you're writing about an author without them wheeling out a rusty old joke: *Isn't the author supposed to be dead?*

In 1967, French philosopher Roland Barthes published an article called 'The Death of the Author'. The title was meant to be provocative. He didn't mean that any particular author was dead, or should be dead. What he proposed was that instead of treating a text – a novel, a film, a poem or artwork – as if it was a holy message handed down to us by an 'Author-God', and assuming that the critic's job was to decipher what the original creator meant by it, we should shift our focus to the multiple possible meanings created by each reader.

In theory, then, we shouldn't have to ask Lisa about her intentions, or try to make connections between her books and her biography. We could look for recurring themes, patterns and motifs, and interpret the novels as if they were dreams, expressions of her unconscious concerns. We might notice the number of characters named after animals, for instance – Bird, Lamb, Wolfe, Fox – a Lula and a Lulu, and two girls called Scarlett, one a toddler, one a teenager, in *After the Party* and *The Night She Disappeared*. (Lisa's youngest daughter has Scarlett as a middle name.)

We could compare the immersive, euphoric descriptions of taking ecstasy in *Thirtynothing* and *I Found You*, the rose bushes planted to commemorate a dead girl in *I Found You* and *The Night She Disappeared*, the two men tied to radiators in *I Found You* and *The Family Upstairs*, and the fascination with foil chocolate

37

wrappers that unites Nadine in *Thirtynothing* and Lorelei from *The House We Grew Up In*. We could note Cheri's toast-coloured tan and vanilla hair in *After the Party*, and the 'vanilla hair and darkly toasted skin' Lucy from *The Family Upstairs* admires on women in the south of France. We could consider the sinister fistful of brunette hair uncovered by Freddie in *Watching You* and Ned in *A Friend of the Family*, *Thirtynothing*'s passing reference to amnesia after a house fire that becomes a major plot point in *Melody Browne*, and the paintings that play a key role in *Ralph's Party*, *Before I Met You* and *The Night She Disappeared*, occupying the start, middle and most recent stages of Lisa's career to date.

(In the latest draft of Book 20, she includes the image of 'things that I cannot discuss . . . buzzing in particles through my mind', and I wonder if I helped to put it there by praising her 'charged air filled with small particles' from *Watching You*; but they are also in *Vince and Joy*, as 'burning particles of his intent floating round the flat, like tiny fireflies'.)

So while contemporary literary theory does not actually pronounce a post-mortem on the author, it does provide tools for constructing perfectly good readings in their absence, which in most cases is entirely practical. But when you have the author right there with you, it's hard to resist asking about intentions and making those connections, even if they're wrong. Siobhan in *Ralph's Party*, for instance, 'hadn't really worked since losing her job as a technician at a fashion college in Surrey'; Lisa studied fashion illustration in Epsom. Lisa 'can draw quite well', according to one interview; Ralph, in her first novel, is a painter. And you couldn't get much closer to 'Jewell', surely, than the heroine of *Ralph's Party*, Jem/Gem? Surely that was deliberate.

'No,' Lisa says kindly but firmly, shaking her head with the tone and expression of someone who wants a stranger to leave them alone on a train. 'Definitely not deliberate, no. Definitely not deliberate.'

'But you've said you were like Jem. Jem, gem. And a gem is a jewel, right?'

'Yeeeahh,' says Lisa. 'Yeah! No.'

In that moment, she looks quite relieved that we're on Zoom, separated by many miles.

Reading back diligently through her work, I develop a further thesis about Lisa's attention to details of clothes and décor, which I feel must be related to her training in fashion illustration. I take substantial supporting notes as evidence. Each book includes lengthy accounts of a character's current outfit – cut, style, fabric, colourway, brand – which in turn tells us about them, their circumstances and often their state of mind. In *After the Party*, for instance, Jem . . .

> . . . was wearing a yellow sundress with a shirred bodice and shoestring straps and apple-green Havaianas flip-flops and her hair was tied up messily on top of her head. Underneath her sundress she wore a bikini. It was a bikini she had not worn for almost five years and, at some points during the weeks following the births of both her children, had thought she would never wear again.

Her former housemate from *Ralph's Party*, making a surprise cameo in the sequel, has one colour in common with Jem, but they're otherwise opposite: Cheri is, as we saw, 'tanned to an improbable shade of toast, vanilla hair, long shapely legs, Prada sunglasses, a leather shopper hanging from the crook of her arm. She wore tight black jeans and a fitted sweater in pale apple green.'

Style choices confirm Nadine's independent quirkiness in *Thirtynothing* – 'a stunning redhead in a blue crushed-silk dress wearing red 1950s plastic sunglasses and butterflies in her hair' – and the effortless off-duty elegance of Libby's work friend Dido in *The Family Upstairs*:

> Dido greets her at the door in wide floral trousers and a black vest top. Her hair is held from her face by large red sunglasses and she is barefoot. Libby has only ever seen her in clumpy work shoes so it's a surprise to see two small, white, perfectly pedicured feet with rose-pink nails.

Again, there's a single element in common – red sunglasses – but the ensembles could hardly be more different, and they convey an immediate sense of the individual.

This attention extends to interior décor, described with the expertise of an estate agent. Toni Moran's living room in *Vince and Joy* is structurally identical to that of Joy's parents, 'but felt completely different'.

> Instead of damp wisps of nylon net hanging across her windows, she had folds and flounces of thick oatmeal jacquard. Instead of fields of ancient, patterned carpeting covering her floor she had shiny beech-effect parquet. And instead of a solitary hanging light bulb housed under a dusty paper shade she had rows of twinkling halogen lamps embedded in her ceiling.

Bethan's 'babymoon' bedroom from *The House We Grew Up In* demonstrates her recent discovery of who she is as an adult, while accepting and embracing aspects of her eccentric mother through items salvaged from the family home: 'the trio of cameos of fat-bottomed cherubs in porcelain frames, a few gilt-framed oil paintings of indeterminate heritage, a couple of fussy bugle-bead-trimmed table lamps'. Her temporary apartment in Sydney, she now realises, 'wasn't a room. It was a stage set. A doll's house. It was where I lived when I was pretending to be a person.'

Millie's eye for design in *A Friend of the Family* – 'Victorian tasselled lamps, a dramatic *chaise longue* in raspberry velvet, Afghan fur rugs, abstract paintings, framed sepia photographs, a brown suede pouffe' – is a major aspect of her appeal to the London brothers Tony and Sean. Libby in *The Family Upstairs* sells upmarket kitchens. Leah in *31 Dream Street* dresses bedrooms in bubble-gum pink for a client's daughters, while her neighbour Toby revamps his life by refitting his house with expensive sofas and flashy bathrooms. And in *Watching You*, it's Nicola's soulless, careless approach to her family home that begins to reveal her true character. The details build relentlessly throughout our exploration of the house. There's 'an overhead light that gave out a cruel yellow glare . . . institutional, uninspiring, bleak'; and 'a bench . . . with a pile of old newspapers hanging off it and washing drying on a radiator: underpants scrunched into small stiff twists of fabric, a tired, drooping bra'; then:

> . . . a faded blue sofa . . . an old piano . . . a chrome floor lamp, a small gilt-framed mirror above a fake-stone fireplace, a high-backed chair in the window that looked as though it should be in an old people's home.

Interior design confirms a character's inner life, and Nicola's is cold and colourless. No wonder Joey, the closest person the novel has to a heroine, decides 'she didn't like this house. And she didn't like Nicola.'

The detailed outfit inventories aren't restricted to female characters. Even as far back as *Ralph's Party*, men are quickly rated by their wardrobes: in Jem's flat, Smith's 'nice grey suit and a pale lilac suit and tie', and Ralph's 'foul baggy grey jumper . . . and a most unbecoming pair of vaguely obscene-looking longjohns.' Classically hunky Vince opts for 'a black Fred Perry tucked into black gabardine peg-fronted trousers,' while Paul in *Then She Was Gone* is distinguished by . . .

> . . . shirts that looked conventional at first sight until you realised that there was a contrast trim of Liberty print inside the collar . . . cufflinks that appeared to be tiny dog heads . . . A flash of geometric-printed silk sock inside a handmade shoe.'

He and Floyd bond over their matching Paul Smith accessories: 'Twins!'

It was this detail, in fact, rather than the more enigmatic mentions of shirred bodices and bugle beads, that drew me into Lisa's descriptions of outfits and interiors. I wore Paul Smith socks before I began to read her work, but I have a horrible suspicion that I ordered two shirts with contrast Liberty-print cuffs and collar after finishing *Then She Was Gone*, inspired by her fictional character's wardrobe.

At the end of this research, I presented her with what I felt was a compelling portfolio of evidence. Surely this fascination stemmed from her training as a fashion illustrator?

'I'm not sure I pay any more attention to this kind of thing than most of my female contemporaries,' Lisa mused. 'I think most women write with an innate eye for details of this kind, whether they've had a fashiony background or not. It's how women recognise each other, I guess, by their styling quirks; how they decorate their houses.'

I was wrong again. The clues, to be fair, were right there in the text. Nadine in *Thirtynothing* thinks: 'Women tend to appreciate the innate sense of style with which she puts the disparate elements of her wardrobe together so that they form one definitive and pleasing look', while men find it 'as easy to understand as an ancient Flemish dialect.' Tony, in *A Friend of the Family*, 'had never really been a detail person when it came to women', while

Joy has always 'compared hairstyles and nail polish and heel size.' And in *After the Party*, Jem assesses Ralph's new woman-friend Sarah by forensically examining the bracelet she's left in his bedroom. 'It is very light, cheap, probably cost a few quid from River Island. She holds it to her nose and breathes in – it smells of skin.' I'd assumed that my own interest in labels and tailoring had made me at least semi-fluent in this fashion dialect, but Lisa's characters are natural experts, having grown up with the language from an early age.

Secretary-with-a-Cinderella-story was, Lisa remembers, the main marketing hook used to sell her brand at the start of her career. But there was another theme that kept cropping up in her early interviews: recently divorced woman escaping abusive marriage. I haven't heard about that yet, and don't want to ask her directly as it might seem rude, so I google instead. After learning about 'Bestselling Author Lisa Jewell's Perimenopause Symptoms', I find an article that summarises *The Third Wife* in relation to her upbringing. 'Essentially', says the *Belfast Telegraph*, 'it's about the emotional carnage left by a man who keeps walking away from the family unit. Coincidentally, Lisa's own father left their family home when she was 21.' She takes up the story herself:

My father, Anthony, was a textile agent who sold fabric in the West End and was away a lot. He was very glamorous. When he first met my mum, he swept her off into this big, social world.

When there were three of us [Lisa has two sisters] my mother was happy to let my dad go off and be glamorous and exciting. He wasn't particularly successful at parenting. His style wasn't very good. He was a strict disciplinarian, flying off the handle, thinking his children should be little soldiers who line up in a row and do as they are told . . .

All that glamour and jet-setting was just a backdrop to him abusing his freedom and having affairs.

In *The Night She Disappeared*, teenager Scarlett's father is coldly distant, working in the City while retaining 'a pied-à-terre in Bloomsbury.' Scarlett assumes he's having regular affairs: 'Rich old men get mega muff . . . I don't care. It's just old people stuff.' And there's a constant background threat of abuse buzzing between the younger couple, Tallulah and her controlling boyfriend Zach. It seems a running theme. I ask her about it, cautiously.

'Hm,' says Lisa. 'I think I've written some of the loveliest, loveliest men in fiction. Genuinely. Particularly in my romcoms, obviously, but also in my thrillers. Gray and his dad in *I Found You*. Aaron and Josh in *Invisible Girl*. Freddie in *Watching You* and Joey's lovely redhaired Viking boyfriend and her twin brother whose name I can't remember.'

Actually, Joey's brother Jack is ten years older than her, but I'm deeply impressed at the way she remembers all the other names; she reels them off like close friends, family members and familiar frenemies.

'I've also written some vile, cruel women: Noelle in *Then She Was Gone*. Birdie in *The Family Upstairs*. The casual cruelty of Lorelei in *The House We Grew Up In*, Meg's sister sleeping with her husband . . . the ultimate betrayal. The daughter in *The Third Wife* who sent the horrible poison-pen letters to Maya. Dylan in *The Girls*, drugging and beating her teenage nemesis in revenge for taking her boyfriend. Nikki Lee in *Watching You*. Utterly, utterly revolting! And of course, pregnant Rebecca who kills Nikki Lee. I think making a heavily pregnant woman a violent killer of another woman is pretty subversive.'

It's a comprehensive, convincing answer. We leave it there, for now.

But just one more thing. Lisa has two daughters, born in 2003 and 2007 respectively. In 2010's *After the Party*, Jem's daughter Scarlett is three years old. *The Girls*, published in 2017, centres on two sisters, one of whom is just transitioning from tween to young woman. In *The Night She Disappeared* (2020), Scarlett is eighteen. Even I can do that kind of maths. Surely those novels were influenced by the experience of being a mother to daughters, and watching them grow up?

Yes, she says, admitting freely that *After the Party* was a direct reflection of her marriage after the birth of her second baby, while *The Girls* was inspired by her communal garden, full of 'free-roaming children'. 'I think thirteen-year-olds are incredibly, incredibly dark. One second you're a child, and the next you're a threat.'

'You'd have to know thirteen-year-olds, to write that book,' I suggest. 'I mean, I haven't known a thirteen-year-old since I was thirteen.'

'Yes, absolutely, absolutely.' At last we're agreeing. 'The age of children is really important when I write a book. They have to fit into the story. They can't be just random children. They have to be really spot-on.'

'I wonder if your girl-characters are getting older, though, as your daughters get older? Subconsciously.'

'Yeah. And in *Invisible Girl* you've got Saffyre who's seventeen and Georgia who's fifteen . . . which is obviously keeping up with that pattern.'

'I noticed the same in Martin Amis,' I begin, ready to discuss the baby Marmaduke in 1989's *London Fields*, and the twins Marius and Marco in 1995's *The Information*, but Lisa leaps in.

'Martin Amis!' she shrieks. 'That's who I was trying to remember.'

'I was going to say!' I protest. 'But I thought you would have known, if you meant Martin Amis.'

'Exactly! Exactly. Yes, that's exactly whose name I'd forgotten.'

And that fills in the previous blank: *The Wonderful World of Dave*, if it had been published in 2009, would have announced Lisa Jewell's shift into a Martin Amis style.

It's doubtful whether the two authors have ever been grouped together before. Amis has been described as 'aggressively competitive . . . a warrior of words, in battle against the forces of mediocrity, as represented by the journalist, the genre writer, the hack biographer, all of whom he remorselessly slays'. Lisa's work, on the other hand is praised as 'more full of warmth than a duck-feather duvet and just as gentle'.

But they do have elements in common. Lisa's earlier novels, in particular, find humour in grotesques, and in the body horror of extreme hangovers and illness. On the first page of *Thirtynothing*, Dig wakes up, finding that his head 'appeared to have had a large shipment of ball-bearings dumped in it overnight, while his blood felt as if it had been transfused with silica and come to a grinding, desiccated halt somewhere around his temples'. Here is Amis's description of Gregory's flu in *Success*: 'I awoke with a body full of heavy water, as if my internal mass had condensed overnight.'

Terry, in *Success*, enjoys 'a spectacular hawk in the gutter'; the equally grim expectorations of Gervase, in *A Friend of the Family*, are described using the same evocative word: he 'wandered towards the washbasin in the corner of the bedroom, leant down over it and in one practised action hawked up the contents of his lungs'. Amis pushes language further into the baroque and is prepared to reduce his characters to carnivalesque monsters for comic and linguistic effect, but there is a similar fascination with, to paraphrase Lisa's description of Amis's work, the ugly behaviour of young men in London, and the indignities of ugly bodies.

Even when these young men tidy themselves up, the process is described with a similar creative indulgence. Nadine imagines that Dig would have 'made an extra-special effort tonight, polished his teeth, perfumed his neck, deodorized his trainers, combed his eyebrow, shined his hair.' Effete Gregory, in *Success*, tells us: 'I'll brush my hard and brilliant teeth, poke fun at my gypsyish hair'; while his unfortunate half-brother Terry needs long minutes of brushing and sponging to prise his eyes open and shift the 'dry paving of dust' from his mouth every morning.

The concept of a character writing a novel is also very Amis – *The Information* centres on a rivalry between authors – and Amis appears surprisingly often in Lisa's fictional world. Freddie, in *Watching You*, is obsessed with *The Rachel Papers*. Joy remembers seeing the film adaptation at the Odeon Haymarket, one Valentine's Day. One of the clues uncovered by Ana in *One-Hit Wonder* is a letter from Kingsley Amis to his friend Philip Larkin. But there is one Lisa Jewell character whose direct address most closely echoes the 1980s Amis style, somewhere between Gregory's prissily aloof confessions and Terry's pathetic neediness:

> And so then what? What happened between then, sixteen-year-old me in my underwear on a nylon coverlet in a cheap hotel room watching the news, and middle-aged me now?
>
> Do you want to know? Do you care?
>
> Well, I got a job. I worked in an electrical repair shop in Pimlico. It was owned by a mad Bangladeshi family who couldn't care less for my back story so long as I turned up to work on time.

(Terry in *Success*: 'I do a job . . . (Do you do one?)'

There was a cute boy there. I'd caught his eye when I sat in reception. I waited outside the office until lunchtime and then I caught up with him as he left the office. His name was Josh. Of course. Everyone's name is Josh these days.

I took him back to my flat and cooked for him and fucked him and, of course, because I was only using him, he fell totally in love with me.

(Gregory in *Success*: 'People always want to fuck me far more than I want to fuck them.')

Lisa's character is called Henry Lamb, the charmingly creepy, creepily charming anti-hero of *The Family Upstairs*: and he's about to come back.

Henry and His Fans

18 February 2021

'I am Henry Lamb. I am forty-two years old.' The words below are blurred by a sepia Instagram filter; but those two sentences were enough to make 'everyone lose their shit,' Lisa says, 'as if Harry Styles had just posted about a One Direction reunion.' This was the first glimpse Lisa's fans had of the sequel to *The Family Upstairs*, and the crowd went wild.

In our first conversation, Lisa told me, 'I never write for readers,' but she nevertheless feels a need to manage her brand, which of course involves a dynamic with her fans. 'I am professionally bound now to have a social media presence,' she tells me, 'and, for the most part, I enjoy it.'

'I read an article about a year ago, just at the point when my American publishers were trying to get me to really dig deep into social media, and there was a line in it that said authors who perceive themselves as a brand are the ones who really become successful. And I thought: Oh, maybe I should perceive myself as a brand. But I just . . . can't do it. Unless the brand is just being me.'

'I mean, that is a brand.'

'Yeah. Yeah. But I can't be one of those people who puts a filter on and pretends I'm having a perfect life. Though I don't know if readers of female domestic thrillers have any pre-conceived idea about what the writer of such a book should look like.'

'Well, think about Marian Keyes,' I suggest. 'Her slogan is *Trust Marian*. Like a big sister figure.'

'Exactly. That's the brand. And she has not messed with her brand. She hasn't blurred any lines with genre. And she's intense online. She just puts her arms out to the reader and pulls them to her bosom. I can't quite go that deep with it. But I think *you* know by now that you can trust my intentions when I write a book. I think I'm a trustworthy writer.'

'Umm,' I say, dragging the word out for far too long. 'I think your shifting between genres makes you a different sort of proposition as a writer.'

'Well, perhaps for those readers who've been with me from the start,' she says a little sharply.

Slightly chastened, I move on, casting back to her earlier comment. 'You don't write for readers, you said. Your last rewrite of *The Night She Disappeared* brought it up to an internal standard of quality, where *you* were satisfied it was good. But doesn't quality depend on the reader? Or do you have your own sense of whether a book is "good", independent of sales, reviews, feedback and so on? Is a book really finished without readers?'

'Right,' she says flatly. Sometimes my conversations with Lisa feel like a chat with a friend. This doesn't. 'Well, I'm still feeling a bit itchy about *The Night She Disappeared*. It's going off to the copy-editor next week, and when it comes back I want to add a few more layers on to the layers.'

'Really?'

'Yes, because the plot with Sophie and "Dig Here" was such a neat idea, and I think I can make it work a bit harder. So with this one, I'm feeling that it's not finished yet, but quite often, by the time it goes to the copy-editor, it's finished. Unless the copy-editor thinks it's not finished, and that there are lots more issues to address, in which case I carry on.'

'So you change a novel right up to the end?'

'Oh, yeah. Yeah, but it's kind of finessing. It's like a lump of clay, and you've turned it into a bird, then it looks like a bird, and it clearly is a bird, but you know you could make it better.'

'So there comes a point where . . . not that you think it's perfect, or good enough, but . . . you think: This is ready now?'

'Ready!' Lisa enthuses. 'I think *ready* is a really good word. Good enough would have done, but ready is much better.'

So *ready* is a matter of Lisa's satisfaction with the work (as long as her copy-editor approves). Her sense of a novel's quality comes from within, independent of how it sells and what her fans might think; an author-centred standard of value, very different from the reader-focused model proposed by Roland Barthes (but then, Barthes was writing about the French novelist Honoré de Balzac, who died in 1850 – he never had the opportunity to ask Balzac whether his work felt finished without a reader).

According to Barthes and the many scholars who have continued his approach to literature and culture since the 1960s, I – the one holding the published novel – am the most important figure, not Lisa at her word processor. My reading of a text matters, not hers. I've been told that for years. Barthes said it forcefully, proposing that any text is comprised of multiple writings:

> . . . but there is one place where this multiplicity is focused and that place is the reader, not . . . the author. The reader is the space on which all the quotations that make up a writing are inscribed . . .

The meaning of a text, he concludes, lies not in its origin (the author) but in its final destination. But my interpretations, like those of reviewers and online fans, don't seem to affect Lisa's own effortlessly confident belief that she knows the truth of her work. Rather than the democracy of meaning proposed by the last fifty-odd years of literary criticism and cultural studies, this is a hierarchy based on the common sense that Lisa is right because she wrote it, and others are wrong because they misread it. Her own authentic understanding of each novel is kept distinct and separate, like an original artefact stored at home, while the multiple alternate interpretations that circulate in the world are, at best, like cover versions and bootlegs. The academic theory of authorship, audience and meaning that I've trusted throughout my entire career as a student, lecturer and professor simply doesn't work when I present it to an actual bestselling author.

I try one more time, clinging to the structures of familiar theory even as she dismantles them: not with malice, more with bewilderment.

'What I mean by saying is a book finished until someone's read it . . . I, and millions of other people, have completed the book with our reactions, our responses. Do you know what I mean?'

'. . . Nnnnyeah,' Lisa says carefully.

'Like, you've finished the book, but . . .' I'm struggling, running dry of ideas. 'But I've got my own version, if you see what I mean.'

'Yes! You've got your own version of the book.' She's happy to agree that, but it's as if I'm a toddler presenting her with a scrawled drawing of *The Family Upstairs*; fascinating and endearing, in a home-made sort of way.

And yet she does seem to care about feedback, whether it's the generous *Late Review* response to *Ralph's Party*, or the way her books have been sidelined by the broadsheets into round-ups of 'chick lit' and 'crime', or a Mumsnet thread that picked apart supposedly implausible aspects of *I Found You*, or a critical Facebook group.

'So the other night I was just flicking through my phone, at about midnight, and I stumbled on to this Facebook discussion, where someone had started off by saying, I'm thirty chapters into *The Family Upstairs* by Lisa Jewell and I just can't get into it . . . is it worth me persevering? There were sixty-eight replies to this woman's question. And I blithely went in, thinking: Well, some people are going to say they didn't like it, and some people are going to say, No, I loved it, stick with it, it gets really good, keep going. And basically, of the sixty-eight replies, sixty of them were going nah, I didn't like it either. Couldn't get on with it. Boring, ridiculous, didn't know what was going on, two of the characters had names that began with the same letter . . . and it was kind of jaw-dropping. Obviously, I know that lots of people don't like it, and I know that it's got a certain number of one-star and two-star reviews on Amazon, but to see this massive body of negative opinion . . .'

'I'd hate that,' I offer. But she's not wounded, hurt or haunted; she's baffled.

'It was the fourth-bestselling book in the country last year, and loads of people absolutely loved it, and I get all these messages from people saying it reignited their love for reading. So the people on Facebook read that book . . . and it was a different book. And that's a really hard thing to get your head around. How can it be a good book and a bad book at the same time? How can it be gripping, and yet boring at the same time? It's the same book. It was a bit of a headfuck, that.'

We have stumbled back on to the same page. One of the classic articles of audience studies, the catchily titled 'Tendency Systems and the Effects of a Movie Dealing with a Social Problem,' written by Charles Winick in 1963, collates very different responses to the Frank Sinatra film *The Man with the Golden Arm* and concludes that for the various diverse members of the audience, 'it would appear that the movie was almost a different movie'. The concept of one text with multiple meanings is something I've embraced and accepted for decades. It hadn't struck me that for someone in Lisa's position, this would be a paradox like Schrödinger's Cat – *how can something be good and bad at the same time?*

'I think that's something you can't think about too much, as a writer.' She shrugs. 'You can't be trying to write books for those sixty people on that thread. You can't. You have to write the book for your most enthusiastic reader. And make it a book that they will love.'

It seems a wonderful, warm place to leave things, and we say goodbye for a week; but Lisa dwells on the subject, then mails me several days later with a follow-up to our earlier discussion. She doesn't consider herself an academic by any stretch – 'I hated learning,' she tells me, 'and only passed six O Levels, in a school where ninety per cent of girls passed nine or more' – but her commitment to *thinking*, to the re-examination of ideas and rigorous, deep reflection, makes her more impressive to me than the majority of philosophers.

> The conversation we had about failure and me being terrified. What I was trying to express, not very well, is that what I fear is letting people down, not failure per se. The terror is of writing a book that people don't like. At this point in my career, as successful as I have recently become, I'm now at the very bottom of a tall house of cards, holding it all up; above me are my readers, the ones who use money they work hard for to buy my words because they have a certain expectation of the experience of reading those words. Above the readers are my publishers, the ones who invest in me, work hard for me, use me to support other areas of the

business that are less profitable. Also tucked into the house of cards is my family, who I support financially. So that is the terror, that I do something wrong and the book is not good and the readers are disappointed and the publishers lose money and I stop making money and the whole house of cards collapses.

This brings us neatly back to the idea of success (and *Success*). Sean London, in *A Friend of the Family*, has won an award and a considerable advance for his debut novel, but is tormented by the fragility of his situation:

> . . . suddenly he'd remember how precarious this 'happiness' he'd achieved actually was. It all hinged on being 'successful' – and being successful wasn't like being a man, or being tall. It wasn't guaranteed for ever. Success could be taken away from you, just like that – or rather it could *slip away*. And where would Sean be without this 'success', without the aura that being 'successful' conferred upon him?

Lisa's anxieties are less selfish than Sean's. Rather than personal failure, she fears letting people down, and feels a tremendous sense of responsibility to all the people who choose to spend their own hard-earned money on her work. Despite her strong sense of authorial ownership over her characters and plots – contrary to what Roland Barthes might tell us – I was struck by Lisa's compassion for and connection to readers in this further explanation. She owes them a debt. They deserve to have their expectations met.

And now I do believe her. Lisa Jewell is genuinely terrified.

Characters Flat and Round

In 1927, Trinity College, Cambridge, welcomed E. M. Forster, who was by that point celebrated for *A Room with a View*, *Howard's End* and the more recent *A Passage to India*, to speak about 'Aspects of the Novel'. His lectures – vastly informed but perhaps surprisingly informal – were published as a book in 1927, retaining their witty, engaging style. One of their key legacies, and an idea we still frequently apply today, is the notion that characters can be 'flat' or 'round'. Mrs Micawber from *David Copperfield*, for instance, is flat enough to be summarised in a sentence: 'I never will desert Mr Micawber.' She says it, she sticks to her word, 'and there she is'. Becky Sharp, from *Vanity Fair*, is 'round . . . she waxes and wanes and has facets like a human being,' while Dickens's 'Pip and David Copperfield attempt roundness, but so diffidently that they seem more like bubbles than solids.'

Occasionally, says Forster, a flat character can pop into roundness: Lady Bertram, in Austen's *Mansfield Park*, breaks from her consistent formula at one point and surprises the reader: 'the disc has suddenly extended and become a little globe.' We can apply the same ideas to Lisa's work.

On the original front cover of *Ralph's Party*, upstairs flatmate Cheri is depicted as a Jessica Rabbit-shaped silhouette, and as a character she rarely escapes that role. Her primary job in the novel is to be a temptress, a *femme fatale* who can be placed in men's way to lure them into a new plot development, like a useful piece in a board game. But she starts to struggle against her two-dimensionality when she sees the advantages of being 'famous for being good, not for being a bitch . . . she'd be a heroine, everyone would love her.' The superficiality is still there, but her motivation shifts just enough to suggest a sense of change, like a non-player character in a video game who suddenly decides to go in a different direction, giving the illusion of independence. In Cheri's final appearance we see her wondering at 'the joys of goodness', with 'a look of surprise, gratitude and pleasure slowly pinkening her face.' She has not become a fully rounded character, but she has perhaps evolved from a flat cartoon into a CGI animation.

Smith, by contrast, is reduced in the finale from a protagonist with the same complexity as his flatmates Jem and Ralph to a slapstick stereotype, a clowning, gurning figure of fun. His behaviour accelerates from gentle comic drama to farce:

> He slammed his drink down on the bar, threw himself to his knees and grasped Cheri's hands in his. 'Oh, God, Cheri! I love you. I've always loved you!' His voice rang out around the room; he didn't care who heard! . . . Smith slavered wet kisses onto the backs of Cheri's hands.

As the dialogue becomes crammed with shouty capitals and exclamation marks, and the guests at Ralph's party start to weep, vomit and throw wild punches, Smith is left in abject humiliation, unconscious in his own filth, and the tone of the novel has altered to the extent that his friends laugh rather than sympathise. Smith has been flattened into a *Viz* caricature, the butt of gross humour.

One of the strongest aspects of Lisa's sequel, *After the Party*, is that it gives Smith breathing space to fill out again, to inflate and expand. If the end of *Ralph's Party* turned him into something from a crude 1990s sitcom – Rik Mayall in *Bottom*, or Martin

Clunes in *Men Behaving Badly* – *After the Party* plays like an adult drama, starring the older Mayall and Clunes: designed for them to show off their subtler acting chops. Here are Ralph and Smith in their final scene together:

> They both leaned back then, their beers held in their laps, their faces lit by the evening sun, two decent men, no longer best mates, but at peace with themselves and with each other for the first time in eleven years.

Fade to black. Roll credits over an acoustic cover of Coldplay. The tone is entirely different, and the narrator seems to quietly observe the characters rather than shove them hastily into place, pull them into funny positions and put words in their mouths. And to her credit, Lisa still feels bad about what she did to Smith, decades ago: 'The only character I feel I really let down was Smith in *Ralph's Party*. He'd been much more nuanced and "real" in my first version of the book, but I ripped it all away from him in the rewrite . . .' (So there were regrets woven into the fairy-tale origin story? I'd have to tug further on that thread in future.)

Of course, characters also get to know each other better during the course of a story, whether through romance, detection or the hybrid between the two that typifies Lisa's novels. Ana, investigating the leftover traces of her sister in *One-Hit Wonder*, finds that Bee is 'growing in her head moment by moment, turning from a two-dimensional cartoon character into a real human being'. And when Joy begins dating George, in *Vince and Joy*, he gradually reveals new dimensions; perhaps too many.

George starts off as an appalling prospect, an unattractive geek – 'whichever way she looked at it and however hard she tried, he just wasn't her type' – but reveals endearing quirks over the course of the evening, to the point where Joy realises she's open to seeing him again.

. . . she noticed that he had a tiny dimple on his left cheek. And as she noticed this, she also noticed that she was actually enjoying herself here in this restaurant with this man with the strange hair and the John Major glasses . . .

Now he evolves from a throwaway figure who could have been good for a single bad-date scene into a fully fledged character. We learn about him as Joy does, through the accumulation of detail:

> Joy discovered that George was an Aquarian, that his mother was dead and his father was a distant and unpleasant memory, that he'd bought his Stockwell flat with his mother's inheritance, that he'd just split up with a long-term girlfriend whom he described as a 'complete psycho' . . .

This is just a backstory info-dump, of course, but we also build a sense of George through glimpses of his behaviour. 'George had a Mr Whippy with a Flake in it, proclaiming, possibly disingenuously, but certainly charmingly, that he'd never had one before in his life and expressing great excitement at the prospect.' From the slightly old-fashioned language that describes him, as well as the behaviour it describes – the prose could almost be Austen, apart from the Mr Whippy – we start to see, and enjoy, an eccentric Englishness, one which could perhaps be played by Benedict Cumberbatch in a romcom role, or Eddie Redmayne at his most awkward. George declares:

> 'I'd go so far as to say that you're the least pointy girl I've ever met . . . I'd describe you more as . . . more as . . . delicately, *spectacularly* pretty – like a beautiful Meissen teacup. If that makes any sense.'

By now George has gathered a kind of Lewis Carroll whimsy

about him – an odd magic, perhaps, but a long way from John Major. 'He really was a funny-looking fellow [Joy decides], gauche, unfashionable, middle-aged in his manner and appearance, yet so switched on to the modern world. He was a walking dichotomy. And Joy had absolutely no idea what to make of him.'

Joy's pleasant confusion is not discomforting for the reader. We are used to this sort of puzzlement in a romantic comedy. We might guess from the title *Vince and Joy* that George will not turn out to be the main love interest by the final pages, but we might expect him perhaps to excuse himself charmingly when he realises Vince and Joy are meant for each other, and to find his own happiness with one of Joy's friends. This doesn't happen.

George continues to evolve beyond the point where a classical romcom character usually stops, until the accumulation of contradictory details becomes hard to process. Joy next visits his flat, which is furnished with 'a very small television balanced on a huge cardboard box, two walls of bookshelves constructed from unpainted chipboard and some blue stripy wallpaper with a sheen to it.' The place is freezing. The toilet is 'so icy cold that it left Joy breathless when she sat down.' Returning to the living room, she finds that he has changed into 'a pair of belted jeans and a thin green T-shirt. Joy missed his smart blue suit already.' George, who has been established as a gentlemanly misfit, then puts on an Arrested Development CD and rolls 'a gigantic spliff'. As Joy says, ' "You just keep confounding all my expectations." ' George responds by pulling out old photographs of himself as a punk.

What do we make of George now? Maybe he could still be played by Benedict Cumberbatch, but in an entirely different, perhaps more sinister mode. A reader familiar with Lisa's previous books might try to make sense of him in those terms – because while *Vince and Joy* is not a sequel, it does exist in the same intertextual network as her other novels, part of what we might call a 'Jewelliverse', a fictional world governed by similar motifs, patterns, attitudes and sensibilities. We have seen, for instance, that Lisa provides clues to her characters through their interior design, and when we enter George's flat with Joy, we might think back, for guidance, to the apartment Nadine shares with Phil in the earlier *Thirtynothing*:

> The flat smelled overpoweringly and depressingly of damp and mildew. No attempt had been made to personalize it or to camouflage its ugliness, other than the rows of rather pretentious and badly composed black and white photographs in Clip-frames which hung on nearly every wall . . .

If furniture reveals character, both men's flats are full of red flags. In *Thirtynothing,* Phil turns out to be overbearing and controlling, robbing Nadine of her confidence, and when we meet him again during another dismal pub date, he spins her contradictory sob stories that she struggles to fit into her earlier impression of him. The fact that his character doesn't quite make sense ultimately finds a simple explanation: he was lying.

So I assumed, at this point of *Vince and Joy*, that George was lying, too. His past must be invented. His suit is borrowed. The photos of him as a punk were faked. When he becomes a snobbish bully – training Joy 'to say "sitting room" not "lounge"', to say "napkin" not "serviette"' – my suspicions were confirmed. He's another Phil, a pathetic man propping himself up with falsehoods. That both Phil and George are reminiscent of Ana's ex in *One-Hit Wonder* – Ana remembers 'a damp flat with a shared bathroom and a six-year relationship with Hugh, the highly intelligent but occasionally overbearing guy she'd lost her virginity to' – only seals the deal.

I told Lisa about my guesses when I was halfway through the book. She said nothing, waiting for me to find out.

I was wrong again. My theories, based on my expectations from Lisa's other novels, made sense, but they weren't correct. It turns out that George isn't lying, though he is unpleasant. He genuinely possesses all those incompatible qualities. He's a cold and controlling man who is also quirky and eccentric, and also likes Arrested Development and gigantic spliffs. George, Joy discovers, 'though he saw himself as liberal and free-spirited, was a stickler for etiquette and tradition'.

To a certain extent, adding layers and details creates a sense of three-dimensionality. Smith, in *After the Party,* gains subtle light, shade and form, like a simple cartoon drawn again as a more detailed sketch. When we leave him, we feel satisfied: we have come as far as we need to with this character; his arc has settled gently to earth, and he is comfortably grounded. But George seems uneasily alive beyond the book. He seems to break through into a fourth or fifth dimension, escaping definition. There is more to him than we see on the page. There is too much of him for a romantic comedy to contain.

Lennard J. Davis makes a similar point in his work of literary criticism, *Resisting Novels*. He uses Flaubert's *Madame Bovary* as his case study, citing her key quality as capriciousness, but almost paradoxically, *consistent* capriciousness. 'If Flaubert had begun to add more qualities to her, her character would have become diluted . . .'

If the author had decided that Emma Bovary also had an interest in neoclassical architecture, Davis points out, she would start to lose her clear and comprehensible form, rather than gain more definition. 'In essence, the feeling that we get that we are watching a complex character is largely an illusion created by the opposite.' Complexity, in fiction, is made up of a relatively small number of traits, easy for the reader to process.

So, George paradoxically became undermined as a character through excess; by having too much character. But there was an explanation. Lisa wrote to me:

> George is an almost carbon copy of my first husband, who
> I met in the small ads at the back of *Loot* in 1990 and who
> I was married to from 1991–1995. And gorgeous Vince is
> a lightly fictionalised version of my first boyfriend. Jem and
> Joy are both the closest I've ever come to writing myself
> autobiographically (which is why they're both elfin and petite
> and dark; to contrast against my own physical appearance).

There's the answer. George feels like too much for the page because he is a real person crammed into the conventions of fiction, and real people are a mess of contradictions. As the poet Walt Whitman put it:

> Very well then . . . I contradict myself;
> I am large . . . I contain multitudes.

I'm also reminded of a couplet by the Swiss writer Conrad Ferdinand Meyer, which I originally encountered in German:

> *Das heisst: Ich bin kein ausgeklügelt Buch.*
> *Ich bin ein Mensch mit seinem Widerspruch.*

It translates as: 'That is: I am no clever work of fiction. / I am a man, with all his contradiction.' Of course, the same applies to women. When I asked Lisa whether abusive men were a running theme in her novels because of her own experience, she deflected with a list of all her kind and generous male characters, and a catalogue of her female villains. But the same type of intelligent, overbearing, bullying boyfriend recurs in *Thirtynothing* (Phil),

One-Hit Wonder (Hugh), and *Vince and Joy* (George), coupled with a young woman who drifts into the relationship because she can't find a good enough reason to say no; and Lisa freely admits that these aspects are based on her life.

Though she's fictionalised and simplified herself into Joy and Jem, Lisa Jewell would not make a good character in one of her own books. She would not be satisfying. There is too much that wouldn't fit; too much that wouldn't make immediate sense. She writes only for herself but is afraid of letting down her readers. She doesn't redraft her prose as she writes – 'I just go, go, go . . . I make sure I don't spend too long overthinking things' – but is prepared to junk plotlines, chapters, sections, even entire novels: 'I have abandoned books thirty, forty, fifty thousand words in and started again or written something else instead.' She cried when writing Ellie Mack's letter from beyond, on the last page of *Then She Was Gone*, but approached the rest of that novel's kidnap and torture with businesslike detachment. ('I can most definitely write about a made-up thing happening to a made-up person without finding it too gruelling,' she assured an interviewer at the time.)

'You care about your characters, though, don't you?' I press her.

'Deeply.'

'I don't want to keep hammering on at this . . .' I am hammering on, though, like a cop trying to break an emotionless suspect. '. . . you've said what you've said, but . . . it didn't upset you when Gray watched his dad die, in *I Found You*?'

'It does now!' she protests, laughing. 'I can't explain why I don't feel emotionally involved in the moment. I think I'm just too busy writing it to feel it. You're telling me that this made you feel a certain way, and reminding me of things I've written, and I'm considering them from this perspective and I think *that's really sad! Those poor people!* But I'm still not really feeling it.'

'And is that what you want? Is my emotional reaction gratifying to you?'

'Fantastic! The bottom line of what I want from a reader is them saying they couldn't put it down.'

'Well, I'm saying I had to put it down. 'Cause I couldn't stand it any more. And then I picked it up again. But I needed a breather in between.'

'I like both reactions equally.'

'I think my reaction is better,' I insist. 'I had to put it down, thinking *I can't believe how bad this is*. I mean,' I add hurriedly, 'bad as in awful, unbearable.'

'I know what you mean.'

I keep babbling. 'That's not my quote about your novels, *I can't believe how bad they are*. I mean this is bad for the characters, I can't bear it any more. So I had to put it down, and then I had to pick it up again.'

'Yes,' Lisa reassures me. 'That's equally good. I don't get that so much.'

We say goodbye; and then a funny thing happens.

' "I googled you after you left," ' headteacher Jacinta tells Sophie Beck in *The Night She Disappeared*. ' "Something about you didn't quite stack up." '

Lisa has started googling me and wants to know more. She is intrigued, but can only find a kind of shell online: a shorthand, almost a two-dimensional cartoon. She remembers me from our first encounter simply as a man in a yellow suit. She doesn't want to just be interviewed; she wants to interview me in return, to have a conversation, to become acquainted.

'I need to humanise and disarm you,' she writes now. It

sounds like a gentle threat: like a nurse warning 'sharp scratch!' as she readies the needle.

> It feels really important to me to break you open into a real human being, because, having thought about this quite deeply over the weekend, this is at the root of who I am as a person and as a writer – I need to humanise people. All people. Anyone who talks to me. Anyone who serves me. Anyone who looks at me. I need to see them and know them.

I don't resist, because I know she's right. This needs to be a two-way process. She needs to sense who I am, as she would with a character, or she can't continue – just as she had to drop Phin from the new novel because she didn't have enough of a handle on him. And this is perhaps the core of all Lisa's novels, whatever the genre. One interviewer calls it empathy: 'Not only do you identify and understand some difficult characters, but you ask your readers to do the same.' 'Yes, absolutely,' she replied at the time, and I can hear her saying that now, after all our conversations.

> I feel sad, for example, that a lot of readers didn't see the two sides to Lily in *I Found You*. I tried so hard to make her nuanced and not just a two-dimensional cold-hearted witch. But the majority of readers disliked her and found her gaucheness and abruptness impossible to get past. I thought she was really funny and just trying her hardest in a terrible situation in a strange country with no cultural cues to help her. And this was why I took the reader straight into the heart of Noelle in *Then She Was Gone*. I couldn't see the point of writing about a person doing a terrible thing unless you could make the reader at least attempt

to understand why they might have done it. Otherwise you're just creating characters to move the story along, not to give the story layers.

The same is true of Henry Lamb, and Smith, and George, and certainly Freddie, who initially comes across as a creepy teenage voyeur in *Watching You*. His revelation about Romola – that she is a person in her own right, with doubts and dreams – transforms him for us, just as it transforms his sense of her. He takes a deep breath and expands at that moment, gaining dimensions; his humanising of her humanises him in turn.

This moment of transformation recurs across Lisa's work: an unmasking, which adds as it reveals. Bernie sees the truth of Gervais early in *A Friend of the Family*:

> His cheeks were slightly pock-marked and Bernie suddenly saw him as the spotty, awkward adolescent he'd once been. The black leather and the tattoo and the dyed hair were just a costume. He was no hard man, she thought, just a little boy, like her boys, like *all* boys.

Gervais then breaks down the barriers that surround the other male characters. To Sean, he urges, ' "You're just kidding yourself. Putting on an act. Building walls around yourself . . . what I see is a very scared man who's trying to pretend not to care about someone." '

In *Thirtynothing*:

> Dig thought to himself that tonight was the first time in a week that he'd seen the old Delilah, the tender, vulnerable, scared girl he'd fallen in love with . . . It was her *vulnerability* more than anything that made Dig love her . . . She was like a lost little girl, all alone in the world, full of secrets and pain.

Con feels a similar rush of feeling towards Daisy, in *31 Dream Street*, when she reveals that she has cystic fibrosis.

> Her smallness, her *translucence*, took on a new and unsettling significance in light of what she'd just told him. The milky alabaster of her skin had a hint of blue underlying it and her fine hair looked fragile and brittle. She wasn't a fairy or a nymph. She wasn't a Condé Nast flibbertigibbet. She was ill. Seriously ill.

If this seems to switch one sexist trope – the idealised object of desire – for another stereotype – the fragile invalid and 'lost little girl' – Lisa's later novels make a more sophisticated substitution. Freddie's epiphany involves seeing Romola not as vulnerable and in need of protection, but simply as a human being with mundane teenage concerns like his own.

Owen, the incel from *Invisible Girl*, is obliged to take a training course to rethink his views on gender, and also experiences a revelation. 'He had never, ever had a conversation, an interlude, an encounter with a woman without the primary thought in his head being that she was a woman.' He asks how he can stop. The guest speaker advises him:

> 'Say to yourself, This is a human being wearing a red jacket. Or, This is a human being with a northern accent . . . Or, This is a human being with a problem who needs my help. Own your reaction. Work round it.'

Owen puts it into action (*This is a human being with brown shoes on*) and 'it broke the spell.' He says sincerely, ' "Thank you. Thank you so much." '

And this is one reason that Lisa Jewell could never really write like Martin Amis; not like the younger Amis, anyway, the famous Amis of *The Rachel Papers*, *Success* and *London Fields*. For this Amis, women are best presented flat, like a glossy magazine. His male characters find their desire wilting when they discover any traces of humanity – smells, stains, unshaven skin – and even react with undisguised horror. In *Success*, Gregory is disgusted by a whole catalogue of normal bodily features: 'post-coital tears . . . pre-menstrual pimples . . . a dented backside, tropical armpits', and indeed anything that provides evidence of a woman as a living, breathing creature.

Gregory, like Henry Lamb, is an unreliable narrator, charismatic but not exactly admirable, and the author, while clearly enjoying Gregory's ripe language, also holds him up for mockery. Amis's writing about women during this period – there are similar passages in *The Rachel Papers* and *London Fields* – is knowingly reminiscent of his fellow satirist Jonathan Swift, whose poem 'The Lady's Dressing Room' from 1732 comes disturbingly close to Gregory's attitudes of 250 years later. The poem's male protagonist, Strephon, steals into the private chamber of his beloved Celia. Accustomed to seeing her as a finished article, 'arrayed in lace, brocade and tissues', Strephon is repulsed by what he finds: evidence that women have functioning bodies.

> Hard by a filthy basin stands,
> Fouled with the scouring of her hands;
> The basin takes whatever comes
> The scrapings of her teeth and gums,
> A nasty compound of all hues,
> For here she spits, and here she spews.
> But oh! it turned poor Strephon's bowels,
> When he beheld and smelled the towels,
> Begummed, bemattered, and beslimed
> With dirt, and sweat, and earwax grimed.

Though Ralph's response to having Jem as a new flatmate – he pokes around her bedroom, examining her bras – is arguably no less creepy, we would not find a character in early Amis comfortably listening to the woman he fancies 'peeing, that strange gushing, jerky sound of girl's pee hitting water', as Ralph later does when he and Jem co-habit on friendly terms. And when Con discovers that Daisy needs an unglamorous daily physio treatment to loosen the mucus in her lungs, he volunteers to be trained, even though she protests that ' "it's a bit like going to the loo with the door open . . . Not very romantic." '

Moving from the bathroom and back to the wardrobe for a final example: working-class Terry's clothes are described in *Success* – by his sneering half-brother Gregory – with such contempt that the language descends into racial slurs. 'He favours paint-by-numbers colour schemes – an absurd motley of [n-word] primaries and charwoman pastels.'

Tallulah, in *The Night She Disappeared*, is also working-class. Dressing up for a rare night out, she tells her mum she's going to wear:

'That top . . . you know, the one we got when we were at the Belfry last week. With the hearts on it. With my black jeans.'

'Oh yes,' her mum replies, 'that'll look lovely.'

Tallulah smiles gratefully. She knows 'it's not the most amazing top in the world', but she can tug it down to hide her baby belly; and she keeps checking during the evening, making sure the fabric meets the top of her jeans. There's no contempt or scorn in this account of an imperfect young woman without much money, who can appraise herself as, at best, 'quite pretty'; the author doesn't patronise, or invite us as readers to feel pity at Tallulah's modest efforts. At the heart of Lisa's novels are the characters, and – particularly in her later work – they are all treated with at least a degree of compassion.

The next time we talk, Lisa has a list of questions for me in front of her. She asks about my plans, my regrets, my habits, my tastes. We begin to share stories, one for one, quid pro quo, like something from a folktale; like wary demi-gods or goblins in a Neil Gaiman graphic novel exchanging their true names and histories, like Clarice and Hannibal trading information between the bars of his cell.

One of the stories Lisa tells me is about going into a shabby pub, when she was seventeen, with a female friend.

'Two much older men came and sat with us; they were drunk and scruffy. They started off with all the "hello, lovely ladies, and how are you both tonight" and we could have got up and walked away, but we didn't, we talked to them, we humanised them, we asked them questions, we ended up having a proper conversation with them about their wives and their kids and their jobs and we left and we were all equals. We had disarmed them. And that's kind of my MO. I like to disarm. I *need* to disarm. It's the only way you can get to the true heart of a person.'

I recognise and respect what she wants (*needs*) to do. She wants to make me into a rounded character. She wants us to be equals.

Sequels

Prior to this new book, Lisa 'always swore blind that I would never do another sequel': she told Mumsnet in 2012 that . . .

> . . . I did make an exception with *After the Party*, my sequel to *Ralph's Party*, because it was the ten-year anniversary of it being published and because I thought it would make my publishers happy. And the experience just proved my point to myself. I did not enjoy it. I unearthed two young, happy, redeemed people who had been on their 'journey', learned their lesson, found each other and kissed for the first time and I made their lives hell! In retrospect I wish I'd left them there on the sofa with the rest of their lives ahead of them. And so that is it for me and sequels.

What went wrong with *After the Party*? She's happy to go into more detail, years later, and reveal more bumps in the ride.

'I could tell my publishers were losing interest. My sales had plateaued at a level that was still high, but not enough to not be on their priority list any more. We were coming up for a contract renegotiation, and I just panicked a bit. That's the only time I've done that, throughout my whole career. And I thought, What would they like? What would make them happy? And I just threw it out there. I said, I could do a sequel to *Ralph's Party*. And even as I said it, I was hoping they'd say no.

'And then of course they jumped on it.' She smiles ruefully, looking away. 'And then I was stuck with it.'

She went back to *Ralph's Party* for reference, and 'couldn't read beyond the first chapters. It made my flesh crawl. Like seeing video footage of yourself when you were young and drunk and being a dick.' She appreciated the opportunity to rescue Smith from his flat, cartoonish ending, to lift him up and 'throw layers at him', in her phrase, but that was one of the few pleasures the sequel offered her. In fact, the book was never supposed to be pleasurable exactly, except as catharsis: rather than a romcom, it was an expression of repressed fury, channelled through Jem, about being shouldered with all the domestic responsibilities involved with two young children.

'I think there's a line in there about how *he'd allowed her to become a housewife?*' Lisa looks at me expectantly, inviting me to provide a line from her own novel. I blank on it.

'I don't know if it's exactly that,' I fumble, 'but that's Jem's energy all the way through . . . what happened to her previous self? *Where had the girl gone?*'

'Exactly,' says Lisa generously. 'Exactly.' (In fact, Lisa had remembered the line precisely – Ralph 'had allowed her to become a housewife' – while mine is cobbled together from phrases throughout the book.)

'And I was full of that resentment and anger. So I thought, I'm just going to go in and put it on the page raw, and real. And I delivered it to my editor at the time, and I could tell . . . she just hated it. She hated Jem. She was Team Ralph, which was the last thing I wanted to hear! It's like going to a friend to complain about your marriage, and they take your husband's side.' Lisa's hands are claws as she relives the frustration. 'Can you not see! Can you not see?'

I nod agreeably.

'And she made me rewrite pretty much every single thought or sentence that Jem had or said. So first of all, it was a book I didn't want to write, full stop, and secondly, it wasn't the book I'd intended it to be once I'd decided to write it.'

'So when you decided you'd go ahead with it, you thought, I'm going to do this in an honest way?'

'Correct,' she says firmly, in a way I now recognise as *very Lisa*. 'And then she made me soften it up. It's bitty, it doesn't have a solid narrative arc, and it doesn't take you on the kind of journey you expect to be taken on. I really struggled with it.'

'And that put you off sequels?'

'Oh, yes. I was already off sequels! I'd been asked so many times to do sequels to this, that and the other, and I'd always said I like meeting new people, and starting afresh.'

A sequel, of course, is the opposite. It involves not just a revisiting – waking up stories that have been put to bed and reopening what seem to be comfortably resolved conclusions – but a recap: a brief precis of the last book for readers who either don't remember or were never there. So *After the Party* requires Jem to walk, in the opening pages, past her old flat on Almanac Road, nostalgically recalling the period of the first novel, 'over twelve years ago . . . when Oasis were the most famous band in the country and football was, supposedly, coming home, when she was a child of only twenty-seven'. By the end of the Prologue, she and Karl have reminisced usefully about the night that concluded *Ralph's Party* – 'you have a very good memory,' Karl comments – and it's been made clear how much has changed since that happy ending ('Jem has begun to hate the weekly handover of the children').

In Book 20, the 'previously, on *The Family Upstairs*' task falls to Henry Lamb, who dispatches it, in his first chapter, with characteristic impatience. 'My sister moved in last year for reasons that I barely know how to begin to convey. The simple version is that she was homeless. The more complicated version would require me to write an essay' – or, of course, a novel. He provides a 'halfway version' instead, dealing briskly with the previous book's flashbacks and culminating in the headline that 'she and I are both millionaires.' Only one night, we realise, has passed since the epilogue of *The Family Upstairs*. As it currently stands, it would be a heavy backstory for the opening of a stand-alone novel, and I wonder whether many readers will come to this cold as a brand-new narrative, rather than as a quick refresher of a book they already know.

As we saw with Smith, a revisiting provides the opportunity for a form of revival: an opportunity to lift up flat characters, breathe new life into them and present them more subtly, with more dimension, from a different perspective. *After the Party* also attempts this form of rescue, less successfully, with Cheri, who pops up towards the end with her toast-coloured tan, vanilla hair and Prada glasses. Cheri, though, as I comment to Lisa, was such a stylised character that it's hard to imagine her inhabiting the more complex universe of *After the Party*; she's like a cartoon sashaying down a live-action London street.

Lisa agrees, pointing out the irony that Cheri was actually based on a real person. 'Called Kerry,' she adds, and laughs.

'An excellent disguise,' I remark. 'She'd never know.'

'Oh, but there's another thing about Cheri!' Lisa declares, raising a finger as she remembers. 'She had a whole storyline that my editor made me cut out. Because I wanted her to be three-dimensional. I wanted her to have as much space on the page as the other people in the house. So she had thousands and thousands of words, a story arc that was cut.'

'But the impression I always had, and that you confirmed, was that *Ralph's Party* was a pretty easy ride. I didn't realise you had to delete and rewrite.'

'Oh, yeah,' she says now, as if it was obvious.

'So, after you submitted the full manuscript to your agent, how much work did that go through before it was sent to publishers?'

'Well, my agent made me rewrite the whole ending. There was no party originally.'

I'm taken aback. 'So what was the book called?'

'It was called *Third Person*. As in, third person needed for a flat share in Battersea.'

'That's pretty good,' I admit, though I can't help thinking it's very similar to *Roommates Wanted*, the American title of *31 Dream Street*.

'And she made me rewrite the last third, which took me a good couple of months. Then she got me a publishing deal, and my editor made me cut out all the Cheri scenes. Because they were quite bleak, and dark. Because I hadn't sat down thinking I was writing chick lit . . . I'd thought I was writing a more serious book, so Cheri's chapters were also more serious. She has a terrible, messy abortion, for instance. Did that make it into the book?'

'I don't think so,' I reply, wondering if it was mentioned between scenes.

'There's a scene where she's actually, like . . . losing her baby into the toilet.'

'That definitely doesn't happen.'

'Does it not?' Lisa checks.

'Definitely not.' I push aside the image of a cartoon Cheri in a photorealistic, blood-smeared bathroom. 'So they paid you a small fortune, but made you cut a third of the book?'

'. . . Yeah.'

'They had a bidding war over it, but then said, a third of this book, I'm not sure about?'

'. . . Yes.'

'So, like, we love this, but . . .'

'But we don't love *her*. So can we get rid of her please.'

I sit back, lost for words, suddenly imagining a completely different, far darker novel, and also revising my sense of Lisa's effortless, fairy-tale entrance into publishing; this is more like a Disney princess arriving at the ball, then being told to come back when she's lost weight, cut her hair and found a better dress.

'It's funny, isn't it,' she goes on, as I struggle to process the information. 'Even as a writer, I read published novels and can't get my head around the fact that it didn't always look like that or read like that . . . you just have this strange sort of contract with the book, when you're reading it, that what you're reading is what the author intended. But so often, it's simply not the case.'

I'm in a uniquely privileged position with Lisa's new novel; I recognise that. I am reading what she originally and initially intended, at a point when it hasn't even been seen by her editor. I am the first person to read her drafts after she writes them, watching characters form and sometimes vanish, watching storylines take shape.

But our conversation nags at me. Is Lisa also rewriting her other stories; not just her fictions, but the ones that she presents as fact, about her life and career?

I check my notes. 'Whenever I think back to that period,' she'd insisted just a few weeks ago as I tried to dig deeper into her origin myth, 'all I can remember is feeling like I was in a dream or a fairy tale.'

A fairy tale in which she'd been obliged to cut a third of her first novel, losing thousands and thousands of words. It's true that folk tales can be grim – *Cinderella* originally involved the sisters slicing off their own toes and heels to fit the Prince's slipper – but to me, this seems at least to complicate the narrative of a smooth sailing towards success. Is she misremembering the story? Lisa sets me straight:

> It was exciting to rewrite the ending. I always find it exciting to work big changes into my novels because I always know that I'm doing something positive. This might strike you as a negative, but it never felt negative to me.

I believe her, of course. Lisa and I have a strange sort of contract, too – not a legal document, but an unspoken agreement based on trust. This arrangement will only work, we know, if we are both honest.

I've realised that she reveals the truth about herself in stages, on a need-to-know basis. She puts enough of herself on public display to give a convincing impression of being an open book, but she's more cautious than she first appears. Her 'brand' is an unpretentious shop with everything apparently on show, to hide the fact that the best stuff is in the back room, reserved, I assume, for close friends and family. And of course, this isn't a character flaw at all; it would be ridiculous to criticise her for keeping aspects of herself private. But if I'm trying to learn the deeper truth of Lisa Jewell, how long will it take before I've earned it?

Signs of the Times

Lisa's latest novels deal confidently with teenage slang (peng trainers, among others) and social media – Instagram, WhatsApp, Snapchat, TikTok and Snap Maps – but her earlier work has characters explaining what a modem is and how to download WAV files from 'the net'. ' "Techno-bimbo?" ' Zander asks Bee in 2001's *One-Hit Wonder*, as she marvels at the photos appearing on her screen 'slowly, line by line'. ' "They're websites," ' he informs her patronisingly. The most sophisticated device in *Ralph's Party* is a tape recorder: a 'tiny, state-of-the-art machine' that records for a then-impressive six hours. Even the sequel, set ten years later, surprised me when Ralph brought out a wallet of photographs to show Smith, rather than simply scrolling through his phone; in *Vince and Joy*, two decades before the launch of Tinder, Joy's workmates are overwhelmed by the idea that a girl could find 'love in the lonely hearts' and cluster around her, asking for a picture of her mystery boyfriend. ' "I'll see what I can do," ' Joy promises.

Over two decades, Lisa's writing reflects changes in contemporary culture – not just technology but fashion, décor, music, celebrities, even perfume (*One-Hit Wonder*, in a flashback to Ana's childhood, reminds us of a time when Anaïs Anaïs was everywhere). Most of the anachronisms capture the time of writing – hence the now-naïve, clunky comments about the internet in 2001 – but she set *Before I Met You* deliberately in 1995, 'because I wanted to have the experience of writing about people who couldn't use mobile phones. So there's a scene I really enjoyed where Betty has to go to the library to use telephone directories.' The story, uniquely among Lisa's work, includes an intertwined mystery from the distant past. Betty, investigating her family history in the 1990s, is stunned when her rich boss offers her a mobile, but her step-grandmother Arlette, waiting for urgent news in 1921, relies on telegrams. The Skinnydip phone cases carried by *Watching You*'s teens were the height of fashion in 2018, but will no doubt soon be as retro as a Motorola Razr. Even the development of text speak can date a novel in surprising ways: it's hard now not to read the name Lol, from *One-Hit Wonder*, as a dry abbreviation signifying mild amusement. ('"Ana! Hi! Lol."')

More subtly, background media grounds each novel in its cultural moment: in *One-Hit Wonder*, Patsy Palmer and Ronan Keating appear on the cover of gossip magazines, while *Thirty-nothing* uses *Dawson's Creek* as a modern reference. Brand names can even provide vital clues: a key plot point in *The Family Upstairs* depends on Miller recognising a sock in an empty attic bedroom as bearing '"the *current* Gap logo . . . they've only been using that for the past couple of years,"' and realising that Henry has stayed there recently.

Overseas readers lose a little of this cultural specificity, as the brands don't always translate directly. *Der Fremde am Strand* ('The Stranger on the Beach', or *I Found You*) struggles with Alice's 'Benetton family' and renders it as 'multicoloured' or 'motley', while *Ils Sont Chez Nous* ('They're in Our Home', or *The Family Upstairs*) copes with Libby's taste for French Connection, but flattens TK Maxx and House of Fraser into the far more generic 'furniture shop' and 'beauty products shop', stripping them of their distinct associations. American readers, for whom the biscuits in Lisa's books have to be translated into cookies, and cat food into kibble, may not fully grasp the implications of Robyn's dad, in *The Making of Us,* sporting Clarks shoes and Blue Harbour sweaters, and Lydia in the same novel opting for a Whistles top and Autograph jeans – especially subtle as Blue Harbour and Autograph are clothing lines within the same store, Marks & Spencer, but with completely different connotations.

Some cultural references become objectionably dated, though, rather than charmingly vintage. *The Truth About Melody Browne*, originally from 2009, was released in the US for the first time in early 2021, and rereading the proofs, Lisa remembers she was horrified by a scene in an internet café 'where Melody asks the girl sitting next to her for help logging into something or other' – not because of its quaint approach to technology, but because she described the other character as a fat Chinese girl.

'Ohh.' I wince. 'Yeah, and she talks in . . .'

'Phonetic!' Lisa exclaims. 'Don't even!'

In fact, when I check, the girl is an 'overweight Chinese teenager', but she does indeed advise Melody to '"put in what you want find there"', and how to make her searches more '"acoorut"'. I could sense our shared relief as Lisa confirmed that her hasty American rewrite allows this character to 'talk English, and not be fat. There was no reason for her to be fat.' She's equally embarrassed, now, by 'all the stuff about Siobhan's weight in *Ralph's Party*. I would never broach those issues now in my writing. Even in *The Third Wife* I have a character whose father is constantly describing her eating and weight gain, which makes me cringe.'

Times change, and terminology evolves, and descriptions that were acceptable in 2005 may now read as grossly insensitive. I remind Lisa about Bella, the trans character in *Vince and Joy*, and she braces herself. 'What do I say about Bella?'

'Oh, just things like "an emaciated little creature", and "an ugly little boyfriend who looks like a girl", and Vince says "there was something unsettling about her, something not quite right."'

Lisa, cringing, explains that Bella was based on a character from the BBC reality show *Paddington Green* (1998–2001), who was a 'post-operative transsexual'. 'So I felt that because I was so invested in this TV show, I had the right to be quite . . . heavy-handed.'

'At the time, that was probably a fairly sympathetic portrait,' I suggest. 'But things have just moved on so much.'

There's a balance to be struck, of course, between preserving the language of the time, and respecting the sensibilities of the modern reader. Would it be best to excise all the references to a 'bender flatmate', a 'sad homosexual' and a 'raving shirt-lifter' from *Thirtynothing*, the uses of 'poof' from *Vince and Joy*, and the unfunny pun about 'Bend Dicks' (Lydia's personal trainer Bendiks) from *The Making of Us*? They're a reminder of the thoughtless homophobia prevalent within laddish culture, but they also make Lisa's heroes far less likeable. Similarly, the admiring descriptions of Godfrey as 'a handsome negro' in *Before I Met You* are historically accurate to the 1920s, but they strike an uncomfortable note now, and Arlette's daydream about a trip to the Caribbean with 'two adorable piccaninnies in tow' is well meant, but jars awkwardly, and distances us from her as a sympathetic heroine. At least, we might conclude, Lisa has taken the opportunity to reconsider and update her previous writing when given the opportunity; the question is how far to go, and when to stop. If all the sexism was stripped from a 1970s David Lodge or Martin Amis novel, they would be pretty thin pamphlets.

In 2004, Lisa told *Pop Idol* winner Michelle McManus – somewhat bizarrely, they'd been teamed up for an *Observer* interview post-*One Hit Wonder* – that 'I changed my mind about being a famous pop star when I realised that it meant I'd never be able to get on the Tube again.' Music was 'everything' for her, she tells me, from the age of twelve through her teens; she met her first two boyfriends through the *NME* classifieds, and wrote letters to the magazines and radio 'all the time. That's what I wanted to be, a music journalist.'

The music in her novels echoes my own engagement with pop, and hers too; at the start, the right song means 'everything', but it gradually fades into the background. Radiohead's 'Creep' is so central to *Ralph's Party* that it's almost another character, and the entire concept of *Thirtynothing* was inspired by Pulp's 'Disco 2000'. Dig from *Thirtynothing* has 'different music for different moments', from Travis to Paul Weller, ABBA to Portishead: for really big problems, he turns to James Brown. In *Before I Met You*, John Brightly runs a Soho record stall, and closes his DJ sets with Underworld's 'Born Slippy': he and Betty bond over a contempt for Ultravox and a passion for the Chemical Brothers' new album.

The teenage Lydia, in *The Making of Us*, is content to be known as a Grunger, because 'she did like Nirvana, she did like Alice in Chains and Pearl Jam,' but resists the labels Goth and Greebo; these distinctions are, again, everything when you're eighteen. Later she listens to favourites on YouTube, 'everything from Bowie to Morrissey to Snow Patrol'; in a subtle moment of connection, her half-sister Robyn imagines their reunion taking place to the 'epic' soundtrack of Snow Patrol's 'Chasing Cars'. In *The Family Upstairs*, a pop classic from what Lisa calls 'my period of obsession' is buried under the surface; she based the house at the centre of the story on the mansion in Adam Ant's video for 'Prince Charming'. (The song's lyric 'nothing to be scared of' recurs throughout *After the Party*, too). But by *The Night She Disappeared*, the only music is Mariah Carey's 'All I Want For Christmas Is You', a campy climax to Tallulah's college canteen disco.

By this point, Lisa and I have tentatively shared tracks by email, in a middle-aged version of exchanging mix tapes. 'I'm glad you liked the Kanye!' she writes. 'I did think, oh God, what have I done, after I sent you the link. I was *not* sober when I watched it.' She tells me she's been listening to 'Sweet Disposition' by the Temper Trap on repeat as she writes the new novel, and in return I offer her Delphic's 'Clarion Call'; we share a taste in decade-old indie-dance, which is fortunate because she reveals she was into Spandau Ballet in the eighties, whereas I was devoted to Duran Duran.

With her daughters now in their teens, music now plays an important part in Lisa's life again – it might not be everything, but it's every Saturday night. 'My husband and I get drunk together; it's fantastic. We have two bottles of champagne and watch old *Top of the Pops*, music documentaries . . . it's just all about music. We go off on YouTube journeys, maybe starting with an old Blur song . . . sometimes we realise fucking hell, it's like, 2 a.m. and we're still down here listening to old music! But sometimes the girls come in at that time, and they redirect the music? They don't show us things they like, but they show us things they think we will like.'

It sounds amazing. I glance from the Zoom screen to the baby monitor, checking on my own two-year-old son who went to bed at 7 p.m., and can't quite imagine getting away with 2 a.m. Britpop parties. 'I'll do that in my own future,' I promise her.

No Plan

4 March 2021

'I am not a planner,' Lisa told an American interviewer in 2016, around the publication of *The Girls*, 'not even slightly . . .'

> . . . I start with chapter one and I keep going. I don't go back. Every morning I read the thousand words I wrote the previous day, and then I crack my knuckles . . . and write another thousand words.
>
> In theory, one hundred days later I should have a full length novel and it does tend to work out like that most of the time.

The latest chapter of Book 20 flashes back to the first encounter between Rachel Gold and her husband Michael, the man that Lucy, Henry's sister, is going to kill.

'It's really, really, confident stuff,' I tell Lisa.

She grits her teeth. 'In some ways.'

'When you were writing it . . . this seems a very basic question, but when you were writing it, did you know in advance what they were going to say? Had you been thinking about it before you wrote, or were they saying it as you wrote?'

There's a long pause. Lisa seems to be staring hard at me, but I sense that she's interrogating herself, considering the question thoroughly.

'They were saying it as I wrote,' she says finally. 'What particular line are you thinking of?'

'Well, they have that exchange in the chemist, as she's buying the morning-after pill. And there's a flirtatious energy and chemistry between them.'

'Yeah, I do sometimes think about it beforehand, and sit down with a conversation in mind, but with that . . . I wanted it to be in America, and I was going to set a fairly big chunk of it in America? And then once I got to the end of that pharmacy scene, I realised, I don't wanna be in America, I want to come back. So that was what formed their conversation . . . that I wanted it to be really fleeting, because I want to come back to London now.'

'And the dialogue just came to you?'

'It presented itself. Yes.'

'And do you hear it? Do you say it?'

'Yes. Yes. I hear his American accent, and her North London accent, in my head, while I'm writing their words.'

At this stage, the novel has two viewpoint characters, Henry and Rachel, leading us through entirely distinct narratives, at different points in time. I promised Lisa when we began this project in January that I wouldn't interfere with her process, but there's an absence so obvious to me that I can't hold back.

'I don't want to stick my oar in,' I begin, 'but Lucy is surely the connective tissue here.'

'You think she should be in it?'

'She must be what brings them together, even if she's not a major character. And to me, she's really, really interesting, because she can never relax. She's always waiting for a terrible thing to happen. She's waiting to be found out. She can never, ever relax!' It's all rushing out of me now, as if I'm pitching a storyline. 'She's found her happy life, but she can't ever be happy! She's committed a murder!'

'Even though she's got her million pounds,' Lisa agrees. 'And a house in St Albans.'

'Like if anyone ever finds that out, she's gonna lose her kids, which is the most precious thing to her . . .'

'Yes. Yes. Exactly.'

'Anyway.' I stop, getting my breath back. 'That's what I think about Lucy.'

Lisa strokes her chin thoughtfully.

I've not just stuck my oar in; I've splashed it around in the middle of her stream and caused a ripple.

Casting

At the end of *The Night She Disappeared*, the conventional prose switches into transcripts of police interviews, *Line of Duty* style – a storytelling trick I recognise from *Watching You*.

'Yeah, it's kind of cheating.' Lisa smiles. 'It's a really good way of getting across an information dump. You don't have to set up a whole scene, you don't have to describe anyone . . . you don't have to splice dialogue with "he said slowly", or "she cleared her throat" or whatever . . . At the end of *The Night She Disappeared* I just had so much information to impart, and it was getting so huge, that I thought yes! Police transcripts! To the rescue.'

> BROOKER: I'm going to show you a series of photos now.
> JEWELL: . . . OK.
> BROOKER: And I want your immediate response.

'I just took a Zoom call from a Victoria's Secret model,' Lisa writes on 5 March. 'She's married to the Netflix Originals boss, she's a huge fan of mine, and she really, really wants Netflix to film *The Family Upstairs*.'

One of Lisa's best friends, Jojo Moyes, had her novel adapted into the romantic drama *Me Before You* in 2016, starring Emilia 'Khaleesi' Clarke. Perhaps it's time for Lisa to consider who would play her key characters; after all, she's already done some of the casting work by comparing them to celebrities in the original descriptions.

BROOKER: Right. You see that? Jon Gavin, right? Looks like Matthew McConaughey.

JEWELL: Why do I know him?

BROOKER: Matthew McConaughey?

JEWELL: No, Jon Gavin.

BROOKER: Oh, sorry . . . Jon Gavin is Jess's ex.

JEWELL: Who's Jess?

BROOKER: Vince's girlfriend who gets pregnant, in *Vince and Joy*.

JEWELL: Oh, Jon! Amazing Jon. Known as Jon Gavin, because there are two Jons in their social group.

BROOKER: Yeah. So he's described as looking like Matthew McConaughey, right?

JEWELL: Yeah, OK.

BROOKER: And you tell us that Toby, in *31 Dream Street*, looks first like Tom Baker as *Doctor Who*, then after his make-over, like Christopher Ecclestone.

JEWELL: . . . Right . . .

BROOKER: And that Alex in *Thirtynothing* looks like Pierce Brosnan. Lily's husband in *I Found You* looks like Ben Affleck, and Robyn in *The Making of Us* looks like Lily Allen. So . . . this is how I imagine some of your other characters, and I want your reaction.

[*Presents picture of British comedian Steve Punt*]

This is how I imagine Mr Fitzwilliam, the headmaster in *Watching You*.

JEWELL [*anguished*]: No! No. No! Maybe if he had a decent haircut. No, he doesn't have that thing about him, that thing you need to carry off a soft paunch, and losing his hair.

BROOKER: OK. Here is Jem, from *Ralph's Party*.

[*Presents picture of Harriet Wheeler, lead singer of British 1990s indie group the Sundays*]

JEWELL: . . . Oh yeah? Oh, I loved her. She's so cool . . . Yeah.

BROOKER: A bit quirky, spiky . . .

JEWELL: Yeah. I'll go with that.

BROOKER: I don't think you'll agree with this one, but in the scenes where Joy is having a terrible time with George, I suddenly started seeing him as . . .

[*Presents picture of Benedict Cumberbatch*]

JEWELL [*sitting forward with distinct interest*]: Oh yeah, why not.

BROOKER: He's too good-looking, perhaps, but he's got a strangeness about him.

JEWELL: I love his face; I think he's beautiful. But a bit alien.

BROOKER: Well, that was that. I do have an image for Vince, but I'll show you it later.

JEWELL: Oh, I want more now! But your Mr Fitzwilliam was so wrong. I'm gonna find a Mr Fitzwilliam for you.

BROOKER: Do you see him more like Hugh Grant?

JEWELL [*hesitantly*]: . . . More like that.

BROOKER: Is he like Colin Firth?

JEWELL: No, 'cause he's more . . . There's a very specific type of older man that a teenage girl can find attractive. I'll tell you what I had in mind. Did you watch any of the *Educating* shows? *Educating Manchester* and so on? All of these sprawling schools were run by these guys who were simply charismatic. That's what Mr Fitzwilliam was like, a composite of those, though I never really saw his face.

Later that day, she mails me a line-up of middle-aged, smiling men in suits: they look like bank managers from a Barclays website, their arms firmly crossed and eyes on the future. 'I have attached a selection of Tom Fitzwilliams,' she writes.

It's funny that I never saw his face in my mind, just his presence, his girth, his lanyard. He could have been any of these guys. The only fixed thing about him was the moment that Joey sees him hailing a taxi on the street and his shirt rides up and she sees a strip of his stomach, that was an image I had kind of embedded in my mind before I started writing; this guy who was always in the coffee shop where I wrote, every day, then one day he stood up and stretched and I saw his stomach and it was kind of jarring but also amazingly tender. That was a scene I knew I was going to write, before I'd even started writing.

In a postscript, she attaches an image of Vince, or rather, her first boyfriend, who was the direct inspiration for Joy's first boyfriend. It's a faded black-and-white image from another era, like a relic from the coffee bars of *Quadrophenia* or even *Brighton Rock*. Vince, his hair neatly waxed, pouts self-consciously at the camera, caught at the perfect moment between teenage diffidence and adult confidence, while his friends lark around on either side.

I was at Barnet College doing my art foundation course and there was this weird little cafe tucked away in the bowels of a church on the high street; entirely wood-panelled and not touched since the 30s by the look of it. I went in there for lunch with some friends one day and those three boys in that photo, plus the guy who took it, were all sitting there in their grammar school uniforms and their quiffs like something out of an Angry Young Men stage production and it was one of the most extraordinary things I'd ever seen. You know how sometimes you see a vignette that's so perfect you almost think it can't be real, that you've imagined it, all posed like a photo shoot, but it wasn't, they were just standing there like that. I can still see it so clearly. Anyway, I thought I'd dreamed these beautiful boys in the cafe for years and then

I was working in a pub near my house and the blond boy on the right started working there and we went on a date and his friends all came and there I was, in a pub, with the boys I thought I'd dreamed up. I didn't get on with the blond guy, but I did get on with his mate.

As a final touch to this almost-impossible story, I send her the photo I'd already chosen of Vince: a portrait of Billy Fury, one of Britain's answers to Elvis Presley, at the early-sixties peak of his youthful beauty. The similarity between him and Vince – or 'Simon', to give his real name – is uncanny. 'But mine is better looking,' Lisa adds with a wink. 'And a lovely human. I was very, very lucky to have him as my first.'

I can't help wondering what her husband, Jascha, thinks of the novel that so vividly celebrates Lisa's relationship with this gorgeous young man.

'Oh,' she laughs. 'He doesn't read. But I would say, just to give that a bit of context, that the starting point was *imagine if I had met my husband, my current husband, when I was a teenager.* And if we'd somehow not found a way to be together but had found our way back to each other. But I didn't want to write about him . . . I wanted to write about an older teenage couple, and that put me back to my own experience with Simon. So the basic idea of the book was: I'm glad I met my husband when I did.'

'That does add nuance,' I agree. 'That puts a different complexion on it.'

'And after *Vince and Joy* came out, Simon read an interview with me on Mumsnet where I said Vince was based on my lovely first boyfriend. And somebody sent that to him. He wrote to me in turn and said he loved it, it made him so happy, and it was one of the nicest things he'd ever seen, and he was so pleased that I still felt that way about our two years together. But there's nothing there for my husband to worry about anyway. We're pretty heavyweight.'

'It's a good story,' I conclude. And how does she feel, overall, about her work being adapted?

'Well, it would be all about the fun of it, for me. Just . . . the experience of watching my funny little world that I created in this funny little brown room, all by myself, just be brought to life . . . how exciting! I can't imagine how exciting it would be.'

The golden apple of film and TV adaptations was first held out to her in 1998 by her agent Judith Murdoch. 'Very quickly, Murdoch started talking about bidding wars and film rights. She said to me, "It's wonderful it's all set in one season, because it makes the television rights much easier to sell." I thought, Maybe she's a little mad.'

It hasn't happened yet: not really. The Netflix conversation is casual, and she doesn't mention it again. It will happen, I'm certain, but for now, she's still hovering on the outskirts of a major adaptation, still at the discussion stages; she's on the cusp of a different kind of big time.

What Pares Do to Help Their Kids

11 March 2021

'How's your writing going?' I ask Lisa carefully, the following week. 'Are you progressing with it?'

'No,' she says. 'Well, I've written something . . . I think I got as close as I have with this book to a thousand words in a day.'

This isn't very promising, though I don't say that. Her usual rate is 1,000 words every day, not 1,000 on the odd good day.

'What I think might be quite fun', she adds, 'is to show you what a horrible typist I am. Because what I wrote on Friday, I haven't been through it yet to correct it. I just like to keep going, instead of stopping and checking back. Going through again and correcting typos is then a really good way for me to finesse the prose, because it gives me a sort of objectivity. Anyway, I thought this might make you smile.'

'Yeah, sure. Why not.' I don't see what's particularly fun about a few typos.

'I don't think you know what I mean by typos,' she warns. 'But you'll see.'

It starts off just fine. I'm still not sure what Lisa was worried about. Maybe she's a perfectionist.

> Rachel's flat was owned by her father. As was her jewellery business. At thirty-two years of age, Rachel tried not to dwell too much on the fact that her entire existence was a mirage.

And then . . . and then, awfully, the narration seems to break down, like an artificial intelligence losing its power, regressing back to basics, stumbling over simple words.

It had happened so gradually, this relainace on her father's adotation and geneotity, that she hadn't noticed when to had tipped over from being ';what pares to do to help their kids get started in life' to soemtihng she was too embarrassed to talk about.

What? I squint: ';*what pares to do to help their kids*' . . . It's like an illiterate rant on Yahoo Answers, the site where a hapless enquirer famously asked the community 'how is babby formed? how girl get pragnent?' and was answered 'they need to do way instain mother > who kill their babbys.' I almost wish I could phone Lisa immediately, to check on her health. The next sentence recovers, but by the end of the paragraph, the prose has fallen off a cliff.

Her jewellery business was making money but was not yet in profit. She could fool herself that it was in profit once a month when her allowanace arrived and tipped her caccoutns over from red to black. But really, she was at least a year away from making a proper living, and even then it would depdend on everyithn ggoing right and ntohng going wrong.

I stop reading there, out of horrified sympathy, and wonder how the writing reaches its published state from these rawest of materials. Of course, Lisa will go back and correct, but the copy of *The Night She Disappeared* she sent me is also heavily annotated with marginal deletions, additions and notes from her editor, Selina Walker, some of them quite detailed: 'This is where he walks down the tunnel to the body? He doesn't drag Guy down the tunnel like in the last draft. I like the fact that Guy is at the end of the tunnel – it feels cleaner, more straightforward?'

Even this final version from the end of January 2021 – Lisa tells me that Selina is old-school and prefers to decorate a printed-out manuscript with Post-its, so these digital annotations evidence her very last contributions – feels like a conversation between the author and someone else.

Lisa has, of course, told me about the radical changes that editors imposed on *Ralph's Party* and its sequel, and I also know that Ellie Mack, in *Then She Was Gone*, was killed at an editor's suggestion; there's an alternate, original ending to the novel floating around online. Would it be fair to say that her editors are co-creators?

'Oh, absolutely. They do timelines, inconsistencies, bloopers . . . they're amazing. What happened to Ellie Mack wasn't someone changing my work, it was someone being a part of it, actually being involved with the writing of the book.'

Lisa's relationship with her current editor is unusual, in that she submits her work in progress directly to Selina rather than via her agent. 'She's the first I've ever had who I'm not scared of disappointing or letting down. I know whatever I send her, she'll take it in her stride. Anything I send her is positive, as far as she's concerned. Even if it's all wrong.'

Somewhere in this process, from the broken flow of words she lays down in her first draft, through the careful second pass to correct and finesse, to the final check and copy-edit, Lisa forms, crafts and refines phrases and images that glint and glow in the mind's eye, and gleam richly in the memory.

In *After the Party*, Jem clinks champagne glasses as the sun goes down in Soho and 'the pretty room was bathed, briefly, in a wash of pomegranate light.' In *Watching You*, realisation flashes through Joey's mind 'bright as sunlight off water'. When Libby gets up for work, early in *The Family Upstairs*, 'there's a kind of pearlescent shimmer in the air'; in the South of France, the sky above Lucy sits 'dark as damsons'. *Vince and Joy* employs a recurring image of Joy drifting in a little boat away from harbour lights as she floats slowly into her toxic relationship with George; a melancholy little motif, reminiscent in its modest way of the green light glowing throughout *The Great Gatsby*, and the 'boats against the current' of its final line. (The comparison is perhaps not so far-fetched: Lucy's dog in *The Family Upstairs* is named after F. Scott Fitzgerald.) Were lines like this there from the start, or did they emerge in the refining? 'All the pretty stuff goes in with the first draft,' she says firmly. 'I never add pretty stuff in rewrites or second drafts. When I refine it's usually to make it sharper, shorter or work harder. Often this can mean cutting out other pretty things.'

There are very occasional clunkers, too, which survived the editing process. 'Arlette felt a bubble of warm feeling rise up through herself,' from *Before I Met You*, is inelegant. 'Inside Maggie's head was the sound of shattered dreams and a broken heart,' from *The Making of Us*, sounds like an eighties pop lyric, and not in a good way. But as I suggest to Lisa, good storytelling and great prose are not always the same thing. Just as the simple, suggestive drawing of comic book panels can convey rhythm and pace more effectively than intricately painted pages that demand admiration and slow the action, so the startlingly original insights of a stylist like John Updike would not suit the high-octane plot of a Lee Child. Poetic descriptions and literary flourishes sometimes work against a story, drawing attention to the author and the writing and lifting us out of our immersion in character and drama. In a thriller, the main job of the prose is to serve the plot, not to be decorative and to invite readers to linger on its elegance.

'Absolutely,' says Lisa. 'Absolutely. I was going through the manuscript of *The Night She Disappeared* recently . . . there were so many bits of writing that I thought I could have done so much better. They could have been polished and honed until they shone. But I know that everyone who's read that book has read it so fast, and been so caught up in the story, that they would never have noticed.'

Lisa has now been writing Book 20 for over a month. At 1,000 words a day, every weekday, she should have hit 20,000 words by now. She's completed 5,000. And the last section is scattered with what can only loosely be called 'words', words of the *covfefe* variety: *geneotity, caccoutns*.

Meanwhile *The Family Upstairs* has just won an award for selling 500,000 copies, her highest-ever readership. The stakes for a sequel couldn't be much higher.

The Jewelliverse

Despite her international success, Lisa's stories remain distinctly British, or, to be more precise, English; to zoom in further, they are love letters to London.

'London, thought Ned, staring at the back end of a used-car depot through the misted-up window of a black cab. Look at it. Just look at it.

'It's so beautiful . . .'

Ned's surname, shared with most of the characters in *A Friend of the Family*, is London: a coincidence they have to consider when weighing up marriage, or christening babies. 'Amanda London . . . it's got a sort of post-modern charm, hasn't it?' (Indeed, it sounds like someone from a Martin Amis novel, alongside John Self, Lionel Asbo, Keith Talent and Nicola Six. *Invisible Girl* comes close, with its character Cate Fours.)

Although she does venture into the south – 'the wilds', as Tony London puts it in the same novel – Lisa's home territory is clearly north of the river. She reserves her coldest contempt for Surrey and its borders, where I currently live and work: in *Vince and Joy*, Norbiton is somewhere Joy had never 'thought she'd find herself doing anything other than driving through', but it serves as the venue for a dreadful Chinese meal with George, a direct echo of Lisa's experiences with her first husband. 'I had to go on a train that way a year ago,' she says now, 'and when it pulled up at Walton-on-Thames, my blood . . . just . . . *chilled*.' So not South, or West, but North and East, and above all, Central.

Even more specifically, Lisa's novels seem to have their heart in Soho – it's where both Bee and Betty, from *One-Hit Wonder* and *Before I Met You* respectively, discover themselves as young women – and we could even pinpoint the key location on Google Maps: Berwick Street, somewhere between Reckless Records on one side, and its vinyl rival Sister Ray on the left. 'The centre of the universe . . .' thinks Betty, 'neon lights glistening on oily puddles, the alleyways and mysterious doorways, subterranean dives and shabby-looking people with secrets.' Soho lives and breathes in Lisa's novels; there is a sense of authentic geography, with real streets crisscrossing and branching off, leading elsewhere. Jem in *Ralph's Party* walks from Chinatown to Shaftesbury Avenue, as the Soho streets assume their 'night-time air of temptation and provocation', and years later, in *After the Party*, revisits her old haunts of Brewer Street, Lisle Street and Greek Street, searching for a small door in the wall that leads to an exclusive club.

Of course, Lisa's stories visit other places: Bury St Edmunds and Tonypandy, St Albans, Guernsey, and further afield to Sydney and the South of France. *Watching You* is set in a fictional neighbourhood of Bristol, and *I Found You* in the invented seaside town Ridinghouse Bay; both novels open with a map, as if they were fantasy epics (Lisa sketches them herself, and they are passed to an artist for a polished redraft). But these other places feel more like stage sets – as Beth in *The House We Grew Up In* describes her Sydney apartment – detailed interiors that end at the front door of a house, exteriors that fade away just around the corner; maps with only blank space beyond their borders.

When Lydia and Dean in *The Making of Us* return to her former home, a Welsh council estate, we concentrate on a single flat and its immediate surroundings, which are described in queasy detail (a bin 'filled to overflowing with squashed pizza boxes, empty cans and a balled-up nappy'). The area beyond is a vague, grey reel of buildings – 'shops give way to terraces and the terraces give way to sprawling estates' – and that's all it needs to be. These isolated locations feel like video-game environments, where the developer has only bothered to create fully textured models of the places the player will interact with; Lydia, Dean and the reader won't go beyond the flat and its forecourt, so there's no need for more than a backdrop surrounding the estate.

Mapping the places in her head, Lisa says, is like 'drawing a dream', and in the process realising that not everything connects rationally, and that some areas are unfinished. In *The Night She Disappeared*, for instance, while she has a clear sense of where Scarlett and Tallulah live, 'I don't know what's on the other side of the village!' She puts her fingers to her temples, like a medium trying to conjure it. 'I have no idea. The bus that takes Tallulah to college comes from . . . a mysterious land. So I picture the bus trundling through this village, past the Co-op, on to the common, picking Tallulah up' – now she's staring into space, and I know she can visualise it – 'and then on to the A-road, and then the big roundabout, and on into town. But I don't know what's beyond the Co-op.'

In Lisa's London, we know what's around the corner, because we can check how Greek Street connects to Lisle, Berwick, Brewer and Dean, and where they lead. But this is still Lisa's London, not the real London. Because Lisa's London, an over-lap of fiction and reality, also contains the imaginary Almanac Road, where Jem, Smith and Ralph share a flat, and Toby's house on Silversmith Road, or *Dream Street* as the title dubs it. In Lisa's Soho, Britpop idol Dom Jones lives on the corner of Berwick Street and Peter Street, where Gosh! Comics sits in real life. Who? You know, Dom Jones from the band Wall, who split up with Cheryl Glass from Blossom and got together with Amy Metz from Mighty? Don't worry if you haven't heard of them: Dom Jones, his exes and his former bands are, of course, Lisa's invention. In fact, she's created an entire miniature music industry. *Thirtynothing* features a girl band, Pesky Kids, and a pop sensation, Fruit, while the Adam Ant-style group from *The Family Upstairs* is called the Original Version.

But things get complicated. Dom Jones ('cockney/mockney art school dropout and darkly gleaming rock-and-roll super-nova') is clearly a hybrid of Damon Albarn and Liam Gallagher, but Oasis also exist in Lisa's fictional universe: Ana mentions them in *One-Hit Wonder*. Ana's sister, Bee Bearhorn, was born from Lisa's (hilarious, with hindsight) misapprehension that Betty Boo was dead; but the real-life Betty Boo is also name-checked in *Before I Met You*. This is a world where people are thrilled to spot Robbie Williams and Fearne Cotton, where Tamsin Outhwaite and the girls from S Club are the standard of female beauty (in *A Friend of the Family*, anyway), but where Jem works with Philip Samuel, the fictional actor from a fictional soap called *Jubilee Road*.

Are all her novels set in the same fictional world? Lisa says no, but I spot a connection and seize on it geekily: Electrogram Records features in both *Thirtynothing* and the otherwise unrelated *A Friend of the Family*. This is surely evidence of a 'Jewelliverse', I enthuse to her: interlinked like the Marvel movies, where characters could cross over, where – taking their relative ages into account – Jem could hang out with Joy, and Sophie Beck could meet Henry Lamb.

'I see where you're coming from,' Lisa says slowly, as if she doesn't much like where I'm going with it. 'But I don't really know what to do with that. No.'

She did, she admits, dare to break the boundary once (I'm assuming Electrogram Records was an unconscious repetition, though I maintain it still counts as proof) by introducing Ken, from *The Truth About Melody Browne*, as a minor character in *The House We Grew Up In*. 'I felt like God,' she says, awed by her own power.

Perhaps persuaded by my enthusiasm, she promises that 'I'll find a Jewelliverse Easter egg of some description for Book 20. This would be the perfect place to put one.'

Hearing Voices

There are people in my kitchen constantly but they're not mixing me cocktails or shucking oysters, they're not asking me about my day, they're using my panini maker to make what they call 'toasties', they're making hot chocolate in the wrong pot, they're putting non-recyclables in my recycling bin and vice versa. They're watching noisy indecipherable things on the smartphones I bought them and shouting at each other when there's really no need. And then there's the dog. A Jack Russell terrier type thing that my sister found on the streets of Nice four years ago scavenging in bins.

Henry Lamb continues to dominate the story, his prissy voice instantly recognisable – a cross, for me, between the Amis character Gregory Riding, who places similarly snobbish inverted commas around 'coffee', 'tea' and even 'Terry', and uptight Niles Crane, from the American sitcom *Frasier*, who also has to tolerate his slobbish dad's Jack Russell terrier.

Lisa is still struggling with the challenges of writing a sequel; about how to welcome new readers and encourage them to read *The Family Upstairs*, while not risking a clumsy information-drop on long-term fans who are familiar with the previous story. 'It's a weird balance to strike,' she observes, and she is falling back on this powerful character as her guide. 'I've decided I am just going to let Henry lead me on this one.'

'I feel he just writes himself, doesn't he?'

'Yeah, he totally did. So I'm going to have to let him do that again. And I'm gonna have to let him manage the whole thing, really. It's gonna have to all work from his point of view, first and foremost, because I think I might be a bit lost otherwise.'

'Henry is almost like a place you enter, isn't he,' I muse. 'Henry is like a mindset. He's so fully formed.'

'Yes! I hope he doesn't start dragging things down because he's so intense.'

'He's almost too pleasurably snobbish, and he needs another aspect to balance it.'

'Exactly, which he had, because when we got to know him in the last book, we got him from the ground up, as a sweet boy, whereas with this, we're hitting the ground running with him as quite a nasty, snobby, bitter person.'

'He's holding the floor here, isn't he . . . he's able to present himself and the world to us in the way that he wants us to see it. You know . . .' And I adopt a firm, deep voice. 'My name is Henry Lamb. These things they call "toasties" . . . and so on. So anything else about him would have to be shown to us through other people.'

'He needs to be peeled back,' Lisa agrees. 'Particularly so that readers who are new to him can learn how to like him.'

Henry is the most overwhelming first-person perspective in all of Lisa's novels to date: more domineering than Noelle in *Then She Was Gone*, or Saffyre in *Invisible Girl*. But there are many other voices throughout those nineteen books: a cacophony, a polyphony. Lisa hears them in her head, 'and I'm not going to dress it up and make it more pretty.'

Most obviously there are the renditions of various accents, some of them less than subtle. Have a listen.

' "Well, yes, I'm pretty sure because I've been up to the clinic at Llantrisant, like, and they turned me inside out and upside down and hung me from the ceiling and there's nothing wrong with me . . ." ' (That's Glenys Pike in *The Making of Us*, who is Welsh.)

' "It is a tragedy. A clever, caring, good man and one tiny mistake – and *pouf!* Everything turns to dust." ' (Marc Blanchard in *The Making of Us*: he's French.)

' "So . . . where you bin hiding, Mr Ned? Why you leave your mother on her own for so long, eh? Your mother, she bin pining – pining pining pining." ' (Mickey, the Greek restaurateur in *A Friend of the Family*)

More complex is the way that Lisa's third-person narration is shaped by the character it describes: the world is filtered through their consciousness, vocabulary and terms of reference, giving a slightly different tint to each perspective.

Take Lily, for instance, in *I Found You* – abandoned by her husband, stranded in a Britain which to her is a foreign country. Her agitated presence in the story breaks the prose into stilted staccato, often followed by a rushing, run-on sentence.

> She also knows that Carl has a sister. Her name is Suzanne. Susan? She's much older than him and lives near the mother in the place beginning with *S*. They are estranged. He hasn't told her why. And he has a friend called Russ who calls every few days to talk about football and the weather and a drink they really should have one day soon but it's so hard to organise because he has a new baby.

We can hear Lily in this paragraph, hear the way she would speak to the police about her husband's disappearance, and perhaps hear her Eastern European accent, too, even though the prose is about her, rather than by her. Compare this with the very different voice of Bernie, the proud mother from *A Friend of the Family*:

> A nice house, a happy family, a few quid in the bank. All she'd ever wanted for her boys was that they be good boys. And, if she could blow her own trumpet for a moment, she'd done a bloody good job on them. They were fine, fine boys, her boys, each and every one of them. Of course every mother thinks her sons are perfect, but hers really were. She honestly couldn't fault them.

While this is Lisa Jewell narrating Bernie, it is Bernie's cadences we hear; Bernie's rhythms and repetitions, her banal but benevolent reflections on life and family.

Gender is also subtly signified. While most of Lisa's descriptions of décor, clothes and hair are informed by her own obvious expertise and interest, when she writes a male character's response to a woman's appearance, the terms of reference are much more basic. Robyn from *The Making of Us* 'tied her hair up into a messy sideways-leaning bun', with the everyday accuracy of a young woman, but Flint's reaction to Ana's ponytail in *One-Hit Wonder* has a caveman simplicity. 'It looked nice. Off her face. Gave her a sort of ballerina look.'

This third-person narration that adapts to the specific person it narrates is particularly interesting when *Before I Met You* shifts back to 1919. Arlette's story seems suddenly to sit up and mind its manners, assuming a more poised, period address.

> As the tight corners of her mind slackened and billowed, she felt herself strangely cocooned. It was as though this was a place where nothing bad had ever happened, and Leticia was a woman to whom nothing bad had ever happened, and while

she was here, in this room, with this woman, all would be well for evermore.

This is not the same style as Betty's story from the same novel, and it is certainly not the narration we are used to from Lisa's earlier, curry-and-flatmates work. It might remind us more of Virginia Woolf in its immersion in the flowing tides of a young woman's consciousness:

> How fresh, how calm, stiller than this of course, the air was in the early morning; like the flap of a wave; the kiss of a wave; chill and sharp and yet (for a girl of eighteen as she was then) solemn, feeling as she did, standing there at the open window, that something awful was about to happen . . .

That was *Mrs Dalloway*, from 1925, and we might also consider Joyce's 'The Dead', from the 1914 collection *Dubliners*, as Arlette's story takes place almost precisely between those dates. In the opening lines, we meet a very different Lily to the one in *I Found You*:

> Lily, the caretaker's daughter, was literally run off her feet. Hardly had she brought one gentleman into the little pantry behind the office on the ground floor and helped him off with his overcoat than the wheezy hall-door bell clanged again and she had to scamper along the bare hallway to let in another guest. It was well for her she had not to attend to the ladies also. But Miss Kate and Miss Julia had thought of that and had converted the bathroom upstairs into a ladies' dressing-room. Miss Kate and Miss Julia were there, gossiping and laughing and fussing, walking after each other to the head of the stairs, peering down over the banisters and calling down to Lily to ask her who had come.

Our impression of this busy household at Christmas is, again, subtly filtered through the characters who occupy it:

> It was always a great affair, the Misses Morkan's annual dance . . . Never once had it fallen flat. For years and years it had gone off in splendid style, as long as anyone could remember; ever since Kate and Julia, after the death of their brother Pat, had left the house in Stoney Batter and taken Mary Jane, their only niece, to live with them in the dark gaunt house on Usher's Island, the upper part of which they had rented from Mr Fulham, the corn-factor on the ground floor. That was a good thirty years ago if it was a day.

This colloquial rhythm is reminiscent of Bernie's in *A Friend of the Family*: it is not Lily, or Kate or Julia, or Mary Jane who speaks, nor any named character in the story – it is certainly not Gabriel, the protagonist, who has yet to enter – but we are caught up in the gossipy voice of an imaginary guest, giving us a quick low-down on the situation in the language of a middle-class Dubliner from the 1910s. It is not Joyce's own voice – he plays too precisely with language to make the lazy mistake that Lily was 'literally' run off her feet – but neither is it Lily proclaiming 'I was literally run off my feet.' Joyce dips in and out, giving a sense of the characters' outlook, status, personality and education by restricting or expanding the third-person narration.

Did Lisa immerse herself in the literature of the teens and twenties before writing Arlette? If not in Joyce, then Woolf, perhaps (Arlette secures two 'heavenly' rooms in Bloomsbury), or Dorothy Richardson, Katherine Mansfield, Jean Rhys?

I should have anticipated her reply.

> The 1919 storyline was, as is the case with so many things I've written about that might appear on the page to have

been deliberate choices, a complete fluke. The book was meant to be about only Betty. And I just couldn't make it work. It was flailing about and felt stodgy. So I did a brainstorm with an editor I had at the time (she only did this one book with me) and we talked and talked and I found myself saying, 'I could write about Arlette? Maybe mirror Betty's story, when she was the same age as her.' And the editor said, 'Yes. DO THAT.' And so I went off to start writing it and of course found that it would have been 1919 when Arlette was that age and I had no research to go in with, just vague ideas based on period dramas I've watched over the years, and jumped in and made it up as I went along.

I adjust my expectations. Did she perhaps read her friend Sophie Kinsella's *Twenties Girl*, with its superficially similar theme? 'I have not read Maddy's *Twenties Girl*.'

I should have remembered. *'I am not a planner, not even slightly.'* There was no plan and no research. Lisa's background reading into the phenomenon of 'gang stalking', which features in *Watching You*, is taken from the first website I found when I googled 'gang stalking'. Her description of Lucy testing a fiddle in *The Family Upstairs* – she 'quickly plays a three-octave A major scale and arpeggio, checking for evenness of sound quality and for wolf notes or whistles' – feels like it's been written by someone else, because Lisa asked her friend who plays a fiddle. If you stop in the middle of *Invisible Girl*, as Cate Fours does, and look up the 1970s housing estate in Hampstead, as Cate does, you'll find exactly the same information that Cate does, not exactly copied and pasted to the pages of the novel, but closely paraphrased. (On the other hand, a quick google reveals that another Cate, the actor Cate Blanchett, is not actually 'very very small' as described in *Watching You*, but five foot nine.)

I am, it's fair to say, a planner. I have all my lectures written for the next academic year, and my research projects sketched out for the next five. I have had a plan in place for this book since its first chapter. So when I first read Lisa's novels, I naturally projected my own habits on to hers, and imagined I was finding my way through an intricate maze constructed by a master architect. Now I realise she's in the next room, throwing up walls, arranging furniture and briefing the characters a moment before I walk in. It doesn't diminish her as a writer – both approaches involve a great deal of skill, of course – but it's a revelation I'm slowly adjusting to. She doesn't draw up a detailed blueprint and study the schematics, nodding in satisfaction before carefully laying the plot down, brick by brick; she's a fluid and organic improviser, making it up as she goes, one step ahead of us, storytelling by the skin of her teeth.

Suspense

In 1962, French New Wave film director François Truffaut, celebrated for the youthful freshness and flair of movies like *The 400 Blows* and *Jules et Jim*, conducted a series of interviews with the far more established Alfred Hitchcock. His aim was to present a new side of the director, to break him out of his reputation as a light entertainer, a showman who made popular thrillers, and to explore Hitchcock's craft. The parallels with this current project are entirely coincidental.

'There is a distinct difference between "suspense" and "surprise",' Hitchcock explained in his gravelly, rubbery voice, the East London accent still intact despite years in Hollywood. 'I'll explain what I mean.'

> We are now having a very innocent little chat. Let's suppose that there is a bomb underneath this table between us. Nothing happens, and then all of a sudden, "Boom!"

This would be a surprise to the observer, but nothing more. However, Hitchcock then goes on to discuss a suspense situation. In this imaginary scene, not only have we witnessed the bomb being placed before he and Truffaut entered, but we also know that it will go off at one o'clock. There is a clock somewhere prominent in the background, ticking off the seconds towards the hour. We want to shout at the two men, to stop them from chatting, to warn them about the threat. By the time the bomb goes off, the viewer has enjoyed not just fifteen seconds of surprise, but fifteen minutes of suspense.

We can see Hitchcock's idea at work in the scene from *Sabotage* (1936) where a boy unknowingly carries a bomb on to a crowded London bus. We know it will explode at 1.45 p.m., so Hitchcock cuts regularly to clocks on the street, building up the tension of the countdown, and even shows us a close-up X-ray of the bomb inside its cannister, its cogs ticking steadily towards detonation. Every innocent chat, every interaction with the bus conductor and fellow passengers, every slight delay to the journey becomes unbearable because we have information the characters on-screen don't, and we want to scream a warning.

Hitchcock dealt in bombs, ropes and knives. Lisa is more comfortable with knickers stuffed in a handbag – walking shamefaced through Soho after an ill-judged night with pop star Dom, Betty in *Before I Met You* bumps into her friend John Brightly, and senses him taking in all the details of her rumpled, smudged appearance, to the point where his gaze feels like an X-ray, detecting 'even the bulge of her balled-up knickers in her shoulder bag' – but the principle is the same.

This technique, where an object seems to glow and pulse from its hiding place, is used more extensively in *The Night She Disappeared*, which builds Hitchcockian suspense from the presence of an engagement ring in a pocket.

The setting is the local pub. Zach, Tallulah's abusive on-off boyfriend, has invited her out for a special meal. Tallulah, who has fallen in love with her charismatic new friend Scarlett, is secretly planning to finish with Zach. To make matters worse, Tallulah suspects that Zach plans to propose to her this evening. She has arranged for Scarlett to be in the pub too, as back-up. Zach has no idea.

With this premise in place, every innocent detail becomes unbearably loaded with meaning. There's champagne ready on the table. Zach pulls out Tallulah's chair as she goes to sit down.

He insists she should have whatever she wants, money no object. Tallulah demurs, and they squabble mildly over the price of the sea bass.

He rolls his eyes at her affectionately and she sees his hand go to the pocket of his trousers as he's done a few times since they left the house and she knows that that's where the ring is and her mouth feels dry and she thinks, Why is she doing this? Why has she let it get this far? She is going to humiliate him and crush him and all of this, this golden summer night of champagne toasts and chivalry will curdle into something unbearable and cruel.

Scarlett and her posh posse clatter into the romantic scene, and Zach bristles: Tallulah 'can feel Scarlett's eyes burning upon her, but she keeps her gaze fixed on the menu. The words swim before her, meaninglessly. Cannellini. Jus. Anchovy. Rigatoni. Chorizo.' We can see it cinematically: a point-of-view shot of the menu, blurring out of focus.

The situation escalates. Zach picks up on Tallulah's tension; Scarlett intervenes to sabotage the date. Innocent objects – a seafood platter, a sticky toffee pudding, a truffled chip – become props in an unspoken conflict as the energies of the three key characters converge and clash across a pub table. Tallulah feels 'strangely like something, somewhere is on fire and it's already too late to put it out.' Scarlett invites them back to her house for a pool party. Sitting in the car as the night carries her powerlessly along on a new course and events tumble out of her control, Tallulah 'can feel the outline of the ring box in Zach's pocket against the back of her leg', the invisible item pushing its way to the front again, almost as if we see it in X-ray.

And then finally, when Zach and Tallulah stand face to face, it's revealed.

He releases one of her arms and dips his hand into the pocket of his trousers, pulls out the small black box and shoves it against her breastbone so hard she can already feel a bruise start to form.

'Ow,' she says, rubbing at her sternum. 'That hurt.'

'Open it,' he snarls.

She inhales deeply and unclicks the fastening, then stares in numb horror at the tiny nub of diamond glittering at her under the low halogens. There it is, she thinks. There it is. The reason for every last dreadful minute of this evening.

Just a petty, cheap ring glinting in harsh light, but it's acquired a malicious little presence like a character in its own right, as deadly as Hitchcock's bomb.

Lisa, it is fair to say, favours build-up over climax. After several pages of painful suspense, the physical violence that concludes this set-piece is over in four plain sentences. She can describe violence vividly, agonisingly – *I Found You* is relentless in this respect – but prefers not to; her focus is on the emotional impact, the broader meaning of each act.

'They have a fight, Gray and Mark, and I remember, that was one of the most boring scenes . . . trying to describe a physical fight between two men, in words. It was like *and then he did this with his elbow, and then he brought his arm down, and then with a slice . . .*' Lisa stabs dutifully at the air then tips her head back like an exasperated teenager. 'Oh God, so boring.'

'I know what you mean,' I reply, 'but to me, it's not the actions that carry the power of it. It's the fact that Gray can't defend his younger sister.'

'Yes,' she agrees firmly.

'It's an emotional thing. It's not actually about the fight.'

'Yes.' My intensity has intrigued her. 'Do you have a younger sister?'

'No,' I say with relief. 'I think if I did, I wouldn't be able to bear reading it at all. It did my head in, as it is. But I suppose when you're writing it, you're thinking about the mechanics, not about how bad you can make the situation for each character.'

'No. I know what I need to make happen over each paragraph, and then I just need to put the words in order to make that thing happen.'

She takes a similar approach towards sex. The most detailed description is in her first novel, as Karl tries to initiate an encounter with his partner, Siobhan. It features sweaty licking, coarse hairiness, and a vocabulary of 'moist', 'ripe', pungent' and 'angry', all from Karl's perspective: the passion is one-sided, and Siobhan soon tells him to stop.

This unnervingly vivid scene is followed by the no-holds-barred celebration of first love in *Vince and Joy*. And since then, Lisa has largely 'drawn a veil', in her phrase.

'It's mostly about flirting and anticipation, isn't it?' I confirm.

'Absolutely.'

'And sexual activity more in service to character and emotion. People who shouldn't be doing something. Like Mr Fitzwilliam, and Joey . . .'

'Sexual tension is what's interesting to write about,' she says firmly. 'Sex isn't.'

Mr Fitzwilliam and Joey are one example of many. We could also cite Jem and her new dad-friend from the playground, Joel, in *After the Party*; the slow burn in *Before I Met You* between Betty and her two very different love interests, Dom and John; the will-they, won't-they, is-he-gay-or-isn't-he between Lydia and her trainer Bendiks in *The Making of Us*; Libby's gradual attraction to her journalist friend Miller that builds beneath the thriller plot of *The Family Upstairs*; the forbidden flirtation between Beth and her sister's husband Bill in *The House We Grew*

Up In ; and Tallulah and Scarlett's affair in *The Night She Disappeared*, its intimacies vaguely, tastefully described through images of melting gold.

In *The Family Upstairs*, Libby and Miller's budding romance is wrapped up through a hasty flashback, a brusque 'He'd silenced her with a kiss.' In *The Night She Disappeared*, Tallulah sleeps with her ex, Zach, primarily because he offers to look after the baby the next day: 'And I could do his morning feed and let you have a lie-in. Yeah? Wouldn't that be good?' It's tempting, and soon, enticingly, his joggers are around his ankles in the back garden.

In both these cases, the emotional motivations and the consequences of the act are what matter to Lisa; the mechanics of what people do with their bodies are not the point. The sustained focus instead is on small, ambiguous moments, decisions that change the dynamic, often subtly, and tiny but significant actions that switch the romance plot on to a new potential route. I was pleased with myself when I noticed that Beth, hearing Bill's key in the lock, 'stiffened slightly . . . touched her hair and cleared her throat . . . rearranged her legs, crossed them, then uncrossed them again,' and realised immediately what it meant, and what was going to happen between them.

Rachel, in Book 20, shares a lot with her author in this regard. When Michael turns up at her flat with flowers and champagne, she . . .

> . . . took him out for cocktails because if they opened the champagne now they'd be having sex within twenty minutes and she wanted to enjoy the lingering experience of a proper date, the building up of unbearable sexual tension, before they crossed that line.

And then when he mentions his son over drinks, and his eyes film with tears . . .

. . . she felt the encounter shift into another gear, a shift that seemed as if it might impinge on the unspoken promise of inevitable sex that had laced every moment of their previous communications, but might also take them somewhere else, somewhere completely unexpected, somewhere grown-up and real.

That other place is far more fascinating to Lisa.

Lucy

25 March 2021

A fictional young man in a tight grey suit clutches a folder. He holds out his hand.

'You must be Lucy,' he says. 'Lovely to meet you.'

At the start of her sixth chapter, Lisa has introduced a third viewpoint character, Henry's sister Lucy. 'I wrote six hundred words today,' she tells me happily, 'my first since the eleventh. It feels like a novel now I've got my third perspective in place.' It's all starting to come together, and she reassures herself that it's still March, just about. I'm delighted too, because I felt the novel needed Lucy to join the two strands about Henry and Rachel; if not now, then later in the story.

And then I read the new material and I'm not sure what to think. Instead of sparkling as it should, it feels flat.

When we started this process, I asked Lisa if she'd mind me commenting on her work in progress. She thought about it for a moment and decided 'no . . . I was wondering if it would risk interfering, but it's not as if I'd care what you think of it.' It was an early glimpse of the no-nonsense, no-frills Lisa: pragmatic, honest and amusingly brutal.

Something has changed since, though, because when I tell her now that I have some thoughts on the work to date, she asks me to hold back and keep them to myself. Which is probably for the best, because it's my turn to be worried. We are 10,000 words into the book at this point, and there's no tension. There's recap, introduction and consolidation. There are flashbacks to how a new character met a dead character. There are people preparing to move and people preparing to leave. It's an effective set-up. But that's a lot of words for a preamble to the main plot.

I check back. In Chapter One of *The Family Upstairs*, ordinary Libby opens a letter and suddenly 'owns a house in Chelsea . . . the proportions of her existence have been blown apart.' By the end of the first chapter of *I Found You*, Alice has rescued a nameless stranger from the beach, discovered he has no memory, and invited him, against her better judgement, into her family home. On page six of *The Girls*, young Pip finds her sister Grace unconscious and half-naked in their communal garden. *Then She Was Gone* begins by grimly telling us that Ellie Mack, the girl we're about to meet, will soon disappear, and that all her teenage happiness will be over: 'Youth. Life. Ellie Mack. All gone. All gone forever.' On page two of *Invisible Girl*, Saffyre Maddox, her heart pounding and leg bleeding, strides out 'towards the man, towards danger . . . [her] fate left wide open.' *The Night She Disappeared* warns the reader even earlier, before the story begins, with its nightmarish flashforward to Tallulah, trapped in the dark tunnel beneath Scarlett's house, imagining spiders crawling over her. By contrast, the three characters leading Book 20 seem, after 10,000 words, like comfortably-off, confident and attractive people dealing with minor issues like annoying siblings and enigmatic love interests.

But I don't say anything. Not yet.

Thresholds

As we saw, a surprising number of Lisa's characters are aspiring or even fairly successful novelists. A surprising number of them, too, come into a large and sudden sum of money, as she did when she was signed for her first book.

When we are told the details of a character's windfall, interestingly, it's considerably less than Lisa received for *Ralph's Party*. Jack, Robyn's boyfriend in *The Making of Us*, had 'just sold the film rights to his first book for tens of thousands of pounds'. Sean from *A Friend of the Family* is paid £50,000 for his second novel. Toby, in *31 Dream Street*, inherits £62,550 in cash from his elderly tenant. Nadine, in *Thirtynothing*, is promised £40,000 for shooting the Ruckham's Motor Oil calendar, 'a commission that will send her earning potential on a quite unbelievable trajectory, straight to the stars'.

But the amount doesn't matter. It's what it means that matters. Lydia, in *The Making of Us*, invents organic odourless paint and sells the brand to Dulux 'for a lot of money': the deal is left vague, but her income enables her to spend £27.99 without blinking on a bottle of Gewürztraminer, 'as though money had lost its context, had been stretched out of shape. This, she assumed, was what it was to be rich.' Libby in *The Family Upstairs* refreshes her phone after selling the mansion and finds her bank balance at 'a stupid number . . . too many zeros, too many everythings'.

It's the transformative effect of all those zeros that matters. Like Lisa with her first publishing deal, Libby can't stop wondering if the inheritance is a 'big wind-up'. Every landmark in her life before she opened the envelope has been shifted on to a larger scale and made to seem small. Her £1,500 per annum salary rise, the MAC eye shadow she'd treated herself to as a reward, the hen weekend it had taken her six months to save for – the little joys that 'gave the flat surface of her life enough sparkles' all become insignificant. In a single extended sentence, reminiscent again of Henry James in the thread it traces through an individual's consciousness at the moment of realising, of *knowing* – Lisa captures the collapse of Libby's familiar structures.

> Libby feels her seams loosen and begin to come apart at the thought that she need not be here, that the sturdy ladder she's been gripping on to for dear life has just dissolved into a heap of golden coins, that everything has changed.

> Her friend and colleague Dido exclaims: ' "Oh my God . . . So you're basically a millionaire?"

' "I guess," ' is Libby's reply. The amount doesn't matter. It's about what the money means.

And money is just one means of transformation. It can come about through a released memory, or a revelation, or a small but significant decision that pushes a character firmly over a line and sets them on a new path. As Libby signs the paperwork, 'she feels very strongly the import of this moment, this invisible turning in her life taking her from *here* to *there*.' That crossing of a threshold recurs throughout Lisa's books.

Delilah in *Thirtynothing* is brutally violated, and gazes at the smudged silver polish on her toe, 'a reminder of the last thing she'd done . . . while she was still happy. Because, even as it was happening, Delilah knew for sure that she was never going to be happy again.' In the same novel, Nadine turns anticlockwise through a park at Primrose Hill, and the omniscient narrator wryly tells us that . . .

> . . . what Nadine didn't know when she made that seemingly trivial choice was just *how important* it actually was . . . little did she know that fate was about leap [*sic*] into her path and change the course of her life for ever.

Bernie, just before she meets Gervaise, the eponymous *Friend of the Family*, gets the feeling 'that if her life was ever going to change it would change now, during one of these brief windows of possibility in her otherwise structured existence'.

Megan in *The House We Grew Up In* recalls walking up a staircase, pushing open a door and discovering her brother's body: 'Eight small steps between *now* and *then*. Between what she knew and what she'd grow to wish she'd never known. Between the past and the future, between a small moment of peacefulness and the worst moment of her life.'

Laurel, Ellie Mack's mum from *Then She Was Gone*, vividly remembers the tiny niggles in her life – her weight, her hair, her husband – which shrank into insignificance when her daughter went missing:

'And then the police had arrived.

'And then the thing began.

'The thing that had never ended.'

In *After the Party*, Jem reflects: 'A moment. That's all it could take sometimes. Just one, brief, shimmering moment and everything could change, just like that. So it had been four months ago when Ralph had told her about finding God.'

Ralph's spiritual revelation – 'it was almost as if a voice that had been living deep inside him all his life was finally making itself heard. It was almost like discovering the truth of himself' – brings us back to the original meaning of 'epiphany', which David Lodge, in his series of essays titled *The Art of Fiction*, describes as 'literally, a showing . . . now loosely applied to any descriptive passage in which external reality is charged with a kind of transcendental significance for the perceiver'. In this category we could group Joey's realisation – 'an image flashed through her mind, bright as sunlight off water' – and Freddie's breathtaking vision of Romola as 'a human being looking at him . . . a skinny girl in a new town and a new school'.

Before I Met You, set in 1919, forgets about the Spanish flu epidemic. (Author-friend Jenny Colgan wrote to remind Lisa, and she retroactively inserted a couple of mentions.) When Lisa writes about September 2001, she is interested in the ups and downs of Vince and Joy, Jess and Jon Gavin's relationships: the attacks on America and their consequences are even less significant to the novel than the Napoleonic Wars were to Jane Austen's romances. The face masks in *The House We Grew Up In* and hand sanitiser in *The Making of Us* are precautions for people visiting new babies, rather than responses to a virus. She has made a firm decision not to write about the current global pandemic. 'I'm gonna write books set in 2019 . . . for a long time.' She's determined that whatever happens in Book 20 will wrap up before February 2020.

'Couldn't it be done?' I ask. 'With Covid?'

'It just makes me feel queasy,' she replies. 'I don't want to set it in aspic, I don't want it to be there forever in my books. I don't want to be flicking through one of my books and be like, Ew, mask! Ew, social distancing! Ew, Tier four!'

'So if you don't write about it . . . you don't have to remember it.'

'I don't want to revisit and think about it, so, yes.' But she recognises that lockdown has indelibly shaped our own dynamic, and in turn, this project. 'We're getting to know each other at a time when nobody's really forming new relationships.'

Now this unique period is coming to an end, and we are crossing a threshold ourselves. The reopening of cafés and restaurants has been announced. I've finished reading all of Lisa's back catalogue – nineteen books, which I estimate conservatively at over 1.5 million words – and she needs to focus on her new manuscript, which is lagging behind schedule. We set a date to meet, in May. There's a sense of conclusion, or at least a break.

'Part two', she writes to me, 'has definitely begun.'

PART TWO

Capital

I meet Lisa in London on a Friday afternoon at the end of May. It's not long after the reopening of restaurants and pubs. The streets are crowded with masked people and the Tube adverts collectively urge a cautious optimism – 'Welcome Back', 'Let's Start Again' – like the mise-en-scène in the final, hopeful shots of a disaster movie.

It is our second-ever meeting. Lisa is the first person I have hugged, outside my most immediate family, in fourteen months. I give her a printout of my writing about her to date – what she now calls 'our book'. She's read the first 20,000 words already.

'I love it, but I think you focus a bit too much on money,' she suggests.

I open my iPad and scroll down the questions I've brought to ask her. They are all about money. I close the iPad.

We're in the Groucho Club on Dean Street, in Soho, right at the heart of the Jewelliverse. The Groucho! In *Before I Met You*, it's a dreamworld, 'an experience that Betty would never forget'. She walks in with Britpop star Dom Jones, and 'Faces opened up like lotus blossoms at the mere sight of him, doors were held open, drinks were bought before being ordered. It was as though the club were a dark room and Dom was a light bulb.'

In the Groucho, Lisa goes to the bar and says she's booked a table. The waitress asks for her name. I frown at the waitress. This is Lisa Jewell!

Back in September 2020, Andy Martin and Lisa proposed the Groucho for our first rendezvous. I was secretly relieved when they changed the plan. I've only been to the Groucho twice before, as the guest of richer, more successful friends, and turning up to meet Lisa and Andy there would have felt like stepping into the deep end of a pool with two strong swimmers. I confessed this to Lisa later, and added that I'd never even heard of Soho House, the second members' club she was now planning to join. She had to check that I wasn't joking. I wasn't joking.

'I'm surprised you seem so wide-eyed about members' clubs,' she said. 'You strike me as absolutely a members' club kind of guy.' This is flattering but far from true. On the other hand, she's not nearly as blasé as she first seemed about this kind of media-celebrity lifestyle. 'I remember getting my Groucho membership card and my Groucho key fob and it being such a buzz, such a high, I was almost tearful.'

She doesn't come from money, any more than I do, and she's also used to feeling uneasy and outclassed when surrounded by effortless, easy privilege. She has financial capital – something she's constantly grateful for, and never takes for granted – but she still feels the lack of a different type of capital; what the theorist Pierre Bourdieu would call cultural capital, or the subtle social expertise that can't simply be bought. I outline the concept in an email. She considers it, then writes back.

'I realised that even though I am a member of the Groucho, I absolutely do not feel as though I belong. Not at all,' she reflects:

So I'm wondering why I want to be a member of a club that doesn't feel like a club and I think it really, for me, feels like owning a little of what you call capital. Owning a slice of Soho, of the establishment, of history, staking my pole in the ground somewhere, to say *I have been here*. It doesn't bother me that I don't feel like a member – and, like you, I always feel a little awkward on arrival, a little nervous walking through the bar, worried that I'll sit in the wrong place or do the wrong thing. So I absolutely get all of that. The most out of place I have ever felt was during the brief spell that my elder daughter spent at a private primary school when she was four. It wasn't even a fancy private school. But I felt so uncomfortable around those mothers, those women. I was thrilled when she got a place at our local state school and I could take her out of there! Then, because she was clever, we put her in for the 11+ at a posh girls' school across the road. She passed the exam and was called in for an interview and we walked into this mahogany-lined room, with all these posh mums who all knew each other from all the posh extra-curricular activities their kids were doing, and I felt like a slug. Couldn't wait to get back to the gritty comfort of the lovely state primary school.

I open the iPad again and turn on my voice recorder.

'I want to ask you a few questions,' I tell her. 'About money.'

'. . . Yeah,' she says finally, warily.

'When I was growing up,' I begin, 'my overriding idea about being rich came from Matt Goss, from Bros. Because he said in a nineteen eighties interview that he bought new socks, every day.'

A longish, puzzled pause. '. . . Yes.'

'How d'you feel about that. You could do that, would you do that?'

'. . . No!' she exclaims in shock. 'I don't even wear clean socks every day.' She hesitates. 'Is that nasty?'

I don't want to be impolite. 'Isn't it?'

'I just don't like waste.'

'Well, it's not waste to wear clean socks every day.'

'No, but he's saying brand-new, and then throw them away. And I know people who do this.'

'You know people who do this?' My voice rises in pitch. I feel like I'm one remove from Matt Goss.

'I don't *know* them, personally. I've heard of other people who wear a pair of socks and throw them away. To me it's wasteful. To me, an equivalent marker of being rich might be . . . upgraded travel?'

I consider for a moment. 'I read someone saying . . . who was it?' Was it another celebrity interview? 'Saying that once you've gone Business Class, you never want to go back.'

'It was Henry,' she laughs. 'Henry Lamb.' He'd announced it in one of the draft chapters from Book 20. I'm so immersed in her work that it's merging with real life, and we talk about him for a while as if he was a mutual acquaintance. I decide it's time to admit that I bought two shirts based on Paul's from *Then She Was Gone*: 'conventional at first sight until you realised that there was a contrast trim of Liberty print inside the collar'.

'So I had them made, inspired by one of your characters.'

'You had them made? How much did that cost?'

'Two hundred and fifty pounds each. Savile Row.'

She rears back in shock. 'Two hundred and fifty pounds for a shirt? I only spent two hundred and fifty on the dress for my fiftieth. My wedding dress only cost a grand.'

Time for my next question. 'I stayed in a hotel a couple of years ago, Green Park area, down the road from Fortnum and Mason. And I was walking down the road, and I see an advert for a café, and it said thirty-nine-pound lobster baguette.' We're halfway through a shared bottle of Picpoul de Pinet at this point, drinking on empty stomachs, and my speech is becoming more South-East London by the second: 'thirty-nine *paaand*.'

Lisa shakes her head firmly. 'If I was going to spend thirty-nine pounds on an item of food, I would want to eat it in an environment that highlighted it. Calories to me are a precious commodity. Any calories that I bring into my body, I want to be worth it. I'd rather just not eat.'

'Speaking my language,' I agree. 'I'd rather drink.'

'Absolutely.'

'I'd rather have wine.'

'One hundred per cent.'

We clink glasses and decide not to order food. The questions are going well now. I move on to the next.

'I think your readers are going to be really interested in your views on this,' I assure her, presenting a news story from my local paper. 'Burger and fries . . . one hundred and twenty-nine pound. It's covered in gold dust. Would you buy it?'

'No!' She squirms. 'No. None of these things. It looks mouldy. It looks like it's been discovered in an abandoned flat.'

'The owner says it's the Ferrari of meals.'

'Well, I wouldn't want a Ferrari either.'

I close the iPad. We crack on with the wine. By the time we finish the bottle, the remaining barriers between us seem to have blurred. The inevitable polite debate about who'll pay is resolved when the waitress tells Lisa her membership account is hugely in credit as a reward for the club being closed during lockdown, and the surprise gift of free wine cheers us even more. We rise and bob together, as if carried by a warm current, towards the stairs. Lisa muses that this project would never have worked if she didn't feel comfortable with me, but 'we like each other very much.' There's a wonderful simplicity about it, an almost childlike directness and lack of disguise, which feels like an arm slung around my shoulders.

On the way to the exit, I ask her lightly if she's the most famous person in here.

'No, because that was Natalie Appleton,' she tells me a moment too late, when we're already in the foyer. I half turn, my mouth gaping open, glancing behind me. I watched All Saints' 'Never Ever' video again on YouTube last week, and the Appleton sisters' celebrity seems more immediate than usual.

'I can't believe you didn't tell me when we were in there,' I hiss, too excited to ask how she knew it was Natalie and not her sister, Nicole. 'We can't go back now.'

'Yes, we can.' She takes my arm and steers me into the bar again. 'White T-shirt.'

And there, smiling in profile, tanned and radiant, is a real-life 1990s pop star. We enthuse as quietly as possible, fizzing with fandom for a few seconds, then scuttle out to the Soho street. I have to go home and help put my son to bed; Lisa has to find a Victoria's Secret and return some bras for her daughter. We hug again and she kisses her hand and waves it at me as if granting a blessing, and then we split up to return to our respective family lives.

But for a moment there, it felt a bit like being rich; it felt like sinking lazily into syrup while letting Pop Rocks buzz on your tongue.

St Albans to Cornwall, Botswana to Chicago

29 May 2021

Lisa has sent me the latest update of Book 20. It's now 20,000 words long: she wanted to 'hit 40,000 by July', and it's nearly June, so she's in danger of missing her own deadline.

But there's good news, too. On page fifty-five of the draft I'm reading, it snaps into shape, the tension suddenly tight, like a slack chain catching on the story's spinning cogs. Until then, Rachel had been cautiously exploring her new relationship with Michael – a doomed relationship, because we know he'll end up dead in a kitchen – and Lucy had been baking fairy cakes for a school sale, 'her head full of houses and Henry'. Her coldly enigmatic older brother had finally, after finishing his recap of *The Family Upstairs* for new readers, set off on his hunt for Phin. Things were progressing steadily, but at a leisurely pace.

And then startlingly, in a single moment, worlds collide, stories collide, timelines collide. Rachel walks out of her separate flashback narrative into the present day, and straight into Lucy's path.

' "Lucy Lamb? My name is Rachel. Rachel Rimmer. I think we need to talk." '

'*She can never relax,*' I'd insisted to Lisa at the start of March. '*She's always waiting for a terrible thing to happen. She's waiting to be found out. She can never, ever relax!*' And I'd got what I wanted. Lucy's new life is thrown instantly off-kilter, into panic. She flees with her kids, as she did in the previous novel, and soon she's huddled with them around a small table in a Cornwall B & B. Marco, now old enough to swear at his mum, resentfully sums up the situation: they've relapsed, within hours, to their old existence of temporary lodgings and constant tension.

' "Why is this happening all over again? Just when it was all going OK. Just when you got your inheritance and we were going to get a house and be normal. Why?" '

Because it had to happen, to transform this into a thriller. The precarious equilibrium needed to be disrupted. As Lucy's plans were knocked off course, I felt as though I was reading a Lisa Jewell novel again, racing ahead for the story, rather than dutifully studying it.

Except now, I can mail the author.

> Now it can be told, perhaps – at an earlier stage I was slightly concerned about the lack of obvious drama, but now those fears are quashed for me. So I think if I was reading it as a novel, I wouldn't have gone through that phase. Reading the first sections very much bit by bit, it felt like a long period of establishing characters and quite comfortable situations, apart from the initial phone call about Michael's death, which we move swiftly past into flashback. But perhaps it was a long period in terms of the *real time* during which I read it.

'It did occur to me', she replied, 'that maybe I'm doing a disservice to my book by giving it to you in such spaced-out chunks.' She's right: it's inevitable, unfortunately. The process of examining her novel in progress, chapter by chapter, though it affords me that unique, privileged position, does risk undermining pace, rhythm and tension.

'She has no masterplan,' Lisa tells us about Lucy. Meanwhile Henry confesses that ' "I'm following my instincts here, entirely. I don't have a game plan. I don't have any kind of plan really." '

This lack of strategy unites the Lamb siblings, but it's also the truth about Lisa. I felt my lip curling sceptically when Henry tells us he's not going to Botswana after all, but Chicago. I could suddenly see through him to his creator. That's not Henry's decision, I thought. That's Lisa not wanting to write about Botswana after all and sending him on a different, more convenient route, ditching the Chobe Game Lodge plot that's been in place since the end of *The Family Upstairs*. After all that, she's decided it would be easier not to write about Africa.

'"It's all a bit last-minute,"' Henry admits. '"And frankly, I'm rather glad I don't have to go to a game reserve in Africa. It's not really my idea of a good time, whereas Chicago very much is."'

Again, if I was reading the novel as a finished piece, with no knowledge of Lisa's methods or previous intentions, I would have accepted the change without even noticing; but that isn't the situation, and so I interrogate her because I can.

'I just didn't want to write Botswana,' she confirms immediately. 'I always had this fantasy that I would go there, as research, but obviously that wasn't going to happen. And now I'm backing off from Chicago, too. I'm thinking I'm gonna reset it somewhere else. I was planning to put it somewhere more small-town. I've made it very clear that Henry's worked very hard to find someone who might have a connection to Phin, but I think it's just been too easy, given the size of the city.'

'But he's not just going around every gay bar in Chicago. He's going around the gay bars that Phin would appreciate, in Chicago.'

'Yes.'

'He's getting into Phin's head, working out where he would go. He still has to check – what? – a dozen bars, or twenty or something?'

'Yes.'

'To me, that's fine. It narrows it down to gay men with a certain amount of money and privilege, in their forties. I imagine that's a relatively small circuit. He asks two hundred people. And Phin's really good-looking and has an English accent. People would remember that.'

'So, you think I could leave it in Chicago? It would make it easier.'

'I think it's fine.'

'OK.' She sounds relieved.

'What's ironic is that when I was reading *The Night She Disappeared*, what I enjoyed and appreciated was how well it all fits perfectly, like clockwork. So it's an achievement that you can make it up as you go along, and it still fits.'

'It's a jigsaw puzzle.'

'But people don't usually . . . make up a jigsaw puzzle as they go along.'

A pause, then she laughs triumphantly. 'They do! Lee Child does. And Ian Rankin does. I would say from my experience of doing panel events with authors in the genre, the balance between planning and making it up as you go along is fifty-fifty.'

I'm surprised, though naturally I take her word for it that she's not the only one who writes this way. But I also wonder if she's the only contemporary thriller author whose new novel is being shaped, however subtly, by someone like me: a shadow at her side.

She also has Selina, of course, as usual; though again, my presence in the mix has changed things, prompting her to share her work in progress with Selina at an earlier stage. 'I never normally give her anything to read until I break for the summer holidays, but since you'd seen it, it felt fair that she should see it too,' she wrote to me.

She liked it very much but cautioned me not to focus too heavily on Henry and his back story; she thinks he is rather crowding the narrative and taking over and I think she is 100% correct (though I always think Selina is 100% correct!). She said Rachel is the most interesting person in the story thus far and she needs room to breathe and shine. So I will prune back Henry, or maybe even save him up a bit for later. I also want to introduce a shadowy fourth character, one that I will know the identity of, but the reader won't. Someone from the first book. I wonder if you'll guess who it is.

The new novel still doesn't have a name. We've kicked around *A Family Reunion*, *The Family Reunion* and simply *Henry Lamb*, which I like for its echo of *The Silence of the Lambs* and its sequel *Hannibal*. But now, suddenly, she has a new idea for a title that itself carries with it an entirely new plot twist, as yet unwritten.

Birdie's Bones.

In-between Days

3 June 2021

Between my and Lisa's face-to-face conversations there are emails, filling the gaps.

Our correspondence began almost a year ago, in July of 2020, when I cautiously sounded Lisa out about what felt even to me like the slimmest suggestion of a possible book idea, and she replied cheerfully but even more cautiously. Like Jim and Lorelei in *The House We Grew Up In*, who write to each other for months (but never meet), we both relaxed slowly into it over time, gradually lowering our guard, and the prose style reflects our changing relationship. Exclamation marks crept into the business chat, and then capitals, and smiley faces, and now we even have a small set of in-jokes and familiar references. If we make a performance of erasing a phrase, as if redacting and retracting it, we use a ~~visible crossing out~~, which reminds me of the philosopher Jacques Derrida's concept of terms *under erasure*, but which is also common on Mumsnet.

Lisa frequently refers to my project as 'my/your' book, or 'our' book, and I sometimes wonder if she's just kidding.

Often she tells me what she's done that week instead of writing more about Henry, Rachel and Lucy, like a long, rambling letter to the teacher explaining why she hasn't started, let alone finished, her homework. In early June, she relates:

After my exciting double members' club morning on Wednesday (Groucho/Union) I was back in Soho on Thursday morning to meet Alison Owen and her production team at Soho House on Dean Street. Alison is Lily and Alfie Allen's mum so it was double, treble media/lovey/wonderful. Then two more Zooms this week with two more production companies and today a long chat with the TV guy from Curtis Brown to discuss strategy.

Interwoven with all this gallivanting I have written a 1000-word piece about my trip to India with my mother in 1998 for *Good Housekeeping* magazine, a 500-word letter to independent booksellers to go into the special new Indie editions of *The Family Upstairs* (they have orange spines as apparently Indie bookshops don't like yellow. And also rather more high-end author quotes. I have attached so you can see). I have written 400 words for Amazon about what's on my bookshelf. I have signed nearly 2000 bookplates for the UK indies (with another 3500 for the US waiting in the wings) and 500 tip-ins. I've written blurb for the UK sales team for *TFU2* as they are already busy getting ready to sell it in. I have written the first of what will be monthly newsletter updates for my new and improved website. That was 600 words. I have done an Instagram live with a big US blogger to promote the paperback publication of *Invisible Girl* in the US. I've written 35 individual thank you cards to the big UK book buyers to go inside their ARCs of *TNSD*. I've spent an hour on the phone being interviewed about my house renovation for *25 Beautiful Homes*. And it's still six weeks until publication day, which will come with its own avalanche of events/requests/interviews etc.

I understand some of the acronyms by now – *TNSD* is what she and her team invariably call *The Night She Disappeared*, and *TFU2,* which sounds vaguely like an internet insult, is the corporate codename for *The Family Upstairs 2* : what we were calling 'Book 20' before it became *Birdie's Bones*. But I don't know what ARCs are, or 'tip-ins', and I'm not sure if I understand what she means by 'bookplates' in this context. Her descriptions of her schedule seem as distant and starry to me as the social diary of the Duchess of Cambridge: a breathless list of pleasant engagements and flattering requests, though undeniably exhausting.

When I confess I don't recognise her abbreviations and industry terms, she writes back immediately to explain – they are Advance Review Copies and signed stickers or, more elegantly, signed pages that will be stitched into posh copies. She sends me photographs of herself at work: a fat golden pen gleaming in afternoon sunlight on a garden table, a stack of neat labels, an autograph that reminds me of Princess Diana's looping, girlish hand. It doesn't really dispel my impression of publishing royalty.

The following week, she updates with a postscript and further instructions.

I deliberately gave you that run down of the 'busy stuff' in my last email as I thought you might want to use it, in fact probably *should* use it. I'd like readers and writers who are also readers to have an insight into what else the job entails, that it's not all entertaining the whims of your muse and speaking sagely in bookshops. I've not been quite so busy this week, though I did ask my publicist Najma to line up three Zooms one after the other on Monday morning to 'get them out the way' and then fully regretted it after three solid hours of talking about myself. Tomorrow I have an Instagram Live with my Finnish publisher and then that is it for this week.

You probably should *use it.* Sometimes I wonder whether she really is writing this book, rather than me.

She sends me cover art and blog pieces, behind-the-scenes trivia – her daughter drew the pictures in *The Girls*, and narrated Pip's sections of the audiobook – and industry gossip, some of it labelled 'top secret for now, obviously: not for your/our book'. Sometimes, to satisfy her curiosity about my life, I send her family photographs, which she comments on succinctly but beautifully, captioning scenes from my past and presenting them back to me from her own perspective; almost as if she's transforming them into moments from her own fiction.

'You're like a character in one of my books,' she muses unnervingly at one point:

> You are like a lot of my characters. You are like Freddie in *Watching You*, wanting an architect's view from up high. You are Henry maybe, or Floyd from *Then She Was Gone*. Both of them lift parts of their outward personas/images from others – Floyd dressing like Laurel's ex, Henry becoming Phin. If I were writing you, I wouldn't have decided yet where you were headed and would be leaving your personality open for any possibility, good or bad. This is why I'm keen to get to know you and keep asking you cheeky questions. My instincts (normally so clear) are firing off in a dozen directions and I don't know which ones to follow.

I sit with this observation for a while, turning it over in my mind. It feels like a jagged rock, jabbing uncomfortably at my sense of self. Either it doesn't fit, or I don't want it to fit.

To take my mind off it, I do what I often do, and spend some money online. I find a Paul Smith sale and buy a new pair of socks, thinking about Matt Goss. There: I have agency. I can choose things for myself. I'm not like a character in one of Lisa's novels.

It's only when the socks arrive that I realise their colour was described as 'damson', and that I chose them explicitly because of that line I liked from *The Family Upstairs*. 'There is a storm brewing over the Côte d'Azur; it sits dark as damsons on the horizon, lying heavy on the crown of Lucy's head.'

I'm writing a book about Lisa, but maybe, in a way, her books are also writing me.

Birdie's Bones

Amazon is helpfully recommending that, based on my previous purchases, I should pre-order *The Family Upstairs 2*, due out in a year's time.

I have it in front of me, as a Word document. At the moment, it's officially called *Birdie's Bones*. 'Enjoy that while you can!' Lisa tells me, knowing all her books have carried temporary working titles that never made it to the cover.

And I do enjoy it. The story has been transformed into something that feels far more like my own sense of a novel; something that feels deliberate, intricate, planned, rather than character strands Lisa is chasing like wild horses, reining in and riding briefly before jumping to the next, second-guessing where they're racing to. The chapters have been spaced out with gritty new material – vertebrae in a spine, perhaps, or tough gristle between the existing parts – that discovers Birdie's bones on the very first page, before Rachel has even picked up the phone, and travels with them through the forensic process as they tell us, and the police, their story.

It's an intriguing, chilling subplot, reminding us of events from *The Family Upstairs*, but from a completely different perspective. Birdie's bones, we learn, have been submerged in river water for a year, but they were concealed for two decades prior to that, and only recently moved from their hiding place. 'Traces of foliage in the plastic bag. Traces of cobweb. Some insect matter.

Some fabric fibres. Possibly from whatever the bones had been wrapped up in before they were transferred to the plastic bag.'

These sections are short and the prose is clipped, more anonymous and transient than the fluidly chatty style we've become used to with Rachel, Henry and Lucy. The bones pass swiftly from teenage mudlark Jason and his archaeologist dad to DC Saffron Brown to her DCI, Samuel Owusu. Birdie's bones provide an undercurrent, a secret history, a detective plot that, all of a sudden, is going on – and has been going on, retroactively – behind the backs of our main characters. While Henry is playing amateur gumshoe in Chicago, charming his way into Phin's former apartment and ramping up his English accent to the max – ' "Would you mind, terribly . . . ?" ' – the skeleton of the first woman he murdered is being investigated back in London. Already, now, we have a fourth character in Birdie, and this is before Lisa has introduced the shadowy figure she mentioned earlier; and Rachel, we discover, is more than one person herself.

> She would look at herself in a mirror occasionally . . . and wonder who she was. Was she still Rachel Gold, the ice princess, the ball-breaker, the statuesque brunette who could never find a man to meet her high ideals? Or was she now somebody completely different? Had there in fact never been one finite version of herself? Had she always contained multitudes?

Of course, I borrowed that line from Walt Whitman, earlier in this book, and Lisa read it, and used it back to me in an email – 'Characters must contain MULTITUDES' – and here it is, in the novel itself, having travelled and found a new temporary home.

The novel, too, is now crowded with people and stories. But

it's also full of phantoms, like Phin's point-of-view narrative, which faded out at the airport months ago. In this draft is a sad note of loss:

> (this mini-chapter has literally gone missing. It was about the bones in the forensics lab, Saffron putting them together, discussing the fact with Samuel that there was a bunion etc. I have no idea where it's gone and am quite gutted.)

That's another section that will never be seen in the final copy, like Henry's lengthy updates and recaps, which Lisa told me she was planning to cut; like *Birdie's Bones* itself, if it goes the way of all her other working titles, which haunt the back catalogue like ghostly twins, like the lost half-brother in *The Making of Us*. Lisa lists them for me: *The London Brothers*, *Toby's House*, *The Kids*, *Pretty Betty*, *The Man on the Beach*, *Melville Heights*, *Dark Place*. (And, of course, every title carries with it multiple translations, like alternate-universe variants of itself: she shows me the covers of *On Se Reverra*, *Comme Toi* and *Tous Tes Secrets*, with their lush, dark floral designs, like perfume packages.) *Then She Was Gone* has its never-published happy ending, and *The Night She Disappeared* has a new epilogue, only for readers of the Target edition in the US; for the hundreds of thousands of people who will never see that extra chapter, Scarlett's final conversation with Tallulah in the prison visiting room might as well remain unwritten.

Then there are the novels that were never finished, or barely started: *The Wonderful World of Dave*, Lisa's attempt at Martin Amis-lite, and the idea she pitched to me a couple of weeks ago, which could have followed *Invisible Girl*. It was to be called *The Birthday Twin*, about a *Single White Female* relationship between two women who were born on the same day, with the less successful one fixating on and fangirling over a social media star. 'I definitely want my next book to be about a stalker/life invader,' she explained. 'It's not something I've done before and it's a sub-genre that I love.' It sounded at least as good as most published thrillers. I found myself wishing she'd write it.

In Translation

18 June 2021

I write to Lisa's French editor, drawing on all my memories of
A level language and literature classes, and feeling a little like
Maggie in *The Making of Us* as she composes a letter to Daniel's
twin, Marc Blanchard. Not *The Making of Us*, I remind myself,
but *Quatre naissances et un enterrement* ('Four Births and a Funeral')
with everything but the first word in lower case, following that
confident Continental style. Even the italic lean of French – *le
nouveau roman psychologique de Lisa Jewell* – seems to suggest a certain . . . insouciance, a laid-back attitude, a . . . how you say?
Une façon de vivre.

' "Je vais à la maison de Daniel. J'ai quelques achats," ' Maggie
repeats to herself, preparing to meet Marc. As I write to Aurélie
Charron, I also try to get my head into the right space; the
shrugging sophistication of a Jean-Luc Godard movie. *Eh ben,
alors, je sais pas. Ah ouais, c'est ça.*

Aurélie replies that morning. From France! Perhaps she's at
her laptop outside a pavement café, her fingers curled around a
tiny cup of black coffee as she reads my mail. She lifts a freshly
baked pastry as she scrolls, smiling enigmatically. *Ah!*

'You probably know this Italian adage [she writes]. « Tradut-
tore, traditore», which makes the translator a betrayer.'

Eh! Alors, bien sûr que je le connais, I say to myself. Of course,
of course, I use it every day.

She tells me that the French version of *Invisible Girl* is *Je serai ton ombre*, 'I'll Be Your Shadow', which loses any connotation of Marvel superheroes and acquires the sinister promise of the Velvet Underground song 'I'll Be Your Mirror', just as *Quatre naissances . . .* abandoned the pun in *The Making of Us* and recalled instead *Four Weddings and a Funeral*. (The French cover for that novel was equally misleading: bright balloons against a pastel turquoise sky, suggesting, as Aurelie says, 'a very light and funny read . . . a joyful entertainment'.)

Aurélie's company, Editions Bragelonne, took on Lisa's books from Presses de la Cité in 2018, and marketed them as psychological suspense, dropping the previous codes of chick lit; but they equally had to take account of specifically French codes and expectations, balancing genre convention with national tastes.

> We do not really *translate* the title, we try to *adapt* it in order to make it resonate in the best possible way with our readership. I always try to stay close to the original idea, but I want to underline the silent promise of the emotional involvement by keeping a personal pronoun in the French title (an inheritance of romance novels, but the shivers of romance and crime fiction have to coexist in short titles). To this day, there are only two [of] Lisa Jewell's books without a personal pronoun, but we made the choice to keep it in the French version.

So *I Found You*, *Then She Was Gone* and *Watching You* could keep that personal address – *Then She Was Gone* became *Comme toi*, grabbing the reader even more directly – but *The Family Upstairs* and *Invisible Girl* were adapted into 'They're in Our Home' and 'I'll Be Your Shadow', while *The Night She Disappeared* in French – *Rentre avant la nuit* – means something more like 'Come Home Before Dark', an instruction from a mother to a daughter with overtones of a folk tale.

@AmeliaDisparu, Mimi's Instagram name in *The Night She Disappeared*, should strictly, Aurélie notes, be *Disparue*. I search through my own comments on Lisa's proof and proudly demonstrate that I spotted this too. I write back passionately, fully, drawing on Camus, on Alain-Fournier's *Le Grand Meaulnes*, on *Alice au pays des merveilles*.

I wait for a reply. I keep waiting. Perhaps Aurélie has, how you say, *une vie*, 'a life'.

In the meantime, I buy a Lisa Jewell novel in French and find I can read it for myself, alongside the original.

Quatre naissances et un enterrement poses a distinct problem to translators as, of course, it is set in the UK, but also includes French characters, one of whom can't speak English. So Glenys Pike is fluent in French from the first page, declaring '*Mon Dieu, non!*' but somehow the novel still has to convey that Daniel is 'foreign' and that Maggie struggles to communicate with his brother.

It achieves that end through the device of placing French words in italics and adding '*en français*' afterwards. So Maggie, meeting Marc and discovering that he is bilingual after all – Lisa admitted to me that this was one of her quick changes for sheer convenience – blurts 'Oui' and then '*Oui*', signalling her attempt at French.

But translations into other European languages do gain one extra dimension, with the complexity of a formal and familiar 'you'. In the French version of *The Making of Us*, we can see that Lydia is on friendly terms with Bendiks from the start, but that even after their heart-to-heart, she and her housekeeper Juliette remain at the polite distance of *vous*. Daniel announces to Maggie, after several dates, that he sees her as a good friend – which fits in perfectly with his Frenchness, and his awareness of these conventions – and they switch from *vous* to *tu* accordingly.

Most touching, though, is the first meeting between Lydia and her long-lost brother, Dean. Approaching each other in a wine bar, they talk formally, as adult strangers would, despite the strange intimacy of their conversation. When she asks, 'And you, who do you look like?' the young man lowers his eyes, hesitates, and declares '*A vous*,' retaining the polite address even at this moment of intense connection. Next time we meet them, that distance has gone. Although in some ways translation inevitably involves compromise, in this respect it adds an unexpected poignancy.

How Is It Done?

25 June 2021

Lisa has sent me her latest draft. It is now 36,000 words long. Over the last six months, I have become more blasé about knowing a bestselling author and being able to read her novel a year before its release. I now simply refer to Lisa as 'Lisa' when mentioning her to friends and family, rather than 'Lisa-Jewell', reverently and breathlessly, like an exotic title. I no longer open these Word documents with quite the same awe and anticipation. I think to myself that I will read a bit of this quickly before bed.

Instead, I read the entirety of her new material, and don't go to sleep until I've finished it. This is her first draft, or second if we include the tidying-up that translates it from gibberish into English. When we left the characters last, Marco had just disappeared from the B & B on his own, and Lucy's world was spinning around her, and Lisa had no idea where he'd gone.

> I have no idea where Marco is. Gone To Find Some Answers I would suspect. I wouldn't blame Marco for going elsewhere to find what he needs. Maybe he's off to find Rachel? If there weren't already so many voices rattling around in this book, I'd be tempted to do some chapters from Marco's point of view. But I don't want to end up with an overcrowded narrative (which I think it is already in danger of becoming. I keep thinking I need to do some pruning).

As a reader, it seemed clear to me that Marco must be looking for Rachel. Inevitably we develop drafts in our heads about the next chapter after a cliffhanger, anticipating what might happen next. That kind of educated guesswork fuels online fan discussion every week between episodes of a cult TV drama. But unless she was holding back and playing disingenuous, which seemed unlikely, Lisa had no more idea than me about Marco's whereabouts: in fact, she had less of an idea than me.

It was at this point that I poured myself a strong gin and wrote her a two-page outline headed 'How I Would Finish *Birdie's Bones* If You Died Now', which she received with customary grace.

> Please let me first say how refreshing and amusing I find it that you are happy to use a phrase like 'if you died'. It's the sort of thing that I would do, because I'm not a strong believer in tempting fate, but a lot of people might steer clear of it. It made me smile. Funnily enough, I did once give Jascha the name of a writer I'd like to finish a WIP if I were to die (I was travelling somewhere). It was *I Found You*, I think.

She won't tell me who the writer is.

> I liked what you said about enjoying seeing Henry through the eyes of someone normal and have taken that through to his next chapter. I'm starting to get a feel for Henry's story being an *After Hours/Desperately Seeking Susan* type of set-up, where he gets batted about like a pinball from place to place, meeting interesting/weird people along the way, each one getting him closer and closer to the truth about Phin. Meanwhile the spectre of the police investigation into Birdie's Bones grows heavier in the background. I think, at this point,

that this is going to be a rather strange novel. Almost two novels in one with the Henry/Birdie's bones play-off and the Lucy/Rachel play-off. How the hell am I going to bring them both into land as one? I have no idea at this stage. It will happen, though. I know it will.

She had no idea. She does not plan. She does next to no research. And yet in the last two weeks, Lisa has written 8,000 words, off the top of her head, that hook me until the end of this new section. None of this should be possible. I reread *Watching You* last week and it still seemed like a clockwork mechanism, each piece precisely crafted and inserted in just the right place. Tiny cogs from many chapters back suddenly click into life and connect with others, turning up clues which were planted at the start. I knew Lisa's method when I read that novel for the second time. I knew she'd just made it up as she went along. Nevertheless, it felt not just planned but intricately planned.

How is it done? I am determined to work it out.

For a start, I realise, it's not a single hook but multiple smaller hooks, like Velcro, that keep the reader gripped. On a broader, structural level, having started *Birdie's Bones* with a single, simple arc about Rachel, Lisa is now switching between four full-blown ongoing stories, shifting gear confidently from one to the other like an expert driver building speed as she pulls into the middle miles of her race. Two of these strands, the siblings Henry and Lucy, started together, built slowly – a little too slowly for my liking – through leisurely recaps and scene-setting, then hit the accelerator at the same time and diverged on to different routes, as Lucy fled London and Henry left for Chicago.

Henry's plot has now settled into an entertaining tour of eccentrics, a social spiral that seems to steadily bring him closer to Phin at the centre – if Phin is there, if Phin even exists. (I have suggested that Phin might be more effective, ultimately, as an absence: a Holy Grail that Henry never grasps. 'I had been toying with the idea of Henry never finding Phin,' Lisa agrees. 'Or maybe finding Phin and finding him diminished in some way, so the converse of your idea.')

Meanwhile Lucy and Rachel have crossed paths once, prompting a crisis as Lucy assumes that Michael's murder is catching up with her through his ex-wife. I've maintained for a while that Lucy's fear of Rachel is entirely misplaced, and that they have a lot in common as victims of the same abusive man. Lisa's response is enthusiastic: 'Remember all those weeks (months) ago when I said I'd had my first sliver of an idea for a character arc – that was for Rachel. And it was just as you say – that Lucy is terrified that Rachel wants to put her in the frame for Michael's murder and tries her hardest to keep away from her, whereas Rachel just wants to meet her to befriend her and share stories and, essentially, hear all about how Lucy killed him!'

Rachel's main plotline, of course, takes place in flashback, so the younger version of her, currently on honeymoon with Michael, is living her own separate story: her past and present selves also need to converge by the end. Rachel and Henry are still distant across time and space, unknown to each other and connected only through Lucy. And the forensic study of Birdie's remains ticks away in the background, a bare-bones police investigation that, with each brief instalment, is reassembling the fragments of *The Family Upstairs* into a fuller skeleton that will be able to speak its own truth to the police about Henry's murders. Already, DCI Samuel Owusu has a pinboard of linked evidence:

- Body wrapped in a dark-coloured cotton towel from *Yves Delorme*. A similar towel today would cost around £200. Logo in use between 1988 and 2001

- Minute traces of poison found in hair and body matter, also found in corpses of beetles and flies. *Atropa belladonna* – or deadly nightshade
- Leaves mainly from London plane trees and trees of heaven (often planted along avenues), but also some dead blossom from the PERSIAN SILK TREE, rare in London

As readers, we also play detective with the available evidence, and try to predict where the plot is leading next: my guess is the hippy apothecary Justin from *The Family Upstairs*, who trained Henry in the use of herbs and is the only adult left alive from the house, older now but still perfectly able to spill what he knows to the police.

So, not yet half of the way in – her books sometimes stretch over 100,000 words – Lisa has successfully built a structure that enables her to keep up the same brisk pace across four tracks, some of which occasionally intersect. It's remarkably complex, considering that this all happened organically. I watched it happen. It grew of its own accord, like a living thing, with only minimal pruning and replanting. It started as a solo narrative, with one woman waking up to a phone call. Henry and then Lucy gradually appeared alongside Rachel, neither of them initially intended as viewpoint characters – remember, Phin was there first, before blipping out like an afterthought – while the investigation was added very recently, a retcon that added new material to the existing strands. Lisa is now in a prime position where she can take each episode to a natural break and then channel-hop us between them; at the end of each chapter we're eager for the next part, but then quickly drawn into another storyline. Our pleasure is deferred, but we're also distracted; we don't mind waiting.

But how is that done? I reread again, more closely. Those

four engines driving the plot forward are powerful, but they're proven too: thoroughly tested in Lisa's earlier work. There's a police investigation interspersed throughout *Watching You*, its brittle, no-nonsense interviews bringing us back to the facts of the murder in between the longer, fuller, character-based chapters. In *Birdie's Bones* the interruptions take the form of brief, professional exchanges between DCI Samuel, DC Saffron and their colleagues, but they serve the same purpose. That neat detail about a logo is reminiscent, in turn, of the abandoned Gap socks from *The Family Upstairs*, which Miller was able to date through their modern branding.

Henry's Chicago storyline is also typical Lisa Jewell – the idea of a character carrying out their own amateur investigation recurs across several books from *One-Hit Wonder* onwards. His clever bit of deduction, studying a photo of Phin until he can discern part of a sign in the background – 'a food shop called Organic something beginning with a D. I google Organic plus a D, and a shop called Organic Delightful comes up' – is a plausible version of the *track in . . . enhance* cliché from post-*Blade Runner* police shows, where a tiny reflection is reversed, enlarged and clarified until it reveals a new clue, but it's also very similar to a scene in *Watching You*:

> Freddie had zoomed in on the photo, looking for some clue as to where it might be from, and found half a logo painted on to the inside of the cubicle that looked like the letters URBN arranged into a square. He'd googled URBN and found that it was the Urban Outfitters' logo . . .

(I tried this myself. It works.)

Lucy, a woman desperately searching for her missing child, is a figure we've encountered several times before – most recently in *Invisible Girl*, where Cate checks through her teenage son Josh's internet history, as Lucy does here:

Rachel Rimmer London
Rachel Rimmer Michael Rimmer Murder

And there, at the very top:

Rachel Rimmer Jewellery London NW6

I don't have to check through Lisa's internet history: she provides it for me. If the police got hold of this, they'd start hunting for a high-class serial killer.

Arboreal forensics
Most expensive towel
Deadly nightshade
Persian silk tree London
Skull bone terminology
Tree of heaven
Which insects eat dead bodies
Is a bunion made of bone

Finally, the building tension between Rachel and Michael – unbearable even in flashback, even though it happened long ago and Michael is safely dead – is one of Lisa's fortes, last seen in *The Night She Disappeared* in the scenes with Tallulah and Zach. The arrogant but charming older man, liable to snap from an easy smile to a slap – verbal or physical – and then back again in an instant, fast enough to make a woman wonder if she imagined it, if she provoked it, if it's all her fault, is a familiar figure in Lisa's novels. She's scarily good at writing his type.

So none of this is new exactly, even within Lisa's own work; but nevertheless it grips and engages, even with someone in my jaded position who's read the previous nineteen novels in the past months, many of them more than once.

How is it done? I need to focus down to the micro level. Because that's where it is, I realise: in the details. There are larger, obvious hooks of effective storytelling, the cliffhangers that drive the 'just one more page' impulse, what Roland Barthes called the enigma code; but what draws us into each new chapter and keeps us there is a series of smaller hooks.

Rachel and Michael, for their honeymoon, 'had a small wooden house on stilts over an azure sea filled with colourful coral and *ribboning* fish . . .' *Azure sea* confirms a clichéd expectation: that the sea is a beautiful blue because the vacation is expensive and perfect. It is holiday-brochure blurb. It is an IKEA word: it does a job; it fills a gap. But *ribboning* fish leaps out; it describes not the fish themselves but their weaving movement around the coral. *Ribboning* is a word you might choose if you'd actually gazed down at those fish. Ribboning is bespoke.

We are told of the days before the marriage, when Rachel focused on the 'exact filigree of her antique lace wedding dress, the last inch she wanted to carve off her hips, the precise cut of the yellow diamond.' Apart from *filigree*, which delicately recalls *ribboning*, there is a series of hard sounds here, well-aimed little strikes – ex*act*, an*tique*, *carve*, *cut* – like a jeweller shaping a precious stone, like a woman wanting to slice away a little more flesh from her bones, like a man chipping away slowly at her confidence. Maybe it's accidental, unthinking: maybe it just flows without effort for Lisa when the writing is going well, but there is significant craft in that single sentence, even if it's unconscious.

Yellow diamond again stands out. A writer less concerned with her characters wouldn't have bothered, would have reached lazily for 'perfect', 'sparkling', but Lisa knows Rachel, remembers that she works with metal and gems, intuits that an expert would choose something unusual and distinctive for herself, knows – as Rachel does – that yellow diamonds are technically classed as 'fancy' colours, rarer than white. She has such possession of this character that, during the first stand-off between Rachel and her new husband, she can tell us, as flatly and simply as if she was stating a law of physics, that 'she could not lie. Rachel was incapable of lying.'

And Lisa confidently controls the pace and viewpoint of this sequence too, forcing us to watch every moment of their awkward exchange as it swings between his aggression and her apologies, as if we were there in the little room, cringing as he refuses to let it drop – ' "Well, I'd say it clearly *is* a 'biggie', Rachel." ' Then mercifully she sweeps us through the next few days with a relentless rhythm, each of Michael's snubs dealing another hammer blow to Rachel's pride. 'But there was no more sex. No more sex at all.' And next paragraph, when they're back at home, with the unadorned plainness of a fable: 'Still no sex.'

The honeymoon started in paradise, with sunlight on the sea. It changes in a second. Rachel's single moment of misjudgement causes the atmosphere in the little wooden hut to *curdle and warp*. The pauses become *darkly silent*: her attempts to *lighten* them and fill them with nervous laughter are rejected. Her laughs sound *hollow*; Michael stands *rod-straight, pinched-faced, hard*. Rachel zips the offending sex toys *tightly* into an inside pocket. They return to the *frozen* tail-end of February. Every adjective, every action contributes to that cold, taut anxiety.

We saw above that Lisa analyses atmosphere like a poetic scientist, assessing a mood on the level of 'particles': here she senses 'every atom of emotional energy in the room at that moment' and immerses us in its toxicity. The language is tainted by it; we can't escape it until the chapter ends. And then, a chapter later, in present-day Chicago, she gives us a sour aftertaste as Henry unsettles the delicate balance between a couple he meets in a bar: 'I feel something radiating from the woman, something I recognise, something that almost has a smell to it, a hormonal musk. It's fear . . . The atmosphere between these two human beings is appalling.'

Though we're safely removed from Rachel and Michael's ongoing story here, the scent of male aggression and female uncertainty returns, retaining sick tension in what could otherwise have been a lighter, low-pressure scene, and reminding us of what we're going back to as soon as we're with Rachel again.

She confronts Michael. She has been through hell, wondering and waiting for him to contact her. He's in the kitchen, stirring things pleasantly as if nothing had happened, asking how her week went. She remembers 'the wall of ice that emanated from him, every minute of every day'. '"You went cold on me,"' she insists. That frozen February chill is back between them. But now it's worse, because Michael tries to impose on her – and through her, on us – another version of the story. '"Well, that's your interpretation of events,"' he says neutrally, calmly, and like Rachel, we might even start to doubt the details of the earlier chapter, wondering if perhaps it was her fault after all. He sounds so reasonable, so vulnerable even, like a child rather than a successful middle-aged man.

'I just recall a girl who was disappointed and pissed off because she wasn't going to get to do the things she wanted to do, and a brand-new husband left feeling a little inadequate and scared . . . And then the girl deigns to send a message and the brand-new husband is too scared to think what this might mean and so he goes to the grocery store and buys organic chicken breasts and the most expensive tomatoes he can find and busies himself with the distraction of chopping them all up and making them taste good and the girl arrives and tells the husband that actually, this is all, all of this sadness and fear and worry, it is all somehow, in fact, his fault.'

The singsong repetition, the nursery language – *the girl*, *scared*, *taste good* – the twee third-person account of himself as a *brand-new* husband; it's a spell designed to convince Rachel that she must have been in the wrong. It is brilliantly plausible, and Lisa is effortlessly good at this; or at least, it seems effortless, which is a rare talent in itself. She puts her two characters in a situation, and because she knows them so well, she just lets them speak and writes down what they say.

And this is the key to it, I realise. Beyond all Lisa's craft with language, her instinctive feel for the right words and sounds, what draws me into her stories is exactly the thing that was troubling and unsettling me about them: that they feel organic and alive, as if she is recording events as they happen. Their lack of planning makes them unpredictable and tense. Every scene could pivot in various ways, depending on a change of mood or a random chance. There is a volatility to them. Anyone could die. Anyone could be lying. She doesn't know yet, and so we don't know, and so her stories seem to hold their breath, preparing for potential shocks around every corner.

There are other little details throughout that sell this sense of observed reality. Lucy, searching for Marco, meets a 'young man with a beard and a head of blond curls'. He offers to call his surfing flatmate. The flatmate is called Simmo. We meet that bearded blond man for the equivalent of a few seconds; we never see or even hear Simmo, but we believe that there is a Simmo on the other end of the line. Is his real name Simon, or his surname Simmonds? Is he a local, or a posh boy slumming it, enjoying the beach life? We'll never know, unless perhaps he returns later. But we believe in Simmo, and so by extension we believe this scene.

Henry sees a woman in a bar. He anatomises her in his objective, aloof fashion. 'She looks young at first, and then, as she gets closer, not so young . . . She has good legs in a denim miniskirt and tanned feet in flip-flops. In her hand is a bike helmet.' There is nothing remarkable about this description. We read it and accept the codes for *minor character*, someone who will be serving the plot briefly, offering information, then moving on. But then he stands next to her, and she 'smells of dry shampoo', and suddenly she becomes a person who got ready before she came out to this bar, maybe even got changed, knew her hair needed a quick boost but didn't have the time or energy to wash and blow dry it, and reached for her Batiste.

Lisa's writing may seem effortless, but the easy, lazy choice would have been 'smells of cheap perfume', 'smells of bike oil', 'smells of sun-tan lotion'; something to confirm our first impression and box her up neatly as a minor character, rather than open up a sense of her as someone who existed before this scene. Why did she smell of dry shampoo? If I asked Lisa, I'm sure she'd just tell me that's what the woman smelled of; that's the person she was, that's the kind of evening she'd had, that's the sort of night it was for her. Why is the surfing flatmate called Simmo? Maybe Lisa would shrug and say, 'He felt like a Simmo; I imagined him in his wetsuit, running down the beach that morning, and saw him in a crowded bar earlier that week looking for his friends, and heard someone shouting, "Yo Simmo!", so I decided that was his name.'

After rereading *Watching You*, I had some questions for Lisa. She answered them fully and honestly, of course: some of the twists, she admitted, were just narrative sleight of hand, some of the incidents were just coincidence, some of the details come down to interpretation. But when I asked her whether Tom Fitzwilliam's relationship with his wife was abusive or a consensual arrangement, she turned the question over to Tom. 'Were he real and were you to ask him, he'd probably sigh and say, "I really don't know."' She last wrote about Tom in 2017, but she can still bring him on from the wings for an interview, as if his life has gone on in the background undocumented since the end of *Watching You*, as if he could appear easily in another novel, years later, if there was a story that deserved telling. 'Were he real . . .' she begins, sensibly, and maybe she feels clearly that he's just her creation; but as a reader, on some level, I believe that Tom is still out there.

So I still don't know exactly how she does it, but I know now what she's doing. She is creating a world so casually convincing in its everyday details that it seems to continue when we're not looking. One step ahead of the reader as the plot unfolds, she pulls off the illusion that she's simply recording what happens; and so anything could happen next.

In These, Our Private Lives

8 July 2021

Lisa Jewell is unnerved.

Six months have passed since we started this strange partnership. Lisa, who has put the characters she loves through unspeakable trauma and kept millions of strangers awake in the middle of the night with her relentless, effortless suspense, is worried. Not by her book, at this point – she sailed past her 40,000-word target at the start of July, though she knows she'll have to go back and prune the earlier chapters and has a suspicion she wants to rewrite a few entirely – but by my book. By this book. By that last part in particular.

It started off well. 'I think it's spectacular,' she wrote to me after her first reading.

> Truly. Definitely my favourite bit yet, and your most powerful and engaging writing so far (which is saying something!). Your conclusions and findings about the way I write and why it works are exactly as I myself have been coming to understand over the past three or four books. I genuinely had goosebumps reading it.

To me, of course, this is like Lee Child writing to Lisa to tell her how much he enjoyed *The Night She Disappeared*, as he did last week. But then the following Friday night, with her daughters out and husband at the big house in Kent, Lisa pours a large vodka and writes to me again.

I am, by now, an expert in Lisa Jewell's writing, and I can almost scent anxiety creeping from the pores of this message. One paragraph in particular lets the guard down entirely.

I am aware (sometimes subliminally, sometimes really quite acutely) of what a huge deal this is, what we're doing. Really huge. I am putting so much trust in you. It's quite extraordinary. Everything is quite guileless and raw. I have to assume that you are who I think you are. But I keep thinking you could be anyone.

'But there is the vodka talking,' she adds. 'I will move along.'

In everything that follows, there is a new caution. She holds back in emails ('Let's leave it at that'). I am afraid she thinks I am like Freddie, or Floyd, or worse, Henry, or worse still, someone she cannot place at all, a character I've invented. She is used to sussing people immediately. It's taken her six months, with me, and she still can't get a fix on who I am.

So I tell her, because if she doubts too much, everything is lost: the project depends on trust. I tell her a version of my life story in my next mail. I tell her about my temporary triumphs and my deep troughs, about trauma and therapy, about what I value, what I've lost or let go of, and what I regret. It takes me two days to write. I feel like Clarice giving Hannibal her memory about the lambs: a painful quid pro quo, a necessary exchange. She replies after a few days and seems satisfied. For my part, I worry that I'm providing her with a character for a future novel, selling myself into fiction.

And now she is concerned – only mildly concerned, this time – that I am not painting a full picture of her. In *The Night She Disappeared,* Tallulah's life before Scarlett had, in a memorable line, always been 'matte, not gloss'. Lisa feels I may only be giving the glossy version of her life.

I think it's worth bearing in mind that my 'thing', as a creator of pretend people that readers relate to so strongly, is to show ALL SIDES of them. Good/bad. Shiny/dull. Shallow/deep. We can all be all these things, constantly and concurrently. So while of course my readers want to know about my Instagram life (signing things with a big YELLOW pen in my garden) . . .

It had looked gold to me. Or maybe I'd just said it looked gold because that suited my point better.

. . . they also want to know about my Facebook life (finding things that look like green slugs with furry arms in the bottom of a carton of tomato sauce buried at the back of my fridge). I was thinking about this earlier, actually, as I painted my own toenails with Revlon nail polish in my bedroom (next to a huge pile of my family's clean and folded laundry which I had washed and folded and was soon going to sort and hand deliver if I could ever find the motivation).

'It might be nice', she concludes, 'for you to allude here and there to how deeply unglamorous most of my life is in the telling of my year. Because it really, really is.'

It might be nice. I feel as though I'm being subtly directed by a charming boss, the type who invites you into her office for biscuits and smilingly chides you about just a couple of things she'd love you to do differently.

I point out to Lisa that I've only seen her three times in person, and that the first involved her headlining a glamorous literary salon, the second featured her and Andy discussing the famous authors they both knew, and the third was *at the Groucho*. She can tell me about how she paints her own nails and does the laundry – which, to be fair, is far more than Lydia does in *The*

Making of Us, with her housekeeper and regular cheques from Dulux – but my own encounters with her have been relatively razzle-dazzle.

Lisa doesn't reply, because she's travelled to Hexham with her publicist for her first live event in eighteen months, so I sit at home and stalk her through social media instead.

This is the first time I've looked at her Twitter, Instagram or Facebook. I've weaned myself gradually off each platform over the last few years. I wanted to engage with Lisa as a person, rather than a public persona. But in her absence, this will have to do.

I trail off after an hour, not entirely satisfied. There's surprisingly little to go on; and I can't identify so much difference between the three, given what she suggested about a different sense of self on each. When I report back to Lisa, she explains patiently further.

> Insta is where I put pretty pictures and 'my lovely life' stuff. Insta followers don't want to know that you've had a bad day. Twitter, I don't post anything at all, I merely retweet and reply to readers' tweets. Facebook is my comfort zone. To me they feel like three very distinct and unique representations of my real life. But maybe that's not obvious to the objective onlooker.

What her Twitter has in common with Instagram is the book covers and promotional material. The distinction between her Instagram and Facebook is more subtle, though, and the same images overlap again across both strands, saturated with colour, light and life. Lisa's father in a striped jacket, sitting regally at a garden table decorated with wine bottles and plates of fruit, raising his hand towards her similar blonde sisters like a modern production of *King Lear*. Skies streaked with gorgeous violet and turquoise; the last of the day's sun glowing magenta off the sea at the far horizon. Garden parties, cocktails, groups of friends, some of them tagged with the names of fellow famous authors: Jenny Colgan, Sophie Kinsella, Mike Gayle, whose debut *My Legendary Girlfriend* was another late-nineties hit alongside *Ralph's Party*. Yasmin Boland's birthday celebrations: Yasmin, the friend who made Lisa that bet, decades ago, and set her on the path to success.

A flashback to a 2015 signing with Jane Green, Lisa and Freya North – *Freya North!* I read all her books at the start of the century – looking like another set of blonde sisters. The outside gatherings resemble Hockney drawings from the 1980s – sketches of lipstick smiles, floral dresses, hands clutching glasses of rosé, a surround of lush green leaves. (And then I think: how do I know what Hockney's drawings from the eighties look like, anyway? Because my parents had them framed on the wall of our big house in a rough street when I was a teenager, and perhaps aspired to that sort of lifestyle themselves.)

In between the social snapshots are a form of promotion by proxy. Lisa doesn't push her own work hard – if she does, her tone is giddily, endearingly excited, almost as if she's one of the fans – but her Facebook feed is heavily punctuated by readers' shots of her novels on eiderdowns, on Asda shelves, in B & Bs, on tables with cups of tea and bottles of beer beside them. There's Paul Burston, another celebrity fan, holding up *The Night She Disappeared* on Hastings beach, the location for his own fiction. 'I don't often go book shopping,' announces one reader, 'but when I do, I make it count.' This, I suspect, is the kind of comment that makes it worthwhile.

And then there are shots of the books Lisa's reading, genuinely gripped: she's in bed with Will Dean's *The Last Thing to Burn*. In the background is an out-of-focus open wardrobe and a dresser with deco lamps. It's a relatively intimate glimpse into an author's life — but tellingly, this is the author as reader, placing her on the same level as the people who post pictures of her covers. Next to this is the news about Lisa's Covid jab ('it made me pretty bloody unwell') and a thoughtful report on a recent conversation with her daughters about the effect of porn on teenage boys.

She can't be faulted for her social media presence. It's open, transparent, and unpretentious. If Lisa's online persona is a mask, it's moulded from life. 'I can't conceive of myself as a brand unless the brand is being me,' she told me during one of our earlier chats. If it's all a bit jollier and fizzier than the uncertain, sometimes acerbic person I've grown to know through our correspondence — a bit 'Marian Keyes' perhaps — that's social media for you. We all put on a public front and happy face.

But as a consequence, I can't really see the unglamorous side she was alluding to in her email. Chores and cheap nail varnish are never mentioned, and though I find the story about a gruesome discovery at the back of her fridge, it's from mid-March.

As I troll through her feed, Lisa updates from her book signing. A restaurant table, loaded with fresh starters and sides, with a pretty woman caught mid-grin behind them; sunset striking the angles of a stone church; stained glass panels of autumn leaves tumbling into a fire; a river under steely skies. Hexham, as photographed by Lisa Jewell, looks like the trailer for a Lisa Jewell book.

She seems to fear she's giving away too much, trusting too much. Sometimes I think I'm no closer than I was at the start, six months ago.

Two Hundred Words

It was going so well. Rachel had finally met Lucy, and the first encounter between these two leading women was nothing like either of them had expected; nothing like I'd expected, either. A different kind of writer, who was content to settle for obvious choices, would have opted for a clash between two divas, all arch remarks and sneering looks, like a scene from a daytime soap or perhaps, these days, from *Love Island* : 'Can I just pull you for a chat, Lucy?' The clack of heels, the swish of gowns. That's how it could have gone. But Lisa sees them both as human beings with messy lives, so of course they first come into contact when Lucy is tired and sweaty and feeling old, touching her oily forehead for wrinkles, and the younger Rachel is swamped in a scruffy hoodie, her hair scraped back. And as I'd guessed – I would say *as I suggested*, but Lisa had this in mind from the start – there's little animosity between them, and a lot of potential for an interesting alliance. They're not each other's enemy.

But since those scenes, nothing: or nothing much, which might be worse. Just 200 words of Henry meeting a man called Kris Doll and introducing himself as Joshua Harris. Henry is going to join Kris Doll on a motorcycle tour of the city. They shake hands and sign some insurance forms. Has he ever been on a Goldwing? asks Kris. (I look it up. It's a type of Honda.) No, says Henry. Any kind of bike? Kris asks.

' "Well, yes. Once or twice. Been given lifts, by friends. But never as a hobby. Or as a thing."

' "I don't suppose you can remember the names or the makes of the bikes you've been on?" '

Henry can't remember. Kris says it doesn't matter and assures him that this will be a really comfortable ride.

If this was an article from an in-flight magazine about motorcycle tours of Chicago, I would have flipped ahead already to the movie listings.

Lisa doesn't write anything else all week.

In a year, this novel will be published. Right now, I can't see how its drifting strands are going to come together into anything like a completed story.

Publication Day

Lisa told me a story at the start of all this, and it stuck in my head. She was once invited to join *The Weakest Link*, the quiz show hosted by Anne Robinson, known for her wry put-downs and cutting remarks. Anne, clad in black like a *Star Wars* villain, cast her eye around the circle of contestants and found something disparaging to say about each of them in turn, to audience laughter. And then she reached Lisa. And Lisa looked evenly back at her, and Anne searched her face and found nothing, and was forced to move on.

When I heard the story, I assumed it must be key to the mystery of Lisa Jewell. I was deeply impressed. She'd resisted a celebrity inquisitor. She must have put up such a quick and effective mask that Anne Robinson was thrown back from it, the Medusa's gaze repelled. Now I realise I was wrong. She hadn't given Anne nothing; she'd given her everything. There was just nothing there to use as a weapon.

Lisa turned fifty-three this week and marked the occasion with a Facebook portrait of herself in bed, unfiltered, with her cat sitting on her face, its tail raised to the camera. Three days later was her publication day, also now an annual July event. I wonder which is now bigger for her: her own birthday, or the birth-day of a new book.

Her Twitter feed was immediately flooded with praise from other authors, from her agent, her publisher, from readers who had been waiting months for the release of *The Night She Disappeared*. That annotated manuscript I read as a Word document in January, inhaling it in one addicted session, is now a real object, a book out there in the world. I check its page on Amazon. The novel's score starts off at a stellar 4.5 and remains steady. All that changes is the number of reviews: 38 in the morning; 76 in the afternoon. By evening, 179 people have reviewed it and the 4.5 stars are still intact. Lisa is safe. She's more than safe. Her new novel has been rapturously received by the people she really cares about. (She told me earlier this year that the broadsheets ignored her, and I've discovered that for myself; I pitched a review of the novel to four editors, with no reply.)

Lisa went out that morning to drop off her daughter's two-day PCR test and, she writes, breathlessly, reminding me of *Mrs Dalloway*:

> . . . when I returned the house was awash with flowers that needed to be put in vases, photographed, put on social media and given thanks for and the day just slipped through my fingers as all days seem to be doing at the moment and now it is nearly five and I have to leave in half an hour for my publication dinner at The River Café.

She has written no more of *Birdie's Bones*: social media has consumed what was once her working day. She replies generously to one message, and when she checks again, another five are waiting. And then there are Zoom chats, and meetings about film adaptations, and that's another working week gone, and soon another month.

> It really feels as if it should be August by now. Surely it is? I don't know why time has lost its shape these past three weeks. I suppose I have not had one regular routine week.

And this hot, languorous weather stretches time somehow, makes it feel like a holiday. I still haven't written any more book. In fact I haven't opened the document since July 12th, the day I wrote 200 words.

Her flurried emails to me are themselves publishable prose. Their rhythm and syntax, built around that striking suggestion of time melting like a candle in the summer heat, would make a memorable internal monologue without much need for editing. Each of her emails to me is much, much longer than the 200 words she's committed to her novel in the last two weeks. And it strikes me that there is one rogue element in this year, the year that it's all slowing down and going off track, and that element is me. Maybe I'm the issue. I write back reassuringly that this time next year, she will be enjoying the responses to *Birdie's Bones* as a finished object, and that I'll back off in September to allow her a clear run at the 60,000 words she needs to finish. But part of me feels responsible that my own project of investigating her has disrupted Lisa's schedule.

On the other hand, it finally feels as though it was worth it. One year exactly since I first wrote to her – tentatively, formally – I feel I'm beginning to work her out. I am coming closer to discovering the truth about Lisa Jewell.

It's there in that last email, about walking to drop off her daughter's Covid-19 test and returning to a house awash with fresh flowers. Actually, it's been there in every recent email, which she fills with details of her daily life. That's what she was trying to tell me by mentioning the Revlon toenails and the piles of laundry, in between the meals at places like the River Café and the calls from people like Jed Mercurio. Perhaps it's been there since her first reply from last summer, when she was in the middle of writing *The Night She Disappeared*: '. . . the 40k words written during lockdown in a rented office with a fridge full of Fanta Zeros, the roar of the Finchley Road and birds' eye view of the queue snaking around Waitrose from my window . . .'

I took too long to see the truth, because I was still stuck on my own idea of what a bestselling author's life should be like, *must* be like, and I resisted her gentle prompts, because I didn't want to be directed about what to write or how to think. So I had to work it out for myself, and it took me a full year.

There is no mystery, or not the one I was looking for. I was working in the wrong genre. Subconsciously, I was trying to write a thriller about Lisa Jewell, and a central character so unproblematically nice, so genuinely generous, so contented and undemanding, didn't fit that kind of plot. I was incredulous, during our first Zoom chat of January this year, when she came across as someone who just wanted to keep doing a job she enjoyed, and again and again, week after week, she had to bemusedly bat down my assumptions – no, she didn't have a room full of Louboutins; no, she didn't fly first class – and I still didn't get it. I just didn't click that you can have a beautiful, award-winning Shaker kitchen that features in design magazines, and still feel frustrated that you have to leave that kitchen because your teenagers have stumbled in at 11 p.m. determined to drunkenly cook something for an army of their friends, and that you'll be the one who has to clean that kitchen in the morning. Selling a million copies of *The Family Upstairs* doesn't mean your daughter, who hasn't read a word of any of your novels, won't tell you *fuck off, you weirdo* when you try to take a nice selfie on her last day at school.

I'd read Lisa's fairy-tale success story and imagined that it had transformed her, but it didn't – it gave her some nice things that she gratefully appreciated, but she was still the same person there at the centre of it all, essentially unchanged. And that's why she's still so good at writing about complex human beings, at feeling out people's stories and finding the vulnerable spaces in their lives, about seeing the multitudes of contradictions within characters. Even after reading all her novels, I'd failed to learn that simple lesson myself. I'd encountered her contradictions and interpreted them as clues and started hunting for a phantom truth hidden at the heart of it all. The real truth is that we all contain those contradictions, and that Lisa is, inevitably, just like us, except that she can do one thing incredibly well.

I was baffled by her approach to writing because I could never achieve it myself. Even now I know that *Watching You* emerged organically, with plot points retroactively inserted and character details changed during the process, it still reads to me like a perfectly planned mechanism. Even though Lisa told me about the late afterthought-alterations she made to *The Night She Disappeared*, it still seems to me like an intricate artefact, mapped out from the start on a colour-coded chart. Even though I've seen *Birdie's Bones* emerge as a work of improvisation, with false trails, dead ends and unexpected detours, I know all those uncertainties will be erased within a year, and it will be published as a complete piece, its current cracks invisible.

The simple truth is that Lisa Jewell is really, really good at her job, and wants to keep doing it as well as she can. She remains astonished at the rewards it brings, and appreciative of how kind people are to her. She knows that her reputation rests on her next book, and that every year she chooses to write, she is opening herself up to the possibility of failure. She wouldn't wake up to an empty bank account, of course, or face the bailiffs coming to take away her new house; but there is a larger kind of house built around her, a symbolic house, a tower of responsibilities and expectations, and she knows that every year she risks its stability again by taking out the very bottom layer and rebuilding it, by replacing her former success with a brand-new novel that could fall apart and collapse the foundations. Every year, Lisa Jewell plays Jenga with her life.

It took me a year in total – including six months of intense involvement in that life – to recognise what she'd told me from the start. But I got there on publication day, and I feel I deserve my own reward as I toast Lisa's new novel myself.

I go out to a local restaurant, where I have some sort of spicy Moroccan dish with couscous, and on the way home I have a sudden vision of Aperol as a suitable drink for a blazing July day like this – the idea of a glowing orange spritzer calling to me like a beacon – and back at home my son's paddling pool is still out on the lawn, so I sit with my bare feet splashing in cool water and raise the glass for that first sparkling, sunlit sip, feeling contented as a king, and then I remember.

I put down the glass and go inside and search my Kindle version of *The Family Upstairs* for the word 'Aperol'.

> . . . as Saturday dawns, another hot day with a sky full of nothing but blue, the windowpanes already red hot beneath her hand as she pushes them open, Libby has no thoughts of . . . April's famous spicy couscous salad or of a glowing orange globe of Aperol Spritz in her hand and her feet in a rubber paddling pool.

My plan for a perfect summer afternoon was lifted from a Lisa Jewell novel.

I look up from my iPad. Without warning, the weather has changed. Fat hard drops are hitting the paddling pool like bullets, splashing into the glass where I left it on the garden table, diluting my drink with rainwater.

Author, Meet Editor

'Author, meet editor!' announces Lisa's editor, introducing me to my own.

We are meeting at the flat of Lisa's editor, Selina. It's a Sunday-supplement sort of place, more spacious than most houses. I walked beside a canal to reach it, in the rain. It is still raining; it rains for the two hours I am there, but when I think about the meeting later, I remember brightness, and then realise it was coming from Selina's side of the room. She seems to squint against her own sharp, radiant enthusiasm. I sense that she could politely ruin somebody if they crossed her.

My own editor is half my age. She is Sophie Whitehead, buzzing with eager energy, and is dressed like a *Doctor Who* assistant, in a blaze-orange boiler suit. She has a tattoo on her ankle of a Hockney dog and tells me she is wearing the outfit partly as a tribute to Bowie. We shake hands. She is the first person I've shaken hands with since February 2020. I ask if we can do it twice, just for practice. She obliges.

My book in progress and Lisa's book in progress – which we are here to jointly discuss – are still just Word documents, but *The Night She Disappeared* is now a doorstop on Selina's kitchen table, next to a plate of lemon drizzle cake and another of little vegan tartlets. We each eat one of the vegan tartlets and don't touch the cake. Instead, we talk about various diets, as if we were the teenage girls in *Watching You*. I remark to Lisa that I didn't realise mini-marshmallows were so low-calorie before reading that novel.

It's only the second time I've spoken to Lisa in company – the third time I've met her at all – and what strikes me in this context is her sense of containment and control. She is a constant presence, but she speaks less than me, less than Sophie, less than Selina. She seems to just watch, and listen, and wait her turn.

And my own dynamic with Lisa is striking, too. We sit on the same side of the table, authors opposite editors, and seem sometimes to become – what? – a comedy double act? A sibling relationship? I mention my birthday and Lisa chimes in with the date. 'It was the first thing I looked up about you.' Lisa discusses her recent signing and I pipe up, to Selina's surprise, 'You had a panic attack, didn't you?' Asked about the last six months of our correspondence, we reply together, interrupting, overlapping.

Lisa assures me that I haven't spoiled her progress at all: in fact, she's written another 2,000 words since I told her how much I liked the Rachel and Lucy scenes. She reveals another aspect of her technique. Every few pages, she says, she drops in a 'pop of colour'. This time, with Henry staring out at Lake Michigan, she wanted something for the sky, and stopped to think about it for minutes before picking acid orange.

'Like those bright shell suits young people wear these days,' she says off-handedly.

'That's a bit undiplomatic, Lisa.' I nod at Sophie and her outfit, which almost precisely match the description.

'Oh, I didn't mean that,' says Lisa, and rescues the situation by asking if the boiler suit is vintage. Sophie feels inside for the label, telling us she found it in Leeds.

Lisa sends me the new scene of Henry by the lake, pasted into an email. Even scrolled through quickly and peered at on a tiny phone screen, it's breathtaking.

I am *incomplete*. I have always felt incomplete . . . the sky is on fire and nobody loves me and I love nobody and I am alone, I am so, so alone and Jesus fucking Christ I have to find Phin. I have to find Phin and if finding him doesn't fix me I swear to God I will swim across this lake and throw myself into that acid orange sun and let myself burn to a smudge of ash.

It is a rush of undiluted despair: Lisa at her no-holds-barred best. If I was reading this passage in the finished book, I'd have to close the novel for a moment, sit back and recover. It's like a furnace: as if Henry has opened one of the secret doors in his smoothly polished exterior and let us see the anguished little boy who's still trapped inside, in hell. It had to happen, to give his quest the necessary urgency; to fire up his plot strand into something more than a whimsical little mystery tour.

'Why did you choose Lisa to write about?' Selina leans forward like a friendly headmistress. I start to carefully construct an answer, but by the end of my explanation I'm caught up in my own enthusiasm, not really caring how I come across. The reason I chose Lisa was because of paragraphs like that one, where the intricate thriller plot is briefly forgotten in a moment of transcendence, and the writing strips away a character's artifice, tapping into something truthful, profound and sometimes painful.

The meeting winds down. Lisa considers it a success. I feel like I've been interviewed and probably passed. We exchange polite questions about where everyone is going, and where they're from. Sophie wonders if we can guess that she isn't originally a Londoner, as she has a 'whisper' of a different accent. I scoff quietly. She sounds nothing like a Londoner to me.

'Are you from up north?' Lisa guesses.

'She's from Leeds,' I tell her.

'Is she?' Lisa seems surprised.

'Of course she is. She got the vintage boiler suit from Leeds.' And I can't stop myself from talking. 'Really, Lisa, you should pay more *attention to people*.'

Lisa stares at me for a moment, her mouth slightly open, then sets me straight. 'Buying a jumpsuit *in* Leeds does not mean you are *from* Leeds.'

I was joking – I've rarely known anyone who paid so much attention to people and their nuances – but it doesn't seem the right moment to say so.

Suddenly Lisa's phone rings, and the mood changes again, as if someone flipped the channel. She stands up, pulling her coat on, talking calmly, quietly but clearly like a high-up TV cop who's just received a new lead.

'So sorry,' she tells us. 'Teenage girl emergency.'

Still holding the phone to her face, she hugs Selina and she's out of the door, disappearing into an Uber like a character in one of her own novels. *Lisa Jewell has left the building.*

That week, *The Night She Disappeared* becomes the number-one bestselling book in the UK.

Just Not Writing

12 August 2021

'I have no "writing" news to share with you, as there has been no writing,' Lisa writes:

> But I have signed around 3500 of 7000 bookplates, done a Waterstones Zoom with Shari Lapena, a South African Zoom with Shari Lapena, Samantha Downing and Megan Miranda, a podcast for readers in the American South, an in-depth phone interview with *La Repubblica* in Italy for *The Family Upstairs*, walked the dog for many miles, signed and mailed out some books to readers, paid my tax, ordered and sent champagne to everyone in my publishing team to celebrate being no. 1, written another newsletter introduction, been to Penguin HQ in Battersea to have my photo taken for an article about my five Desert Island books for their website, been a guest on a Zoom book launch for Louise Candlish, posed with photos (taken by Amelie as it wasn't allowed to be selfies) with a plate of American cookies sent to me for my partnership in their book club next month, and answered a written Q&A for a group of Instagram bloggers who had been reviewing the audiobook. So yeah, not not doing anything at all. Just not writing.

Which means that I, in turn, have nothing to write about *Birdie's Bones*. We decide instead to go out for dinner.

The Bengal Lancer

'I read a quote the other day,' says Lisa. 'If you close your menu the moment you've decided what you want to eat in a restaurant then you'll feel more confident in your choice. I always close my menu the minute I've decided what I want to eat in a restaurant, and I realised that this is also how I write. Writing a book without a plan is a long series of making multiple decisions and I make them very quickly and instinctively and then, when I've made that decision, I metaphorically close my menu. There, I think, it is done. That is on the page and that is what it is. It saves a lot of angst.'

Food is important to Lisa, and important to her books. (It's important to her fans, too: one blog, by Tina, reviews *I Found You* by recreating its meals. 'Alice roasted beef and root vegetables and I opted for poultry. Lovely to share over a glass of wine and lots of chatter.') The bet with Yasmin was honoured with a Thai meal at Esarn Kheaw, and Lisa has claimed in interviews that her own showpiece in the kitchen is a 'Thai banquet' for a houseful of friends. Jem cooks chicken jalfrezi and green curry, picking up all the ingredients from Chinatown; Ralph's eponymous party includes:

> Miniature Thai crabcakes festooned with sprigs of fresh coriander, dwarf sticks of satay with tiny little bowls of gloopy peanut sauce, diminutive pink bundles of prawn wrapped around baby

butts of sugarcane, the smallest samosas Ralph had ever seen in his life, saucers of sweet chilli sauce, chopped green chillis, minced red chillis and chilli pickle.

Even in her earliest work, which as we saw can sometimes be cartoonish and crude, Lisa's prose dwells in loving detail on food, taking no shortcuts. In *A Friend of the Family*, 'Sean had prosciutto and figs followed by pappardelle with chicken livers. Millie had risotto of wild mushroom with an enormous rocket-and-Parmesan salad on the side and tagliatelle with smoked pork, cream and broad beans.' The description goes on for the rest of the page. Ned and Ness, in turn, are awed by fancy nibbles: 'a mosaic of spiced crab and marinated tomato', and 'foie gras parfait melba with black truffle.'

Home cooking is, if anything, even more vital to Lisa's characters and their relationships. Jem's curries are the centre of *Ralph's Party*, of course. Daisy, in *31 Dream Street*, introduces Con to organic chocolate, goat's cheese and olives from Borough Market, and in *The Making of Us*, Lydia's Uncle Rod bonds with her over a meal, its preparation described sensually, step-by-step:

> . . . he started rhythmically to untie the chicken, shred herbs, stuff the cavity, rub butter under the skin, slice carrots, peel potatoes and boil water. Lydia watched him hungrily, listening to the words that flowed from him in his sinewy Welsh accent . . .

I haven't eaten with Lisa before, unless you count a tiny vegan tartlet at our last meeting. In the Groucho, I told her I'd rather spend the calories on wine. Tonight, we've agreed to meet at the Bengal Lancer, near Kentish Town Tube, because it features in *Thirtynothing*. A board outside boasts that it has been 'King of Curry Since 1984.' I'm mildly shocked when Lisa tells me she's never been here herself; she just sent Dig here instead, over two decades ago. She has brought 'material', as she promised – not new pages of *Birdie's Bones*, because there are no more for now, but props, which she pulls out of her bag like a children's entertainer.

'A first edition of *Thirtynothing*,' she declares, displaying the kitschy, late-nineties cartoon cover. Flicking through it, she can't find, and can't possibly remember, exactly where this particular curry house features. Fortunately, I have the Kindle version on my iPad.

'What about restaurants? [Dig asks Nadine.] Where shall I take her?'

'What's wrong with the Bengal Lancer?'

'I can't take her there.'

'Why not?'

'Because – because she's Delilah, that's why. I want to take her somewhere special.'

The Bengal Lancer was his favourite restaurant, without a doubt. The proprietor, Archad, was friendly and welcoming, the naan bread was the fluffiest in all of London and, most importantly, they served until midnight. But come on – he couldn't take *Delilah Lillie* there for dinner, could he?

Decent and comfortable, but not good enough for one of Lisa's scruffy, uncertain thirtysomethings, at the tail-end of the 1990s: it's not exactly an overwhelming recommendation. Perhaps one or both of us should have looked up what Lisa actually wrote about the place before we both agreed to trek here: half an hour on public transport for her, an hour for me.

But Dig was right. The naan bread is outstanding: light and buttery, crispy at the edges. It really could be the best in all of (North) London.

This is only my second restaurant meal in eighteen months, and I tell Lisa about the first, which was the previous week and with my former choir friends, in a Surbiton pub garden. It is the quintessential small-town choir, I tell her. It is the ur-suburban choir. Whatever you imagine of a suburban choir, it's that, in every detail, right down to the church hall for rehearsals and the local theatre for performances. But on that night, meeting for the first time in a year and a half, it felt strange and vibrant, as if we'd all been frozen in time and suddenly released. *It's you!* I cried more than once, as if delighted that they still existed. It felt like a reunion of survivors. We didn't shake hands or hug: we examined each other's faces at arm's length, exclaimed at new hairstyles. Without planning it, we'd all dressed in bright, jewel-like colours – emerald, sapphire, rose – as if for a summer wedding, and as dusk fell we were lit by tiny bulbs hung across trellises, woven through climbing vines. There was something enchanting about it, as if we'd all been given a second chance at normal life.

But several times during the meal, I had the experience of watching myself trying to act like a human again, like a social creature; relearning the rituals of turn-taking in conversation, copying other people's responses, and remembering to join in at the right time. I felt as though I was standing behind myself, observing a clumsy puppet. After ninety minutes I was exhausted from the effort and stood up from the table, excusing myself: the first to leave.

In return – because as ever, we share stories, like Hannibal and Clarice sitting opposite each other in a curry house – Lisa tells me about her own experience on the same evening.

She had been invited to a private film screening in Soho, and because it was still a novel pleasure to Go Out Properly, she'd downed a couple of champagnes beforehand and then ordered a double rum and Coke from the free bar. But her mood was out of sync with everyone else; Lisa was energised, ready to mingle, but when she tried to start conversations, they fell flat. Was she out of practice, or were they? Had she misjudged the tone, or simply forgotten how to speak to people? She'd arrived in party mood, bouncy as a helium balloon, but those tiny punctures soon drained her. She told her friend she had to leave, and ducked out of Soho House by 9 p.m., at about the time I was leaving the Prince of Wales in Surbiton.

'I'm not sure that Jojo Moyes has quite the same social cachet as Yvonne From Choir,' I suggest. Lisa laughs, rewardingly, but I realise that isn't the point. They were examples of the same post-pandemic experience, in Central London and Surrey, maybe an hour away from each other. It isn't relevant that one was a premiere of *The Last Letter from Your Lover* and the other was a burger with the most suburban choir outside *The Good Life*.

And I realise, too, that my notion of Lisa's social life as a glamorous cast list of literary stars – Jojo [Moyes!], 'Maddy' [Sophie Kinsella!], Jenny [Colgan!], David [Nicholls!] – is not just misguided but borderline obnoxious. I get my own vicarious thrill from hearing about them, but of course to Lisa they're not celebrity namedrops, they're simply friends, like my Yvonne From Choir and Jo From Choir and Will O. From Choir, always designated with his initial to distinguish him from me. She wasn't telling me a story about being successful. It was a story, like mine, of feeling odd and left out. Lisa's life has many privileges and pleasures, and she knows that as well as anyone, and is humbly grateful for them all; but selling a million novels doesn't insulate you from everyday disappointments and frustrations, or protect you from self-doubt.

There's a classic academic book from my undergraduate

days. It's called *Reading the Romance*, by Janice Radway, who is now a distinguished professor. In the early 1980s, the younger Radway travelled to a small midwestern town in the US and interviewed the readers of popular romance novels – the Mills & Boon type – to explore what pleasures and meanings they took from this critically reviled genre, lower even than chick lit on the cultural ladder. Radway's hostess was Dot, the owner of a local bookstore. Some of the romance fans were wary of an academic coming into their small-town lives to study them: they thought she might look down on them and mock them in print. Dot reassured them. 'Jan is just people!' she said simply, and I remember that line vividly now, decades since I last read the book. 'Jan is *just people*.'

Lisa is just people.

She's brought other material, too: an old-fashioned wallet of old-fashioned photographs from the late nineties, from the publication of *Ralph's Party* and *Thirtynothing*. I leaf through the glossy images, all different shapes like mismatched decks of cards shuffled together, and finally I can believe the fairy tale that overwhelmed her at age thirty.

Or not *believe,* because she'd convinced me at the Groucho, but I can feel it, emotionally rather than just rationally. She looks young and frail – she lost a lot of weight that year, from stress – sitting tensely, neatly, red lips pursed, in a floral dress and cerise cardigan, or stiffly posed in a sleeveless top and combats at a desk in front of a Robbie Williams calendar, looking like a literary member of All Saints, or perhaps Louise Wener from Sleeper. There are the more established authors she didn't dare speak to – Nick Hornby, whose work prompted her to write her first novel, signing beside her at a bookstore as she catches the camera, wide-eyed, with a *THAT'S NICK HORNBY!* expression – and there's her now-husband who barely reads her books: a stoic, solid, classically handsome presence at her side.

And suddenly I can see Lisa as someone I might have known that year, when I was working on my PhD in Cardiff but returning regularly to London; she was shopping at the same stores as me and my gang, no doubt buying the same music, drinking in some of the same pubs. It's not impossible that our paths crossed, perhaps one day in Soho between Reckless Records and Sister Ray. But while I was striding past the posters for *Ralph's Party* on the Tube, she was stopping in front of them for her friends' photos, dumbstruck and ecstatic to see her own name displayed for the entire city.

We finish the curry and jointly count the calories, agreeing to split the bill. (She is instantly, quietly confident about what amount I should enter on my weight-watching app to account for half the meal – 'seven hundred', firmly and surely as if she was telling the time, or her own age.)

When the restaurant owner arrives to clear the plates, we chime and chorus, 'Lovely!'

'You know that book?' He nods at the copy of *Thirtynothing*. A slender, neat man in his forties, with a dark beard speckled grey.

Lisa performs a perfect, startled double take. 'That book? Yes . . . I know it.'

'This restaurant is in that book,' he beams.

There is a brief sliver of a moment in which Lisa could say, 'Actually, I wrote it.' The moment passes and can never be recovered. Seeing it vanish, I step in with an explanation for the prop.

'That's why we've come here. Literary pilgrimage.'

'Lots of books mention us,' the owner goes on proudly, and astonishingly, brings over his own prop, a Mark Billingham novel called *Buried*.

Lisa is still stunned. I have to say something.

'Yeah, it's famous. Even I'd heard of Bengal Lancer, and I'm from South.' The London boy is coming out of me again after a couple of glasses.

'The author of that book', our new friend tells us, 'brought in a copy of it for me.'

'Did they?' Lisa asks incredulously.

'They live around here.' He gestures vaguely.

'I never did,' Lisa whispers to me as the man turns away to tap our cards. 'I never came in here with a copy of my book.' She hesitates. 'Unless I was very, very drunk.'

The owner holds the door open, and we walk out into the warmth, the noise and neon of North London. After such a build-up from *Thirtynothing*, I'm not convinced I've fully experienced the King of Curries. Perhaps it's changed since Dig last visited.

'But the owner did give you a gift,' says Lisa thoughtfully, before we split up and walk in separate directions. 'A strong end to a chapter is so important . . . and he gave you that.'

What Remains

Last time we heard from Henry, he was sitting by the lake, staring at an acid-orange sunset. He's been sitting there for a month now, while Lisa went on holiday – the kind of blissful holiday where the natural light and colour make Instagram filters unnecessary – and then returned to prepare for her American tour, which Covid then cancelled at the last moment. She conducted it from a Marriott up the road, getting up obligingly at Central Daylight Time to Zoom with bookstores across the Atlantic.

So the novel is on pause, its momentum stalled. There are four months remaining in the year; four months until her deadline. We are three-quarters of the way through our process. Lisa is, at most, only halfway through the book. But this time, she doesn't seem remotely worried. Her tone is leisurely. 'I will attempt to get back to *TFU2* next week and maybe, just maybe, bash out the first few thousand words of the "second half".'

I notice that she's calling it by its old, abbreviated title again, and ask her about that. Our pace has slowed too from its former urgent energy into a lazy late-summer routine – we are corresponding once a week now, sitting down to a lengthy email every Saturday evening – and so a fortnight passes before she replies to confirm she's managed another 700 words.

I got to the end of the Henry/Kris Doll chapter and could not make it work in terms of a springboard into Henry's next

203

move. So I turned off my laptop and watched four back to back episodes of *Cooking With Paris* instead. Now it is 5.07pm and I have written no words today at all. I hope to write some when I've signed off from you. But I suspect I won't.

'We are discussing titles,' she adds. '*The Family Remains* looks like a contender. What do you think?'

Immediately, *Birdie's Bones* drops into the list of quirky alternate titles, alongside *The Man on the Beach* and *Pretty Betty*. *The Family Remains* is so obvious and right, it seems to have been there all along, waiting to be found.

Popular

16 September 2021

Since there is no more of *The Family Remains* for me to read, I read around it instead, exploring texts that seem to confirm its shape as an absence at the centre. I read the books that shaped Lisa's life, according to her recent blog for Penguin – Agatha Christie, who inspired her to write page-turners, and Maggie O'Farrell, who influenced her mid-career family novels like *Melody Browne* and *Before I Met You*. And I take part in a survey from the University of Wolverhampton which asks me about my recent reading habits and then questions me about how 'literary' each book is. My list, inevitably, includes several of Lisa's novels.

It strikes me that I have no defined idea of what 'literary' means: just a general sense, a spectrum that runs, perhaps, from Jeffrey Archer on one end to James Joyce at the other. I write to the academics behind the survey to ask what they had in mind. They politely explain that they can't give me an answer because they are waiting for their respondents to tell them, and that the results will be available in a year.

So I look back at the books that shaped Lisa, and realise that – while they're not exactly Archer and Joyce – Agatha Christie and Maggie O'Farrell clearly occupy different positions on that spectrum, from the efficient, plot-driven page-turner to the unhurried immersion in finely wrought language and character, and that Lisa's novels fall somewhere in between.

There are moments in Maggie O'Farrell's *The Hand That First Held Mine,* for instance, that remind me of Lisa's prose – the precise delineation of a crucial moment, when time slows and a character passes, with a sometimes-painful epiphany, from one state to another, realising that life has just changed around them. In one scene, Lexie has arrived at her lover's hospital bed and is told that he died unexpectedly during the night. His wife – the nurse avoids Lexie's eye – has made the necessary arrangements. Lexie asks if she can see him, and gathers her things expectantly, anticipating a yes. Instead, the nurses stand in awkward silence. 'She listened to it. She felt it. She tested its length, its breadth. She could have put out her tongue and tasted it.'

This passage could be written by the Lisa Jewell who focuses on 'particles', on tangible shifts in the atmosphere, who senses the power of repetition to convey the edge of panic: 'a sense that she was all alone, that she had in fact always been all alone, that the corners of her life were folding in and folding in . . .'

But then there are the scenes in Maggie O'Farrell that sit for a whole night in a deserted coffee shop, listening to the cappuccino machine, the click of its chrome casing as metal contracts. The café itself is awake and listening: 'A drop of water falls from the tap, spreads over the bowl of the sink, then trickles towards the plughole.' The only witnesses to this patient scene are cups and glasses, becoming minor characters in their own right as they stand inverted in rings of tepid water.

This, surely, is 'literary' prose: a contemplative meditation, perhaps approaching poetry – though that would be a whole debate in itself – where the interest lies not so much in the scene, but in the way it's described. Most of us do not read a novel to learn about glasses and plugholes, but there is a satisfaction in the sounds – the clicking consonants of the cappuccino machine, the water's abrupt 'drop' and slower 'spread' – and in the sense of life that O'Farrell grants the location as it waits patiently overnight. The language encourages us to linger, rather than propelling us urgently forward to the next page.

There's no doubt that Lisa could do this. It might not be effortless, but she could do it. She wouldn't do it, because she feels she owes her readers the next part of the plot, the what-Henry-did-next, instead of twelve hours watching taps drip in an empty coffee shop.

Somewhere towards the other extreme is Agatha Christie, who, Lisa remembers, was like crack to her as a twelve-year-old. 'I read all her books over the space of a year. What I want to recreate for my readers now is that reading experience.'

Turning from *The Hand That First Held Mine* to Christie's *And Then There Were None* is like being shoved back in your seat by sudden G-force. The prose is a streamlined machine, designed for speed. Characters are rapidly sketched and remain consistent, with no emotional development except that one murders all the others. There is a sense of inner voice, but it is as brisk and efficient as the description of the location and the central players. 'Vera Claythorne, in a third-class carriage with five other travellers in it, leaned her head back and shut her eyes. How hot it was travelling by train today! It would be nice to get to the sea!'

Schoolteacher Vera Claythorne's train of thought, with its banal little exclamations, is distinct from that of older men like Dr Armstrong, who fumes 'Damned young fool!', and dashing playboy Tony Marston, who observes 'Fizzing hot day!', but there is not much in it: they are all Agatha Christie, give or take a few mild swear-words and variations in slang.

These are well-crafted sentences, too, but with a purpose entirely different to O'Farrell's: they have the clean utility of computer code, as if setting the parameters of characters and maps, then running the program through to its conclusion.

Aficionados of the adventure game genre may be reminded of playing 1980s classics like *The Hobbit*, where Thorin tended to enter a room, sit down, wait and sing about gold:

Mr Justice Wargrave allowed his head to nod . . .

He slept . . .

Philip Lombard said sharply:

'Must be difficult to land here in dirty weather.'

Mr Blore was tying his tie.

He thought . . .

The layout, ironically, may recall poetry, but the effect is like a series of line-by-line reports generated by ten avatars allowed to wander an island and interact with the environment and each other. Any sense of internal torment is conveyed with the subtlety of a sledgehammer. Vera flashes back to the tragedy in her past: 'Drowned . . . Found drowned . . . Drowned at sea . . . Drowned – drowned – drowned . . .'

In this respect, Lisa's writing is far more like that of O'Farrell, who describes drowning with unbearable clarity as 'flailing against the cold, muscular clutch of the current', and holds us intimately close to the characters through their suffering, forcing us to experience their trauma first-hand.

Though she aspires to Agatha Christie's addictive qualities, Lisa is far too interested in her characters to treat them like animated pieces on a board; she needs to be fond of them, or at least fascinated by them, because the plot emerges from them, from their responses, motivations and decisions. The only character who comes close to this Christie approach – in Lisa's later work, at least – is teenage Georgia from *Invisible Girl*, most of whose behaviour could be coded in a few lines (enter kitchen, choose snack, chat to Mum, leave) and who, unusually for Lisa's novels, has no arc, and remains cheerfully unchanged by the thriller that goes on around her.

Despite the neon capital letters on her covers, then, and the fact that broadsheet newspapers barely afford her a sniff of attention, Lisa's novels perhaps have more in common with Sally Rooney than Lee Child, while combining elements of both: they are carried forward by pace and plot, but driven by the complexity of people. The stories she prefers these days also fall somewhere in the middle.

I think most of the books I enjoy the most are the ones that sit between both poles: incredibly propulsive, compelling plots and dazzlingly lovely prose. All of them use exquisite language, with dozens of those 'someone just reached into my psyche, pulled out a thought I'd had but never acknowledged and put it into words' moments (another feature of literary prose, I always think).

With my own writing, I write to the absolute top end of my intellect, ability and talents. I write with my six O Levels and a smattering of 'proper' reading in my early twenties. That is all I have. I aspire with every book to write as beautifully as my favourite writers, who all have degrees and awards and serious reviews in serious newspapers. But I am not disappointed in myself when I don't quite get there. I think I'm probably just literary enough.

The Reverse Out

7 October 2021

Agatha Christie mapped out the meticulous architecture of *And Then There Were None* in advance. She admits in the introduction that she only wrote the book after a 'tremendous amount' of prior planning. Her characters may feel like computer programs, a brief list of personality traits allowed to interact, but they follow a carefully plotted path. This kind of coding takes time, patience and testing.

Lisa may model herself in some ways on Christie, but her approach is quite different. If a novel is the mysterious house at the heart of a thriller, Christie draws up and double-checks her blueprint before beginning construction work on the intricate maze of criss-crossing passages. Lisa, by contrast, builds an extension, sleeps in it for a couple of nights, then decides to knock through one wall and dig a tunnel back to one of the bedrooms, as an experiment.

She has written new material, the first chapters in several weeks. The novel was essentially parked up over summer, and when she came back to it in autumn, its engine needed turning over to warm it up. It was a fresh start; it was a cold start; it was a false start.

Henry comes out of his freeze-frame, blinking back to life on the banks of Lake Michigan. 'I clear my throat and straighten my back.' The conversation with biker tour guide Kris Doll croaks into action, almost as if it had never paused.

' "How long have you been doing this?" ' he begins, and his amateur detection continues through subtly searching questions about Kris's past, his bisexuality, his ex-boyfriend. Kris, it emerges, knows the story of *The Family Upstairs*, but he's heard it from Phin first-hand. Like Henry, we are gripped by the reveal – until the conversation is interrupted by a stage direction in block capitals. 'I BEGIN TO WRITE MYSELF INTO A CORNER HERE.'

Three hundred words follow. Three hundred good words. Three hundred words which will never appear in print. Because then Lisa realises she's stuck, and stops.

> Kris takes us back into the city and drops me on the side of the road outside my hotel. I haven't got what I needed from the afternoon (ME NEITHER!!!) I suck in my breath and I say, 'your friend. Phin.

The chapter ends there, without even a close of inverted commas. Then, Lisa rewinds her characters – imagine Henry and Kris raising and lowering their drinks in frantic reverse motion – and sets them running again from an earlier point. The previous conversation about bikers and bisexuality never happens. Instead, Henry comes up with an idea just after Lisa does, and this time the chapter concludes on a cliffhanger, as if it was planned that way from the start.

Lisa's method seems disarmingly ramshackle compared to Agatha Christie's self-proclaimed precise planning; but then, Agatha Christie composed her introduction when the novel was satisfyingly completed, rather than confiding her challenges to a friend halfway through. Lisa's notes are endearingly informal, reading more like a Mumsnet post from a harried parent than the poised overview we might expect.

I was trying to end Henry's acid orange sun chapter on a cliff-hanger and I just COULD NOT so I left it and went and watched the Paris Hilton cooking show and then came back to it the next day and fixed it. So we have a thing. I'm not sure what that thing is yet, but it gives me something meaty to play with when I come to start his next chapter tomorrow.

She has fifty days to finish the novel, and 50,000 words to write. She's struggling a little; groggy with a cold, finding her way through fog. She can't motivate herself to leave the house for the coffee shop where she used to work, and the studio across the street, where she completed her last two writing pushes, is just too expensive for her to justify the indulgence. Her home, however spacious and lovely, is crowded with family. She feels, she confesses, like 'A LUMP'.

But this time, I feel Lisa shouldn't be worried, and I tell her so. After only a paragraph, I'm gripped again by the plot – or not by the plot so much as the characters. I haven't reread the earlier material since July, but I'm immediately right there with Henry as he searches not just for Phin but for something deeper and more personal: a chance for his life to acquire meaning and purpose.

And then we switch to Rachel, and although we know exactly how her story will end because her husband was murdered in *The Family Upstairs*, his gradual transformation in the sequel from charming boyfriend to coldly bullying husband – more dreadful because of the occasional flashes of his old self, the possibility that the relationship could be rescued if Rachel tried to do the right thing – is just as captivating and chilling. It's the detail that sells it: the fact that Michael, short on money and short of temper, has brought home 'the small, pink, cooked prawns, not the big raw mother-of-pearly ones he always used to buy', just before he suggests that, as he passive-aggressively puts it, 'we could start' to share the cost of shopping. The characters are moving within the structures of a bigger, broader thriller plot – a detective quest, a trajectory towards murder – but what really matters is exactly how they get there, and what it means for them as people.

While waiting for Lisa's new material I filled my time with other recent novels, including Marian Keyes' 2020 family drama *Grown Ups* and T. J. Newman's airline-hijack thriller *Falling*, a bestseller of summer 2021. I was gripped by Keyes' character Cara, who suffers from bulimia, when she was trying to resist her nephews' Easter eggs, but left cold by Newman's heroine Carrie when she had a gun to her head and a suicide belt in her face. The contrast was striking, and it seemed to hold a broader, more resonant lesson. If a novel's characters don't matter, everything else loses weight and purpose. The stakes can involve aeroplanes crashing into baseball stadia, and we won't care if we don't connect with the characters; but make us care, and minor crises like bingeing on forbidden chocolate, dealing with teenage kids, an argument over dinner or an awkward flirtation become high-tension drama.

Plot without character is just an empty frame. A flatly predictable protagonist can have spectacular events happen to them and around them, and we will watch them distractedly, like a figure on a distant screen surrounded by CGI; but if an author captures us and draws us in close to her creations, we experience their tiny temptations, challenges and fears as epic spikes of anxiety and triumph. Compared to Marian Keyes' sprawling but satisfying relationship saga in which not very much happens to a group we grow to know intimately, and T. J. Newman's high-altitude, high-concept but ultimately so-what action, Lisa's thrillers fall somewhere in the middle – which could be seen as the best of both worlds.

The Family Remains is, at this mid-stage, typical Lisa Jewell: a man with a dark past seeking answers; a mother protecting her children from secrets; a woman trapped in an increasingly toxic relationship. Rachel's story is, in fact, not so different from Joy's, way back in 2005, and in turn, not so different from the story of Lisa's first marriage, which she related for the Penguin article on novels that shaped her life. 'I married in haste and repented at leisure,' she recalls. Joy and Rachel could say the same, and both could have written the next paragraph, in spirit if not precise details.

> He was incredibly charming and intelligent, and had a very interesting background, but he was very damaged as well. I didn't fall in love with him, but I felt very much that his approval was something I wanted to seek . . . Three months after we met I said I'd marry him; we were married a year later. It very quickly became apparent that he wasn't what I thought he was: he was a coercive controller, and my life very quickly became very small and very limited and very controlled by him, to the point that I didn't have a front door key for our house.

'I can't even remember what I said to displease him,' says Lisa, recalling one particularly grim occasion, 'but he stopped talking to me.' When I asked her, months ago, whether she had a tendency to feature toxic men in her novels, Lisa countered with examples of the lovely male characters and vile women she'd written, but there's no denying that domestic abuse seems to be a theme.

And yet there's something brand-new in *The Family Remains*, too, interrupting the flow of the three main narrative strands. It feels like an experiment. Even the font is different, signalling a different mode of storytelling, and the layout ignores inverted commas, presenting its dialogue baldly, like a play on a starkly spotlit stage.

```
Thank you, Philip, for coming at such short
notice.
    It's no problem at all. I mean. It's
my sister, after all. I can't think of a
better reason to cancel a few plans and get
on a train.
    Take a seat. Please.
```

This is the story that lent the novel its interim title, *Birdie's Bones*: the tale told by the 'family remains' themselves. These knobbly little plot-vertebrae knit together bit by bit into the book's police investigation, which runs steadily and inexorably in the background, and has the potential to undermine everything Lucy and Henry have built up since leaving the family home.

These sections do more than simply build a threat against our main characters. They achieve something astonishing in their brief, stripped-down exchanges: they invite our sympathy for the arch-villain of the previous novel. They remind us that Birdie Evers – Bridget – was a girl with years ahead of her, with talent and ambitions, with family members who still miss her. Gradually, the unthinkable starts to happen. We begin to mourn Birdie.

In a Season of Crime

16 October 2021

Saturday night. I am watching the TV show *Unforgotten* with my wife, Fiona: Nicola Walker as DCI Cassie Stuart and Sanjeev Bhaskar as her partner DC Sunil 'Sunny' Khan, digging into old, cold-case murders and piecing together the bones of buried crimes, returning the dead to their bereaved families.

'She reminds me of Lisa Jewell,' Fiona muses, unprompted, about Cassie. I ask her what she means. 'Kind and compassionate . . . not passively empathetic, but actively curious about people. Intensely interested in people. She wants to progress her characters to a good point. Or at least a fair point.'

I don't tell Fiona that we're only watching *Unforgotten* because Lisa recommended it to me in May. I dig out an old email, to check.

Jascha and I have been working our way through it from the beginning, and he says he can see a lot of my style of writing in it. For example, in this final season there is a character called Ram; a British Asian detective. He's cocky and conniving, he's really harsh and heavy handed, hyper-masculine. Yet, in scenes with his wife, he is so tender and gentle. They've just been told that their unborn baby has Downs Syndrome and they both are struggling with the decision of whether or not to terminate the pregnancy. He would like to continue it, but then, when he realises that his past is coming back to haunt him and he might end up dead or in prison, he starts to change his mind because he cannot bear the idea of leaving his wife alone to raise a disabled child. He cries, and it is totally and utterly convincing that someone who behaves with so little care for other people in the world would care so deeply and tenderly for those he loves. He is the most remarkably complete and believable character, and I already knew before he started crying over his unborn baby that he would be capable of doing it.

In short, he contains multitudes.

As we progress steadily through each series, I see Lisa too, or her approach to character, in Cassie's wondering remark about a killer, 'How is it that I feel sorry for her?', and in the complex, moving depiction of petty liars and conmen, people with troubled pasts; imperfect humans who have made mistakes and tried their best to patch them up.

I call Lisa, because now when I'm reminded of Lisa Jewell I can speak directly to Lisa Jewell.

It's our first Zoom in half a year, and we both look different; her tan is the colour of toast (of course) – 'Well, I am part Indian, you know,' she explains – and my hair has found its way back somehow to 1974-Bowie auburn and blond.

'That Asian guy,' she recalls now. 'I think he was one of the best characters in any of the series. He was so real.'

'Because he seemed such a shit, didn't he?' I point out gleefully, enjoying the memory of his unpleasantness.

'Yeah, but then the way he handled his heartbreak . . .'

'But he's both,' I suggest. 'It's not like, you thought the characters were one thing, and they're another thing instead. They're one thing *and* the other thing.'

'Exactly. Exactly. And you see them flipping over.'

'It's like feeling a sympathy for the villain. And that's what you're doing with Birdie, as well.'

'Yes, it's what I try and do with all my bad characters. Even with Noelle in *Then She Was Gone*. I gave her pages and pages of backstory, but I think because it was all in her voice . . . she was the most unflinchingly bad.'

'And with Michael, as well . . . you don't exactly have sympathy for him, but I understand why he is that way.'

'Yeah,' says Lisa, uncertainly, about the man she created.

'It's because he can't get it up, isn't it?'

A moment's laughter bends her double. 'Yes!'

'It's because his masculinity is undermined. That's why he loses his temper so much.'

'And he lies, too,' Lisa agrees. 'He pretends that he wants to be with a powerful woman, but all he wants to do is put a woman on a pedestal and admire her. He doesn't want her to be powerful.'

'Well, he might not know exactly what he wants, but we can understand why he does the things he does. Because masculinity is so important to him. And that connects with money as well, with him not being able to afford dinner, and having to ask Rachel. That ties in with his performance in the bedroom.'

'Absolutely. Yes. I feel I've written an awful lot of words about floppy penises.'

'Yeah, you have. There was a line about how he needs a paramedic for it. But it's fine,' I assure her. 'It works.'

The silence that follows is on the edge of awkward. 'Good,' Lisa says, just in time.

'So, what do you think you've taken from *Unforgotten*?' I ask, more formally. 'I think the *Birdie's Bones* subplot was directly inspired by it . . .'

'Oh, absolutely. Yes. I will say that without any shame or

embarrassment for stealing things. It was almost that sense of watching it and having a slow realisation that what they do on that programme is not dissimilar from what I do, with these seemingly disparate storylines, and people in different places, who are brought back together by something that has happened, or is about to happen . . . it was that sense of seeing my own structure reflected back at me, and realising that I hadn't adopted it with this book. It was a case of reminding myself what I do. Because I'm writing a sequel. And everything's up in the air, and I'm not following any of my usual rules. So it brought me back to what I do.'

'So you are taking something from it. You're paying homage to it. You're recognising the similarity, and then you're being a little bit more similar.'

'I am, and that is absolutely apparent in the way that I've introduced a proper detective. And this is the first time I've ever written a detective that I've felt anything for, who isn't just a puppet or somebody getting in the way. This is the first time I've written a detective who I'd want to hang out with. And I love him. I actually really love Samuel.'

Lisa had confessed this love for Samuel Owusu earlier in the week, on Instagram – 'I'm very much hoping he will show me the way' – combining the reveal of the official sequel title with a further, disarmingly honest confession to her fans that 'I still have FORTY THOUSAND WORDS of it left to write and have no idea what's going on or where it's all headed.'

There's an unnerving gulf between the image, a flashy publisher's picture of *The Family Remains* as a real, solid object with a hard cover, a respectable number of pages, a subtitle and even a sticker announcing it as a sequel, and the author's text below, with its open admission that the book is nowhere near finished. Somehow, in the next eight months, the two will have to come together: Lisa's uncertain, incomplete Word document drafts will have to become that heavy volume, on sale in shops.

'I honestly . . .' says Lisa now, a finger to her temple and her eyes closed, finding the right words. 'I'm feeling . . .' A heavy sigh. 'I'm feeling quite bad about the book at the moment. Not because I think it is bad, and it's been lovely getting your emails, boosting my confidence a bit that I'm not actually doing bad writing . . . I could be feeling pressurised, which I never normally do feel, but there has certainly been more pressure. I mean, the hype usually starts building from when I've delivered the book, but this is massive, and that's quite a headfuck, really. I'm doing an Instagram Live tonight, half an hour with me just talking about the sequel, and I'm trying to use it as an opportunity. Talking about it for half an hour might be really helpful. I might formulate some sort of idea where it's all headed. So anyway, I'm not feeling good about it, and after I've finished talking to you, I've got to go and write a rape scene.'

'Oh no. Oh God.'

'And I woke up this morning thinking' – she adopts a wryly precise voice – 'what sort of rape should it be?'

'Do you have to do it?'

'I kind of do have to do it. I kind of do. It's because Michael raped Lucy, and so he has to rape Rachel, I think.'

'Oh, God.'

'But I think the Rachel thing is what I'm most concerned about. Because her arc, which had seemed so simple to me when I spoke to you that first time, back at the beginning of the year, is *too* simple, and it's too obvious for the reader what's going on. She's not going to be fussed that Lucy killed Michael, and there's going to be some bonding going on at the end, and the reader's probably wondering why Lucy's scared. Ohh!' she exclaims in frustration. 'I don't know.'

'The thing about Rachel', I volunteer, 'is that there shouldn't be any tension, but I do feel tension.'

'Good. Tension is brilliant,' Lisa says.

'I know exactly what's going on, and we know how it's going on, but the details of it are still horrible to read. The prawns, for instance . . .'

'Wait until you see the pumpkin risotto on the wall.' She shakes her head at the scene she created last week. 'There's all sorts of nasty little things.'

'Well, I really like Zach and the seafood platter in *The Night She Disappeared*, as you know. The details, and the uneasiness, and the ramping up of tension with this guy who sometimes blows hot and sometimes cold.'

'Exactly. Well, I'm enjoying the scenes as I'm writing them, but I don't really know where it's going, or what's going to be a satisfying ending for my readers. What are they going to get out of it? They know that Michael is dead. And they know that Lucy isn't in peril. Because they know it's very likely that Rachel's glad Lucy killed him.'

'Is that the only threat to her?' I wonder aloud. 'Didn't she also have a role in killing Birdie?'

'Well, yes. She helped Henry get Birdie's body up on the roof. I believe. I'm fairly sure.'

'And the risk doesn't just come from Rachel. There's the cleaner, who suspects Lucy had a part in Michael's murder.'

'And you know who else there is? Her landlord in that scuzzy hostel she used to stay in. I always thought he might inadvertently put his foot in it, saying they left abruptly.'

'And the French police were looking for her.'

'I think you're absolutely right, and that's where I've been headed with it, that the threat to Lucy shouldn't be coming from Rachel. And I've got my police in London . . .'

'Well, good police might link the two murders somehow.'

'Yes. Yes! Good, thank you, yes.'

'If I was you,' I begin carefully, 'I would close down the tension about Lucy and Rachel quite soon, because I don't think it can be sustained all that long. And their relationship as allies might be more interesting for the last third of the book. It's not going to be a surprise that Rachel doesn't want to put Lucy in jail.'

'Yes. Yeah. I agree with you, I think you're right. I think that arc, which I thought would sustain Rachel's storyline right to the end, is not strong enough. See, it's all well and good saying oh, I don't plan! And I've got half my readers thinking I'm so clever, because I don't plan, I don't plot. But this is the precise sort of moment when it would have been very useful had I outlined the whole thing before I started and had some idea of the structure of it.'

'Well, that would have been a different kind of approach, wouldn't it?'

'And I can't do it. I'm incapable of it.' Lisa sighs again. 'OK, well, I'm going to go back to my book.' But she's smiling.

Endgame

20 October 2021

The strands are coming together at last, all at once. Samuel Owusu has discovered Cheyne Walk, and meanwhile, Marco and his friend Alf are tracking down Henry through his search history, with lots of 'um . . . um . . . um' punctuating their breathless patter. Even in Lisa's unpolished draft form, it feels like an intense convergence of previously parallel plotlines; your eye skims over the typos, easily piecing together the action: ' "Want anything to eat?" Maeco pulls open the fridge and looks at all the foos that was left there when they disappeared on Friday night which is starting to loks a little sad after five days.'

And in Chicago, Henry has finally spotted Phin. Months ago, in spring, Lisa and I discussed whether this would ever happen. Would Phin remain a phantom at the centre of the book, a golden absence defined by other people's idealised memories of him? Would he be diminished, his glow long departed? Would Henry Lamb, who constructed himself painstakingly as a Phin lookalike, be revealed as a poor man's copy of his lifelong crush, a stitched-together Frankenstein next to Phin's effortless natural radiance?

Half a year later, we have answers. Lisa didn't warn me in advance. For all I know, she might have decided the moment before she wrote it. Henry, looking at himself in the mirror after his sighting of Phin, sees himself anew, with all his retouching embarrassingly obvious – he even blushes in this scene, his cool veneer cracking – as a slightly camp middle-aged man with extensive cosmetic work. Not for the first time, I see myself uneasily in Henry Lamb, and not just because my university password matches his ('Can you even believe that?' Alf mutters, breaking easily into Henry's files. 'I mean, that's like, psychopathic.')

'It feels like we're entering the endgame now,' I observe to Lisa, trying to sound portentous and cool like Dr Strange talking to Iron Man in the last big Avengers movie.

'It isn't, obviously,' says Lisa, 'but as it's the difficult "middle section" which can often suffer from turgidity, I'll take that as a win.'

She's right, of course. But I wasn't entirely wrong, either; all the characters have to be positioned in the right formation before they can enter that last, explosive conflict. And maybe, semi-consciously, I had something broader in mind, too.

'Are you going to keep talking to Lisa, after this project is finished?' my own editor, Sophie, asks me when we meet this week on Zoom.

'It would be weird if we didn't, wouldn't it?' I ask, wanting a second opinion.

'Oh, yeah,' she reassures me. 'That would be weird.'

'But maybe it won't be quite the same,' I add, almost to myself.

As mentioned, I'm the opposite of Lisa: I'm a planner. I've already plotted out the remaining chapters of my book about her, giving each of them titles, and have noted down all the difficult questions I want to ask her before this is finally over. That chapter is called 'Last Words'. It's not far off now.

House of Words

24 October 2021

A year ago, I was on irregular, relatively formal, best-regards terms with bestselling novelist Lisa Jewell. Now I am wandering barefoot around her new house, drinking her wine.

Lisa is out of the country, and I am staying at the big white place overlooking the sea that she was so excited about when we started talking in January. She invited me here so I could carry out my own research into the area around Dungeness, whose towers are just visible in eerie silhouette from the balcony outside her bedroom.

She wrote this house, she realised recently, but not in a book that was ever published. She wrote it many years ago, in *The Wonderful World of Dave*, which she also realised, digging it out and reading it objectively, was 'kind of awesome! It read like the pilot for a really snappy, edgy Netflix show. I had set them all up, this vivid array of people, all primed and ready for DARK FARCE.'

The house appears on an early page, in a flashback to the eponymous protagonist's childhood. You won't have read this book, so it is worth quoting it at length.

Beyond the beach he sees the cliffs, chalky and sharp, jutting out into the sea, one, two, three times, like a concertinaed piece of paper. And there beyond the furthest cliff he sees the house. It looks like a piece of Lego from here, like a tiny piece of cream coloured plastic. It is called Ivy House. He knows it is called Ivy House because they drive past it every summer, on the winding road that brings them here from the motorway. It has peeling stucco posts on the road with a sandstone plaque that says: *Ivy House*. From behind, it looks like a flat cardboard house, with small windows and a small door. But from down here, from on the beach, it looks like a face; tall bowed windows looking out to sea like wide incredulous eyes, as if it has just seen something remarkable. It has a terraced garden that spills down the steep hill towards the beach, with columns and pale grey walls that zig-zag through the land at forty-five degrees. Dave is sure there must be a maze in that garden, maybe one with animals hewn out of bushes and a secret statue in the middle.

Dave asks his mum who lives in the house. 'I've no idea,' she shrugs. 'Someone very rich, I'd have thought.'

'Can we go there one day?' asks Dave.

'Why not?'

'Because it's not our house, it's someone else's house.'

I've never seen a house like Lisa's in a novel. Nobody would write it quite accurately, perhaps not even Lisa. They would make it too spooky, too quirky, too perfect or too pretentious, too luxurious or, given the owner, too literary.

A novel about a bestselling author's house might include the Warhol print in the kitchen and the Klimt reproductions in the attic rooms, the prints of animals captioned with Beatles, Cure and Oasis lyrics, but not the original paintings by Lisa's friend Grace O'Connor: haunting portraits of teenage girls that have the blurred quality of dream-photographs.

A novelist would do the obvious and fill the house with books: but there are only a handful here, including what looks like a Scandinavian *Family Upstairs* next to a bright yellow volume titled *Luckiest Girl Alive*, which reminds me of Lisa, or at least the way she seems to see herself.

A writer imagining somewhere gorgeous would include the basement swimming pool but not the paddling pool inflated under the living room ceiling to catch drips from a hole in the plaster and protect the parquet. In a book, this house would either be sunlit or spooky, not a South of France idyll by day and so foreboding by night that I hesitated to go downstairs, hearing the AI of the home security talking to itself, the computer on the freezer communicating with the computer that runs the lights, and an answerphone message echoing in a distant chamber.

In a novel, the nuances of taste would be eroded. Lisa would have Nutella or the jars of some artisan spread called Noir that I've never seen before, not both. She would have the Dior espresso cup or the Waitrose mugs, not both. Most authors, creating this house in fiction, would decide that the scent of vanilla, linen and rose that airs every room came from something fancier and more obscure than Zara diffusers. But this is a real home, a human home, a family home.

Henry Lamb would never own this home, because he is (at this point, anyway) too cold and too out of touch with what it means to be human and family. His niece Libby – although there's a bottle of Aperol, her signature drink, in the fridge – doesn't have the style, the flair or aspiration. (She's been written out of the sequel for good reason.)

Lucy Lamb, perhaps, if she was allowed to settle and put her mark, with Marco and Stella, on their new house in St Albans, but hadn't yet erased the traces of the family that lived there before, could have a house like this (there are still multiple signs of the previous owner in Lisa's home, not least in the fitness centre he built himself in the basement, in the 1990s. He, too, must be built. I can barely lift his weights, and the dents in the vinyl floor suggest they've not been moved since he left).

Cate in *Invisible Girl*, perhaps, and her son and daughter, once Roan had been banished; or Alice Lake from *I Found You*, with her clan of kids. And maybe Jem – Jem from *Ralph's Party*, who would now be in her fifties. Jem, who, as Lisa's first creation, was always closest to her author, could have furnished and decorated this house, which is still halfway through finding itself, still growing organically to look more like its new owner.

Coming down barefoot to curl up on the sofa in front of the huge plasma, I feel lightly hungover though I only drank one glass of Lisa's wine last night, then realise I'm imagining it because it feels so inevitable: this would be such a perfect house for a party that, in the morning, you half remember a night before that didn't really happen. The retro music from Google speakers, the adult voices growing more raucous, the teenagers disappearing into the dark corners of the garden to cluster and chat. The underwater lights in the pool are fused, so they rely on phone torches, light flickering off wet bodies until the batteries die. The sound of their shouts echo faintly up through the floor: ghost voices from below, drowned by Spotify.

A thriller plot writes itself here – a group of rich kids decide on a late-night swimming session that turns ugly, then tragic – and I almost think there's a novel in it, but then I realise I'm thinking of *The Night She Disappeared*. Lisa's already done it.

I've brought along an old book from my university library called *See Jane Write: A Girl's Guide to Writing Chick Lit*. Its second chapter is titled 'Getting Back at Your Ex and Other Reasons to Write.' It includes a quiz for the aspiring author, inviting her to select her goals and motivations for writing a chick-lit book. These include turning up to your own book signings with a 'handsome, sensitive, mogul husband' while your ex-boyfriend watches in dismay; working all day from home wearing 'fluffy orange sweatpants', and touring New York, Milan and London, drinking Bellinis. 'Cartwheel right over those velvet ropes. You're ready for the A-list, baby.'

None of the answers include a big white house overlooking the sea. That would be too far-fetched even for this naïve, nineties dream of success. But in a very real way, that is what Lisa has achieved, and it started with a twenty-something woman writing something like chick lit at her boyfriend's kitchen table in the late nineties.

Somehow, that young woman who had attended creative-writing evening classes at a Working Men's College put one word in front of another and built a book, and then another book, and those books became bricks that, over twenty-two years or so, became her ownership of a big white house overlooking the sea.

It's a remarkable, astonishing house, but in a way there's no mystery about the process. It was absolutely simple. There were publishing trends and genre shifts and lucky breaks and mid-career doubts, but ultimately, Lisa got here by writing words that people wanted to read. She built the house with words.

Phantom Threads

4 November 2021

As I type at my computer, I hear the front door slam, and then the faint conversation downstairs.

'Where's Daddy?'

'Daddy's in his room right now, working. Do you know what he's doing?

'What?'

'He's writing a story. It's about a lady who writes stories.'

'. . . What happens next?'

I don't know. I haven't received a new sample of *The Family Remains* since mid-October (and it turns out that I won't until late November). Lisa is writing every day, she assures her audience on Instagram – she's in the final phase now, she promises – but I've seen nothing of it.

What I do have are her email updates, which describe revisions of passages and plots that I've already read. The rape scene that, horrifically, ended the previous section is now going to be significantly different from that draft, based on my feedback and that of two writer-friends. 'I write using my instincts almost entirely, and the very fact that I have felt that I needed to ask three people about this was probably clue enough that it wasn't quite right,' Lisa explains:

> Following our chat, I will also change the meeting between Rachel and Lucy outside Rachel's apartment block to her

trying to tell Lucy, without alarming the children, that SOMEONE KNOWS SOMETHING, that the French police have been in touch. And then THAT is why they run away to Chicago, not to get away from Rachel, but away from the French police investigation. So that arc will fade away there and move along to the next perilous thing. I think this will be great. And I am very grateful to you.

When I first met Lisa in autumn 2020, my companion Andy Martin enthusiastically proposed a theory about all the alternate paths writers open up and then shut down whenever they make a choice about plot, character, dialogue or description. It was perhaps a little heavy-duty for an initial coffee chat – the kind of thing Jack Reacher might come out with while hitchhiking, baffling the driver who picked him up at the last turnpike – but I think Andy was right, and Lisa's process has proved it.

At the most minute level, every time Lisa (or any other writer, including me and you) chooses an adjective, other words are considered, however briefly and subconsciously, and then ruled out. More dramatically, every time she decides on a protagonist's direction, whole branches of potential plot come into spectral being like ghosts, and then are swiped out of existence. Sometimes this pruning happens after scenes are completed: we saw that with Phin's point-of-view scene, which could have progressed down its own path, but was erased almost before it began. Drawing on Jacques Derrida's philosophical approach, mentioned earlier, we could imagine these possible plot strands as present-but-absent, choices that were never made, or that were reconsidered but whose traces still hover like phantoms in the text.

So when Lisa writes the line I cited earlier, 'They had a small wooden house on stilts over an azure sea filled with colourful coral and ribboning fish,' we might imagine the alternate words *modest* floating faintly above 'small', and perhaps *a cobalt* above 'an azure', and an inferior adjective like *dancing* above 'ribboning'. Any of these changes would have subtly shifted the meaning and tone. And in another version of *The Family Remains* – perhaps published in a universe one side-step from our own, under the title *Birdie's Bones* – Lucy still runs from Rachel rather than the French police, seeing her as an enemy rather than an ally. And perhaps in another volume, on another earth, Phin still has his own point-of-view plotline. In a third, we'd get Marco's perspective on the hen party at Clemency's house, which Lisa told me she was toying with writing but which I haven't yet seen, if it even exists: it's a Schrödinger's scene. And in another version of the manuscript, Lisa found the Samuel Owusu chapter she loved and lost (it was either deleted or never saved, and she mourns it regularly) rather than having to struggle to remember its details and then rewrite them.

Too science-fictional? Bear with me for one more paragraph. In China Miéville's fantasy novel *The Scar*, a character owns an uncanny weapon called a Possible Sword. When swung, it conjures up and manifests every conceivable way that the arm could move and the blade could strike; watching this warrior in combat is like seeing a man with 1,000 ghost-limbs, a blur of multiples. If we could see all the possibilities that had been raised by and then erased in Lisa's writing process, the result would be similarly uncanny and ungraspable, a volume of hypothetical scenes and might-have-beens, a tapestry bristling with phantom threads.

At one point, Miéville's swordsman explains his technique. 'Precision is the one thing I cannot afford. I must be an opportunist, not a planner. I must fight from the heart, not the mind.'

Write, fight: the principle is the same. The unpredictability of Lisa's novels comes, as I've learned, from the fact that she doesn't overthink, and never plans. As Miéville suggests, this is the technique of an expert, the result of years of training and experience; you can only write using your instincts 'almost entirely' if you know exactly (or almost exactly, almost always) what you're doing.

Meanwhile, I keep waiting to read *The Family Remains*. As I wait, I sometimes ask myself whether Lisa, aware that I've been reading her novel at artificial intervals, staggered and interrupted rather than with the natural flow of a normal reader, is holding off in order to drop the final third on me all at once, and allow me to immerse myself more fully in the story.

Anything's possible at this stage.

Meeting the Readers

Lisa is telling her story again. Not one of her novels, but her own origin story, which she describes once more, happily, as a fairy tale: redundant secretary, drunken bet, three chapters, bestselling debut. 'It was a big deal back in 1999,' she concludes, and her fellow panellists nod immediate agreement.

Lisa is appearing at the BerkoFest Book Festival in Berkhamsted, a pretty town in Hertfordshire that feels to me, because of its medieval heritage, slightly and quaintly miniature; I have to stoop to get through most of its doorways. She is on a panel with four other writers – Rowan Coleman, Katy Regan, Rosie Walsh and Clare Swatman – discussing women's contemporary literature. Lisa had told me it would be a 'girly' event, chilled and informal, with her writer pals. The tone is chatty, self-deprecating, apologetic. I've seen male authors at events like these (they tend to be given their own panels with a single interviewer, like Alexei Sayle's session today, and are not invited to discuss 'men's contemporary literature') and the focus is invariably on the process of writing, rather than childcare, dog-walking and 'faffing about with admin all morning'; not because women prefer to talk about these things, but because men are less likely to be lumbered with them.

It's the first time I've seen Lisa at a public event since Polari, in December 2019, and I find myself checking what she says against what I already know. The fairy tale is, unsurprisingly, almost exactly the same as the version I've heard before, with some added colour details – she slipped Yasmin Boland her draft chapters under the table of a pub, like an embarrassed spy – and valuable context, like the fact that *Ralph's Party* was written pre-Bridget Jones, when Lisa assumed that all female novelists were middle-aged, rather than in their twenties. She also claims that she writes 1,000 words every day, which . . . is true for some months of the year, sure. But then, Lisa's fellow authors admit that they sometimes delude themselves, their intentions falling short of the reality; one of them admits that her entire website, created before she had children, is now 'full of lies', or at least outdated information and wishful thinking.

Shortly before BerkoFest, I read *Plot*, the 2021 novel by Jean Hanff Korelitz. (Lisa did a Zoom with her last week. 'She was so so so nice. I wanted to be her new friend.') The author-protagonist, Jake, experiences sudden literary success, including his first entrance applause when he turns up at a book festival. One of the venues has over 2,400 seats; Jake stares out at this sea of readers, spotting the Kelly green cover of his latest paperback in people's hands and on their laps.

Lisa sometimes has these starry, literary-celebrity experiences herself, but this Sunday lunchtime is not one of them: BerkoFest is more like the modest literary event Sophie Beck attends at the end of *The Night She Disappeared*. We are in the elegant but draughty town hall, and the room is comfortably full with attentive women; I count only five men, not including myself at the back. The women raise their hands politely and apologise when their questions run over time. One of the men, by contrast, shouts out a comment without bothering to wait his turn, and another begins his query for the authors with an anecdote about his own mock exams. It crosses my mind that gender is an important factor here, integral to how Lisa and her panellists write their books, and how they and their books are then treated.

Afterwards, in the green room – the feeling of walking in on the teachers during a school journey, with chairs in a circle and a table of pastries – Lisa gives me an early copy of the next Gillian McAllister thriller (having my hands on an 'ARC' is a huge thrill in itself) and tells my three-year-old son, with great respect, that she is very pleased to meet him. He turns his face shyly into my shoulder.

Tomorrow, Lisa is travelling to another little market town for another panel, but this one is four and a half hours away by train and bus. She invited me to the Bridport Writers' Festival but I dropped out, daunted by the journey. I tell her I'm impressed by her commitment, and I mean it; I hadn't imagined that being a successful author would involve so much work outside the actual writing.

'Oh, it doesn't feel like work,' she assures me with winning, earnest energy, sounding very Lisa. 'No, it doesn't feel like work at all.'

As I lead my son out of the town hall, we walk past a long queue of patient people.

'Are these all for you?' I ask Lisa, knowing her fanbase has increased dramatically over the last few years.

'No.' She smiles. 'They're all for Alexei Sayle.'

My academic background includes audience studies, and for some time, I'd planned to talk to Lisa's readers about her work. Berkhamsted presented a prime opportunity: I could have selected a focus group from that audience in the town hall, given out surveys to the people queueing, or invited fans to take part in interviews. I ultimately decided against it. This was to be a book about the author, about her side of the process, the creation rather than the interpretation and reception. But then a reader came to me, and I couldn't resist.

Magdalena Glowacka is an MA student on the Museum and Gallery Studies programme at my own university. I gave a brief outline of my research to her class at the start of the year, and she approached me afterwards, not sure if she was breaching a boundary, but unable to help herself. Lisa Jewell's books, she told me breathlessly, had both followed and shaped the path of her own life since she arrived in the UK in 1999, the year of *Ralph's Party*. She was twenty at the time of Lisa's debut, and is now forty-two; she had essentially grown up with Lisa. Lisa's writing, she said, had even taught her English.

Of course, we had to talk more. On our second meeting, Magdalena produced a paperback of *Ralph's Party*, its covers soft from multiple readings. 'I couldn't remember how I'd got it, but then I realised . . .' She flipped it over. *Free with ELLE*, said a sticker on the back.

'When I first got here from Italy, in September 1999' – she'd lived between there and Poland for the first decades of her life – 'my English wasn't good at all. So the only things I could enjoy were magazines. And I think that must have been the first magazine I ever bought, when I landed. The book sat on my shelf for six months until I felt confident enough and ready for the challenge, and I just gave it a go.

'And it was extraordinary, because I never thought my English was good enough to understand anything, but as I started reading . . . it almost felt like having a conversation with somebody. It was so approachable. And I felt, within a couple of pages: this is like talking to a friend. This is exactly what I'm doing and experiencing. I was a young girl, wanting to study fashion, working in pubs in the evening, doing Saturday-morning drawing, painting and portfolio classes at St Martin's College . . .

which took me into that world of Soho and Tottenham Court Road . . . and then I got myself a Sunday job at H&M on Oxford Street. Of course, I was in a flat-share because I couldn't afford to pay for more than one bed in a room, so . . . everything in that book was my life. The characters were my friends. Everything was so relatable. It made me feel a bit more at home. This was my world, this was my life, these are my ambitions.'

Magdalena shows me photos: real photos, analogue photos, glossy snaps from the late 1990s. They look just like Lisa's photographs from the year of her debut book launch, except that Magdalena isn't standing in front of an advertisement for her next novel, but cooking in a shared kitchen. I recognise the clunky, stained gas hob – in fact, I recognise the whole kitchen, crowded with labelled jars and miscellaneous cereal boxes, and cupboards that don't properly close – from my own 1990s flat-shares. And then there's Magdalena in 2003, wearing a nice, going-out top and eye make-up, smiling warily in front of a cute card with two cuddling teddy bears. 'Our final anniversary,' she captions it. She's absolutely right. She looks like a Lisa Jewell character. It could easily be a publicity still from a period-perfect adaptation of Lisa's early novels.

By the time she finished *Ralph's Party*, *Thirtynothing* was on the shelves, and Magdalena was compelled to buy it. 'And that was extraordinary because I'd started a relationship with somebody who was part of our group. His grandparents were in Bournemouth, like Phil's, and I'd previously lived in Kentish Town. And the whole dramatic situation of the novel was in Kentish Town. That book reconfirmed why I came to London, at a time when I was starting to doubt myself and wonder if I should stay here. It was all about the incredible freedom of the city when you're young. So as soon as I finished the book, I thought: there was no way I'm going back to Italy.

'And faster than anyone expected, because I was getting so much into reading books, my English improved. My tutors were amazed. I even had to deliberately fail one of my exams to prove that I needed an extension on my language courses, to secure my visa. I was literally eating books now, all because I started with *Ralph's Party*.

'Now, I could analyse every Lisa Jewell novel in relation to my life, but it would take a week. But I can guarantee you that every new book happened to either mention a place, or an event, which links to myself or my life. It was amazing, like finding a soulmate. It was as though her books understood me. For instance, I always felt I should be born in the 1920s, and I felt I was channelling my grandmother, who looked just like me, and then *Before I Met You* came out.

'And then my life got a bit darker,' Magdalena says, looking away with a heaviness entering her voice. 'And Lisa's books got darker. This is exactly when she started writing crime. And every year I waited for her new book to come out, but now, the titles were like summaries of what was happening to me at the time.' I check the titles – *The Third Wife, Then She Was Gone, Watching You*. I don't ask what was going on in Magdalena's life during those years.

'And I always wondered,' Magdalena goes on. 'I know Lisa is exactly ten years older than me. I wonder if we're living similar lives, if I'm doing everything she's done, ten years later. It's as though she's telling me . . . right now, for instance, our family is dealing with an inheritance, and my whole year has been consumed by a big house in Blackpool . . . it feels like I'm one of her characters.' The uncanny synchronicities continue. 'In at least five of her books,' Magdalena insists, leaning forward, 'Lisa describes my mother exactly. And in *A Friend of the Family*, Millie's pregnancy was exactly like my pregnancy. Including the exact weight of the baby.' (I look it up: nine pounds, two ounces.)

Are these really synchronicities, I wonder, or the phenomenon of pareidolia: the tendency to find patterns by selecting some aspects and ignoring others? Magdalena, of course, isn't a blinkered obsessive. She realises that Lisa's books aren't really messages to her as a long-term fan; they're so rich with detail that multiple readers could latch on to different features and apply them to their own lives.

'They're so identifiable, so familiar, everyday stories with humour and wit. I love the way she colours the scenes; it's like you're there. I almost feel as though I'm the one narrating it. But anyone could. I'm pretty sure that's not just me.'

I ask her how much she knows about Lisa's writing process. The answer astonishes me, partly because it's so different from my own earlier assumptions that Lisa's thrillers must be intricately plotted in advance.

'I don't think she plans too much. My instinct is that the stories have so many twists and turns . . . they always surprise. I don't think it's possible to plan all that. I think she wakes up all of a sudden with a new idea and thinks: Oh, I'm going to do this now, and changes it completely. When you read it, it's fresh.'

'I see,' I say coolly, concealing my surprise. 'So you mean, because it twists so much, you get the impression she can't have planned it.'

Magdalena considers, and nods. 'That's what I think, yeah.'

And of course, once more, she's absolutely right.

Seeing France

18 November 2021

Lisa has sent me new material, for the first time in a month. 'Are you doing another progress chapter? I had a thought for this one. It could be called "300 Pages: Seeing France".'

> So, I am at 297 pages and as most of my books are around the 400 pages mark, hitting page number 300 is an important moment in its development. And I've said things about boats and ports before when I talk about writing with no plan; ie, I've boarded a boat but I don't know where it's going or which ports it'll stop at on the way. But what I've realised, thinking more deeply (as this project has forced me to do constantly over the past ten months!) is that each book is much more akin to swimming the channel. I know that I'll get to France eventually if I just keep going but for most of the swim I can't actually see it.

The new material is dominated by a storming Henry chapter, if not the climax then the coming-together of dense, crackling clouds, the build-up to a tempestuous conflict and perhaps, afterwards, to catharsis. Before this year, I suppose – if I can clear my mental slate and imagine reading this fresh, without any knowledge of Lisa and her process – I would have assumed this scene was painstakingly crafted, placed just so in the plot by design and then carefully polished. Now I encounter it as the work of an author who writes 'to the absolute top end of

[her] intellect, ability and talents', who works by feel, guided by instinct and emotional rightness rather than a pre-prepared plan. She doesn't know what she is doing until she's doing it; sometimes she can't tell whether it works until she's finished it, until she can walk away and look back at it in context.

I don't know how I would have explained this Henry chapter to myself before I accepted and understood Lisa's approach, but now, knowing her as I do, it seems impossible that it could have been written any other way, by any other author. Its rush and raw energy, its desperation and anguish, seem to have been poured on to the page with barely any hesitation or self-censorship, to the extent that I can glimpse Lisa in the prose, behind and in between Henry's monologues. When looking at porn makes Henry 'cross', I hear Lisa, although it also suits her prissy, uptight protagonist; when he buys and then gives away a bag of ketamine, I suspect it's because Lisa didn't trust her own experience to write about the drug's effects, and didn't want to be slowed by having to research it. And I hear and see myself in Henry, as I increasingly have – worryingly – throughout this novel, and find myself asking whether I was simply like him from the start, way back in *The Family Upstairs*, or whether he's evolved gradually and subtly during the course of this novel.

But then, we've all had nights like Henry's, surely? Driven by a restless need you can't name, rebounding like a pinball from bar to club to bar, manhandled easily by bouncers and sent on your way, seeing yourself in shop-window reflections and other people's reactions as a staggering, slurring drunk, a lost ship veering from port to port, on its way to becoming a wreck. We've all sent a late-night text (haven't we?) that ends up '*Im dunk adn horn comr adn find em On your big bikr*, with a bike emoji'. (Henry's message to Kris Doll is unfortunately implausible, given the sophistication of contemporary predictive text, but I found it the funniest line so far in a dark novel; and beautifully fitting that Henry ends up writing prose like his author's uncorrected, typo-ridden manuscript.)

There are other overlaps that seem trivial, but which nevertheless resonate like quiet chimes in my head after this peculiar almost-year of sharing so much of my life with Lisa. After cataloguing all the scented diffusers in her big white house, I found myself sourcing them online and buying two for myself, so my suburban home now smells a little like her seafront villa. Henry, in turn, spends seventy dollars on room sprays and scented candles in an attempt to transform his manky Airbnb. I think, reading this: I told Lisa I'd spent too much on a Cire Trudon Ernesto candle this summer. And then I realise I'm just being paranoid and self-centred; Lisa can invent character behaviour without having to draw on my frivolous purchases for her vain, traumatised anti-hero. And then I think: But self-centred paranoia is one of Henry's key traits.

Henry Lamb is forty-two, about ten years younger than me and Lisa, though in some ways he's still stuck in his twenties – still cherishing objects and appearance, still chasing cute waiters half his age. One revelation that's crept up on me gradually during this year is that Lisa . . . how can I phrase this . . . that Lisa, whom I still think of on one level as the girl in the pink dress who'd just written *Ralph's Party*, is not exactly that person any more, and that over two decades have passed, and that somehow she's become the kind of person younger writers like Gillian McAllister look up to for inspiration. McAllister – whose astonishingly accomplished sixth novel Lisa passed on to me at Berkhamsted – was only fourteen years old when *Ralph's Party* was published; she's a long-term fan of Lisa's novels, thrilled to have her work endorsed by a more established writer. Lisa, I realise, is now referred to as the 'Queen of Thrillers'. Maybe she is, startlingly, entering Ruth Rendell territory, on the way to Agatha Christie status.

But, crucially, she doesn't write with the easy confidence that status implies, and that's what gives these passages their necessary energy. This Henry chapter, which accelerates and blurs into stream of consciousness, is nothing like the wryly knowing inner monologues of Joyce's Stephen Dedalus, or even his Molly Bloom soliloquy, whose apparently free-flowing torrent of words bears the careful choices of the author rather than simply succumbing to the energies of the character. It is nothing like the clever exercise in technique that distinguishes David Lodge's *Thinks . . .* , an attempt to capture consciousness – 'is it a stream as William James said or as he also rather beautifully said like a bird flying through the air and then perching for a moment then taking wing again . . . ' – or the eerie metropolitan poetry we encounter when Virginia Woolf dips into Clarissa Dalloway's way of seeing the world. Its quality is quite different and can perhaps be best explained by stepping sideways into another form of artistic expression.

Henry Lamb, again, is forty-two. At forty-two, Frank Sinatra recorded 'Come Fly With Me'. Imagine that song, or better still, listen to it. One verse is enough; in fact, the first two lines are enough. As soon as Sinatra starts to sing, you sense his absolute control over his own instrument. You can relax into his firm, confident grasp, like a pair of hands on your shoulders steering you, guiding you gently into a dance. You feel it in his willingness to stretch out a note for an extra half-second, to pause between words, to playfully delay: listen to him smoothly sliding over the sibilant in 'use' to 'some exotic booze', throwing in some swing for 'a-there's a bar', then bending the pronunciation of 'Bombay'. Two lines is all it takes. You're safe. Sinatra is in the cockpit; settle back, folks, and enjoy the trip.

There's a pleasure in that. And then there's the pleasure in a very different kind of vocal, rawer and less polished, which thrills because it reaches as high as it can, and only just makes it; and even if it falls marginally short, brushing the target with its fingertips, there's still a tremendous power in the attempt. It is the voice of a younger man. Think of the 26-year-old Bruce Springsteen yelling 'the *highway*'s jammed with broken heroes', halfway through the exhausting workout of 'Born To Run', or the 25-year-old David Bowie's anguished repeats of 'Five years! That's all we got!', or 27-year-old Neil Young stretching his voice up plaintively, thinly on 'Heart Of Gold', or nineteen-year-old Tim Wheeler on Ash's first album, his vocals marginally flat but it doesn't matter, because that sound so perfectly suits the teenage naivety and sincerity of the songs.

That, not Sinatra, is Henry's voice; and that, I think, is also Lisa's voice, devoid of arrogance and complacency, writing 'to the absolute top end of [her] intellect, ability and talents', reaching, reaching.

And then at around this point in the process I start to see the outline and I pick up my pace because I've kind of had enough and just want to get there and the closer it gets the more details I see and I start to dream of a warm bath and moules mariniere and a glass of wine in a harbour front restaurant, so now, each day when I come to the book, I am focused and ready and I jump from chapter to chapter much more easily, stop far less for breath, keep going, keep going, France is there.

That's Lisa, but it could almost be Henry.

She is almost there, she tells me. The next time we see Henry may be the last; may, indeed, be the last chapter.

At this exact moment, I still have no idea what will transpire between Phin and Henry, although they are now in a locked room together, and am thinking of leaving Henry for a few chapters and letting the other stories play out. I think that could be quite suspenseful and that maybe what happens in that room could in fact be the final chapter? I'll give it a try and see if it works.

But now, as she grows more confident, I become worried. I have to deliver my manuscript, this book, to the publisher (her publisher) before the end of December. I'm concerned that she won't finish *The Family Remains* before I have to draw a line and decide, perhaps prematurely, that my report is concluded. I can see the destination, too: I can see two figures in a room, at a distance, like silhouettes behind a window in an Edward Hopper cityscape, but they are vague and shadowy. I can't tell if they're embracing or fighting, kissing or trying to kill each other.

Lisa is ploughing ahead now, fully productive, her diary empty of everything but the novel – 'and it is the loveliest feeling, I feel lighter, more limber, more flexible, I feel like a writer when that's all that I do, and that is a very good feeling indeed' – but I may not be around to see the finish.

In fact, her diary isn't empty. We have one more date.

Finale: Polari

1 December 2021

My last meeting with Lisa is at Polari, the literary salon run by Paul Burston, held tonight in Heaven, the famous gay club beneath Charing Cross. The morning after our night out, I'm left with fragments. My notes — emails sent to myself from the club — are like Lisa's drafts or Henry's texts: typo-ridden half-sentences, experimental poetry. 'Irony parallels. Ambulances mean a lot now. He breaks down. A wisp of a waiter barley old enough to drink milk.' I dig out receipts, like souvenirs from a nightmare city, where a large coffee costs £5.90 and £17 gets you two small glasses of Pinot Grigio.

It's been a long time since I drank in Central London, and even longer since my last Polari — almost two years, in fact. Two years since the night that started all this, when I saw Lisa reading from *The Family Upstairs*. That was one of the last parties before lockdown; festivities during a final month of innocence when we hadn't even heard of Covid-19. Tonight has a doomier air. On the train, everyone is masked again, under new government restrictions; people mutter about the Omicron virus and the possibility of another cancelled Christmas.

This Polari event is a special evening to commemorate World AIDS Day, and the speakers recall homophobic discourses of 'gay plagues' from the mid-eighties. We all shake our heads in dismay and applaud with hands sanitised against a genuine epidemic. There are horrifying anecdotes about policemen wearing rubber gloves when raiding queer bars, implying that the community was contaminated and untouchable. Now, people ask permission before embracing. ('Are you doing hugs?' Lisa checks with Paul.) On stage, Adam Zmith reads from his book on the history of poppers, celebrating the pleasures of breathing in deep, while we sit smiling behind our masks. Times have changed, for better and worse, and the new ways of talking and interacting offer a counterpoint to the old.

Listening to the stories of previous decades, I remember a day in 1988 when an older boy promised me he was going to 'take me to heaven' the next time I was in London. I didn't realise he meant the club, and nervously declined. Thirty-three years later, I'm sitting at a table on Heaven's dance floor, next to international bestselling novelist Lisa Jewell, learning about 1920s modernist lesbians. Some futures simply can't be predicted.

This afternoon, before leaving for London, I read, or reread, the most recent 30,000 words of *The Family Remains*, because Lisa wants to discuss them in person. Most of the chapters were familiar, but a few were entirely new; a substantial chunk of the novel, it turned out, had been delivered to my spam folder during late October, when I thought Lisa was deliberately withholding material. I experienced this section out of sequence, as an unintended flashback. Other chapters were unfinished or marked for a rewrite. Some were destined to be cut completely. Lisa confides now that she has two strands plotted out – she knows that Lucy's story will end happily, while another will be 'very sad and might incite tears in some'. I ask her not to tell me; I'll find out, in time.

She asks me, in turn, to fix Rachel's story, which doesn't yet have a satisfactory ending. I do it in twenty minutes, over our first glass of wine. She's grateful and astonished, but to me it seems quite straightforward. I've lived with these characters, as she has, for most of the year now. I feel like I know them. We talk about them as if they are mutual acquaintances, discussing what music Samuel Owusu likes – I suggest Chris Rea's *Auberge* album, she tends towards Ed Sheeran and Adele – and what song Rachel should play for Lucy on the fiddle, in the South of France. At the time of writing, it's Katy Perry's 'Firework'. By next week, that detail may have been entirely erased. Possibilities wink in and out of existence as we talk; phantom scenes and strands write and rewrite themselves. One thing is certain, though. 'You won't see any of these characters again,' Lisa promises me firmly. This is her longest, most complex story – 'It's a mess,' I tell her rashly, 'a beautiful mess, like life' – almost two novels in one, as the sequel begins where *The Family Upstairs* stops; but it concludes here, with no prospect of another volume.

A sense of impending loss now dominates this project, as December begins. *The Family Remains* is nearly finished. Samuel is closing in on Libby and Miller – encouraging our loyalties to shift, as we now root for the investigating detective rather than the heroine of *The Family Upstairs* – Lucy and her children are on the run from the police, and Henry is finally in a locked room with Phin. What happens in that room, Lisa tells me with satisfaction, will only be revealed in the very last chapter. 'Do you want to know?' I hesitate for half a second, and tell her no.

The story will soon be over, and so will my story with Lisa. In her covering note with the most recent chapters, she included a paragraph that reminded me, strangely and a little sadly, of letters I've received at the end of relationships. She couldn't predict whether we would remain friends after this, she mused. *We will either stay in each other's lives, or we won't.*

Perhaps that's why, after another glass or two, I badger her about whether I've shaped the character of Henry Lamb in this sequel. If we're going to drift out of touch once our twinned books are finished, will that be my legacy? Have I been incorporated into her twentieth novel as a lonely, empty antihero, a polished shell of a middle-aged man?

'I honestly can't say,' Lisa tells me simply. She wrote a passage describing Henry's highlighted cowlick, and realised that sounded like my hair, but checked back and discovered that he's always had that style.

'I haven't had a chin shave and cheek implants like Henry,' I point out, starting to shiver. The salon is over, the nightclub closed; we're sitting outside Gordon's Wine Bar on Villiers Street, and the overhead heaters are weak against the December chill. My fingers tremble around a tumbler of Pinot Grigio. Lisa takes off her scarf and drapes it over my knees.

'You might have,' she points out. 'I wouldn't know.'

'I don't spend two hours in the gym every day like Henry,' I protest.

Lisa gently changes the subject. Her next novel, she confides, will be about a stalker, and set in the world of academia.

'I could help you with that,' I offer, teeth chattering. 'I've had experience of being stalked.'

'No,' she says kindly. 'The academic is going to be the stalker.'

I stare at her.

'He's going to be shadowing someone for a year and writing about their life.'

'So it's about me and you,' I stammer, pretending to be indignant, but secretly thrilled. 'Well, I suppose it wouldn't really be about me and you, because however it starts out, it would become your own work immediately, and evolve into a different story.'

'That's right,' she agrees.

'I know a lot about academia,' I offer again. 'If you want any expert advice.'

Lisa looks at me with a kind of restrained glee. 'So I have your permission?'

'Yeah, of course you have my permission. And I'd love to keep reading your work, to be honest. I'd really miss it if I couldn't read your work in progress. And I think I've been quite a good reader.'

'Oh,' says Lisa with happy certainty, as the servers announce last orders and we stand up to make our separate ways home. 'You've been *beyond*.'

The Sense of an Ending

17 December 2021

While I waited for Lisa to send me new material, I began reread-ing the classic French novel *Le Grand Meaulnes*, which I'd first encountered for French A Level, some thirty-three years ago. One line from the opening chapters had stuck in my memory, and it leapt out again because of its perfect correspondence to the date. 'Et c'est là que tout commença, environ huit jours avant Noël.' ('It was then that everything began, about eight days before Christmas.') That evening, Lisa emailed. 'I attach THE BOOK,' she wrote. At the bottom of her brief message was a Word document: the entirety of *The Family Remains*. That's when it ended, then: about eight days before Christmas.

I embarked on this project partly because, after writing exten-sively about the work of David Bowie for most of the previous decade – he died, tragically and inconsiderately, halfway through my research – I wanted to deal with a creator who was still alive, to analyse art in progress and ask the author about it (because even while Bowie was alive, he was, of course, unattainable). The author – Lisa – has held a prominent role in this book, retaining or reclaiming a power that should have been impossible after Roland Barthes's provocative declaration that we should consider the writer dead and buried, ignore their intentions and look to the reader for meaning. At every stage, I've been able to ask Lisa about her inten-tions, and her choices and interpretations have taken precedence.

But during this unique process, Barthes's proposal – that meaning lies with the reader – has also proven true, in ways he could never have predicted. Barthes would never have expected the author to turn to the reader, as Lisa did to me, and confess that she needed to brainstorm the final chapters; Barthes would never have dreamed that author and reader might actually come up with a collaborative plot. Lisa's final chapters present me with a unique, unnerving experience in many ways, not least because I'm seeing my own suggestions come true; the story about Rachel, her dad and Michael is exactly what I sketched out in that twenty minutes on the dance floor at Heaven, made vivid through Lisa's characteristically touching, telling details, such as Brian Gold's choice of cava instead of champagne, and his pretence that he really wants supermarket lilies rather than his usual luxury blooms from an upmarket florist.

I check the scroll bar at the side of the Word document as I read, assessing how much is left; how much time I have with these characters, how much space there is for all their stories to be resolved. I've found myself daydreaming, even actual-dreaming, about the very last scene, the epilogue in which we'll finally discover what happened between Henry and Phin, after Henry pushed his way inside and then denied he'd ever found his target, the object of his decades-long obsession and desire. I've been visualising Chicago cityscapes as I fall asleep, my viewpoint travelling slowly in like a drone camera towards one window, spotting two figures in a passionate struggle. I've imagined kicking my way into that locked-room mystery, days later, and finding a body tied to the radiator – or perhaps two, locked together in a final embrace. The corpse, or corpses, can't be immediately identified: is this dead man Phin or the man who pursued him, who changed his body and face and name so he could pass as his quarry?

'You may be let down by the ending,' Lisa adds, in a cover note. I'd told her my visions of the epilogue, meaning it as a compliment that her novel was occupying my unconscious to such an extent, but perhaps it just added to the pressure on her during the final push. She did consider all my suggestions, she goes on, 'and they were all scenarios I'd pondered vaguely, loosely . . . but I ended up somewhere else'.

I reach the end of *The Family Remains* and I'm reminded of what should have been obvious. It's Lisa's book, after all. She faced near-infinite possibilities, branching paths lying ahead in a dazzling map of permutations, and she made a decision for her characters at each junction, as if navigating her way through a vast game-world, constructing that world with her choices, until she ended up with these conclusions for each of them. It's Lisa's book, of course, except that it's about to go out into the world and become your book, too, open to your own interpretation. As a finished novel, *The Family Remains* will be in your hands.

Right now, though, it's still an unwieldy Word document, overlong and uneasy with contradictions. Some of them can be explained through mixed messages and faulty memories. In *The Family Remains* Henry is described as 'the guy who chained Phin to a bed'. I check *The Family Upstairs*. Yes, as I thought: 'I tied him to a radiator, to keep him safe,' Henry confesses there. Maybe it's a character's mistake – Kris Doll is reporting what Phin once told him – or maybe it's Lisa's slip. Either way, it can still be fixed; because the novel, at the end of the year, is not yet truly finished. It is still a living thing, subtly shifting its form beneath the skin. I scroll back over the current draft and find Samuel Owusu interviewing a man called Oliver Wolfensberger, the current owner of the ill-fated house on Cheyne Walk. I could have sworn that Samuel interviewed a woman in this scene. I search a previous document, from November, for the distinctive surname. Yes: the last time I was with Samuel in this house, he was speaking to Kate, Oliver's wife, and the mansion had been tastefully redecorated in shades of white and grey. Now the rooms are 'stripped bare, the air thick with dust and mites that spangle in the sunshine'. It is a beautiful line, but I still cling to the fact that it was Kate who answered the door the first time Samuel called.

My own sense of this novel, as a witness to its strange construction, is itself of a sprawling house filled with false memories. The structure is firmly in place, but the details change. I can open a door and find it completely different from what I expected, what I thought I knew. In time, the new version will definitively replace the old, but for now, for me, the previous version remains, a stubborn ghost not yet fully erased, its traces clinging to the architecture.

Some of the changes are trivial, some more significant. Reaching the end of the novel, I realised, unnervingly, that the opening scene – or what was once the opening scene, when Lisa began writing – no longer worked with the conclusion. Rachel's reaction to Michael's death was wrong. It didn't make sense in light of what we now knew.

I scrolled to the start of the new version, the finished novel. And as if subsequent events had rippled back in time, sending waves that shaped continuity retroactively, as if the beginning of the story had adapted itself obligingly to suit the ending, I realised that the opening scene had changed, too. It had never happened that way, after all: not officially, anyway.

I kept reading from the start, astonished, with retrospect, by how few of the chapters had been finished during the first half of the year, in that slow climb through spring to summer, and how many in the second, in that downhill rush through autumn towards the end of December. I read it almost like a diary, the characters' lives corresponding to little landmarks in my year with Lisa – ah, that's where we went to the Groucho; that was just after the Bengal Lancer – and its scenes struck me fondly, nostalgically, as if I'd lived through them.

I began to reread *The Family Remains*, and through it I revisited my year with Lisa Jewell.

Last Words

I sent my feedback on the novel's ending to Lisa, and she replied almost immediately. Remember, she told me, that these final chapters are as much in flux as the previous sections you read, and just as open to change. Selina read the novel over the weekend, as I did, and will begin her edits immediately. At this stage, everything and everyone is still in play. Characters who seem safe in the draft could be killed off ('Look at the evolution of *Then She Was Gone* post-delivery'). The only aspects that are truly fixed at this point – frustratingly so – are the events that *The Family Upstairs* set in stone.

In Heaven, I'd referred to the two novels as one big book. I was right, Lisa says now, and also wrong. Writing the sequel, she'd wished she could go back to 'the first 380 pages' – the previous novel – and tweak them, but they remained 'immovable and inflexible. Just having to work with them and around them even as I knew that the second 480 pages would be so much better if I could go back and change elements of the first 380 pages. Really annoying and not as helpful as one might think.'

It's an important point, and I've never seen it voiced before by a novelist, though it's a common problem in serial popular narratives. Superhero comics, operating on the margins of critical respectability, regularly solve this dilemma through the device of *retconning*, changing the past to suit the current story. Batman needs a fresh origin to explain how a character from 1939 can still be thirty years old today? Just commission the currently hot creative team to provide a new 'Batman Year One': their retelling will officially replace every version that's gone before, and only fans will notice.

Lisa pulled this trick herself with the opening scene of *The Family Remains*, rewriting Rachel's reaction to the news of her ex-husband's death; but *The Family Remains* is still wet concrete, rather than set stone, and novels, even popular genre fiction, carry far more cultural weight than superhero comics. Rewriting and republishing *The Family Upstairs* to fit its sequel would be an exceptional, almost unthinkable move, if not entirely without precedent: Tolkien rereleased *The Hobbit* in new, revised editions to better match the more serious, epic tone of *The Lord of the Rings*. But that was Tolkien. Lisa isn't yet in his position. She will have to adapt the sequel to match the inconvenient truths of the original, and it's a compromise she's never faced before: *After the Party*, set eleven years after the events of her debut novel, didn't pose this problem.

Lisa had promised that one subplot would be very sad, to the point of inciting tears. That didn't happen, and left me wondering if I'd missed an emotional cue. Now she explains that she held back from the emotional blows she'd originally planned, pulling her punches. 'When it came to it, it didn't fit the flow and also didn't seem that poignant, so I condensed it down . . . it's still sad, but not that sad.'

'Not that sad' is, ultimately, the emotional keynote for *The Family Remains*, which provides a happy ending for most of the characters. I was surprised – I'd been prepared for the emotional torture of *I Found You*, *Then She Was Gone* and *Watching You* – and so, it seems, was Lisa. Although her choices for the plot strands diverged from my expectations as reader, we both looked at those final chapters and came independently (and reassuringly) to the same conclusions.

. . . it's spooky because just today I was mulling over the thing I made, which I had no idea at the outset of how it would end up, and I did think it had more in common with my earlier books like *The Making of Us* and *The House We Grew Up In* than my more recent books. It needed to end with a closed door, rather than the spine-tingling ambiguity I've chosen to end my last few books with and that gave it a rather solid, happy ever after feel. I kind of think it had to.

I'd scribbled my own notes, at the same time:

She is back to family drama. The 'family' returns. This is *A Friend of the Family, The Making of Us*; happy endings, reconciling, reunions. People get to redeem themselves. The big twist of the epilogue is a joyful return, a welcome visit.

I add those notes to my 'Last Words' document, which I've been preparing for the last few months; the document contains my final questions for Lisa, scheduled for a Zoom call at 2 p.m. today. Unspoken is the fact that I've been left slightly unsatisfied. It's not a problem that Lisa's epilogue was different to anything I'd imagined; that was inevitable. My issue is that the redemptions don't feel entirely earned. Not yet.

In the end, I don't have to say anything, because Lisa already knows. She is so adept at reading people that she interpreted correctly from the absences in my emails, from the gaps between sentences.

She has just got off the phone to Selina, and before we move on to my questions, she takes me through her editor's half-dozen recommendations: deft, decisive cuts which in one case slice three days out of the story and excise Cornwall from the story's map. No detour to Cornwall, and therefore no cameo from Clemency. Not only will we never see Marco's perspective on the hen party, but the hen party didn't take place at all, or not with Lucy there, anyway; I'm so immersed in this universe and its characters that part of me believes it must have gone ahead in parallel to the novel's plot, a little sideline for Clemency that never intersected with the main strands.

'And Selina liked the ending,' Lisa says apologetically. 'Sorry.'

'I didn't say anything,' I protest mildly.

'You didn't say anything,' Lisa agrees with a smile. 'But you don't need to say anything, to say something.'

Over the next twenty minutes she listens patiently while I explain my various uncertainties, only interrupting to gently chide 'Oh, you!' when I pick up on a plot point that she knew was an issue but hoped would slip by. To go into specific detail would involve spoilers – and at this stage of the endgame, it seems inappropriate to reveal too much – but we resolve everything to my satisfaction, and she asks me to put it all in an email. Later that day, I send her a mini-essay confirming our joint solutions. So there currently exists – in my mind, and in Lisa's mind – a hypothetical, as-yet-unwritten version of *The Family Remains* with subtle differences to its conclusion, and even if it never reaches print, I feel we've crafted an alternate ending between us, and I'm happy.

I mentioned that Clemency will be cut from the final edit. As a character, that's true; she may now only appear as a brief mention. But in fact, ironically, it is clemency that dominates those final chapters, and guides the novel's conclusion: clemency in the dictionary sense of mercy. Samuel Owusu, the calm centre of this story, with his deep sense of justice that goes beyond the letter of the law, grants it to the guilty parties. People were killed in the house on Cheyne Walk, he recognises, but they were bad people, and the children involved have surely been punished enough. Both Lucy and Henry Lamb, pursued by their past, deserve to find a kind of solace; and Phin, too, has been on the run for too long, for the wrong reasons. He deserves to return to his family, and they deserve him.

In the end, I realise, it is the children of the present day who rescue the grown-ups of the previous generation. Marco and Stella and Libby – originally named Serenity, the baby born in a house of horrors and discovered with a lucky rabbit's foot in her cot – are the characters who break the cycle of abuse and trauma and bring the family together. Beneath it all, under the barriers that Lucy has built to protect herself, and the façades her brother Henry constructed to conceal himself, there is love; love remains.

An obituary at the novel's close, Lisa promises, will add one final reminder: that Birdie, the foul creature with tiny teeth who smelled of sex and hair, was also someone's sister, and that she is mourned by her brother, who remembers her as Bridget Dunlop-Evers, and that perhaps, although it would be easier to believe otherwise, none of the adults in this story are entirely evil, just as none of them are entirely without blame. It is a mature and in some ways challenging ending; it is a complex, hard-earned ending, its twists born from emotional truth rather than a desire to gratuitously shock. It is, perhaps, an ending that Lisa could only have written at exactly this point in her career.

At the start of the year, she'd told me that if there was any author she'd want to emulate, it would be Ruth Rendell/Barbara Vine. 'She didn't win any awards. But she just wrote consistently good books.' Do you think, I ask her, that you're entering a new phase – now that younger thriller writers like Gillian McAllister look up to you, and you're starting to be called the Queen of Crime – where you're approaching that Ruth Rendell status of a veteran author?

I expect her to demur modestly. But she simply says, brightly, 'Yes.'

I'm slightly taken aback by her open, undisguised confidence, though I don't show it. And I realise immediately, internally, behind my bland reaction, that I'm only surprised by her response because Lisa is a woman. I don't expect a woman – a woman in her fifties – to be so boldly honest about her own abilities and reputation, and that's entirely my issue. I untangle my own prejudices quickly as she talks.

'Definitely,' Lisa is saying. 'I think it's inevitable. Or specifically Barbara Vine, maybe, instead of Ruth Rendell. Given my age, and the point I'm at in my career. I think I've reached that kind of benchmark, with the quality that now comes from my books . . . I'm either going to disappear into obscurity, and I think we can safely say that's not going to happen . . . so I think it's inevitable. And I'm prolific.'

'You're reliable,' I volunteer.

'Yes. And that's what people keep saying about me. *Lisa never disappoints*. And there hasn't been a new Ruth Rendell for a very long time, so I don't see any reason why it shouldn't be me.'

'Well, that's good, isn't it?' I'm still surprised, but this time by her matter-of-fact delivery. 'You say all that without obvious happiness, but that's your happy end, isn't it? Career-wise.'

'Yes!' She laughs. 'It just means that there won't be that weight of expectation I feel at the moment, where the publishing process is like white light, and all the engines keep moving really fast and everything gets really hot, really quickly, and that can't be sustained. It has to chill out. It has to turn into "Yeah, Lisa Jewell's got a new novel out", without it being a big deal every time. And I'm thoroughly looking forward to it. I'm thinking of maybe going down to a book every two years from age sixty, so . . . a book every year for the next six, seven years, and then I can just slow down and become Ruth Rendell.'

'And when do you think the Ruth Rendell status will kick in for you? You think it's started now?'

'I think it's now!' she declares. 'Yes. Someone's gotta do it, why not me?'

'Well, I said I'd be catching you at an interesting point in your career, on the cusp of a new phase, and I was right.' I turn to my next Big Question. 'If you could go back to age twenty-nine, would you change anything in terms of your career?'

'Nooo . . .' Lisa replies thoughtfully. 'Could I be in a better place than I am in, right now? In terms of me, Lisa Jewell, who I am, what I want out of life, I don't want anything else.'

Next question. 'In your big house, on your fridge, there is a digital screen.' I'm proud of my little lead-in. 'And on that digital screen, the date is set to 2038.'

'Yeah?'

'So, where do you want to be, in 2038?'

'I was born in sixty-eight. So, I'll be seventy. That's neat. I'll write my books, and a load of elderly readers . . .' She stops, raising a finger. 'That's the point, isn't it? When I stop picking up new readers. Is there going to be a point at which the only people who buy my books are the people who are buying them now, in 2021? We shall see.'

I move into my quick-fire round.

'Is this novel officially in the Jewelliverse? Is there any reference to your other books?'

She strokes her chin. 'I could put an Easter egg in anywhere, couldn't I. Well, there are Easter eggs for *The Family Upstairs*, obviously.'

'You could add a street name, I suppose. You could mention Silversmith Road, the real name of Dream Street.'

'I've never specified the name of Henry's street!' she exclaims.

'He could live in the same street as Bee Bearhorn, who also lives in Marylebone. Do you like that?'

'I do like that.' I'm grinning as if I've just opened a surprise present. Next question. 'Is this the first Samuel Owusu novel?'

'Yes,' she says with pleasing certainty.

'It could become a series, like the Hither Green Detective Agency. Because he's not exhausted as a character, is he?'

She agrees. 'There's so much more to know about him.'

We're running out of time. I scheduled an hour for our meeting, as I did for our first Zoom chats in spring of this year, which now feel impossibly distant, although we're back in the same cold season, under a similar threat of impending lockdown. We have two minutes left.

I realise that we're coming to an end, and also that the chapters I planned that would lead to this point read like a slow, extended goodbye – 'Finale', 'The Sense of An Ending', 'Last Words' – as if I was preparing myself, step by incremental step, for this moment when we'd hang up on each other and the process would officially finish.

'Would you do this again?' I ask her.

'I would happily do this again. I *won't* do it again, because I think it's a one-off, but that's the only reason I wouldn't do it again. And I should also say that Selina noted a certain quality, a higher quality of writing in the book . . .' She runs her hand through the air, pinching her fingertips together as if catching an invisible skein of *quality*. 'And I do wonder if I wrote *up* to you a bit. Because you have a high opinion of my writing.'

'I'll take that.'

'So I think we can attribute some extra gloss and extra style in the book to my experience of sharing it with you.'

'I like that very much.'

The exchange of symbolic gifts is over. Our hour is up. I drag out the final seconds. 'Bye for now,' I tell her. 'We'll obviously talk again.'

Lisa lifts her hand in farewell, and it feels to me for a moment as if we're both on the decks of opposite ships that are about to drift away from each other.

'I'll write,' she says. Of course she will. Of course Lisa will write.

She smiles, and her 'Bye' is so faint it's little more than a breath, as I press the button to cut the call.

Afterword by Lisa Jewell

On this day last year, my diary contained the following appointments:

- Sugar vet 9am
- Zoom with Will 2pm

We were in full lockdown. My children were both off school and I was using a rented studio flat across the street from my house to edit *The Night She Disappeared*. I was worried about my daughter's guinea pig, Sugar, who was losing her fur. I was also about to start an intense, year-long project with a man I barely knew, one that would involve him following the progress of a book I had barely started to think about.

A year is a long time.

Fast-forward to today: lockdowns are a thing of the past and I have reclaimed my kitchen table as my workspace. *The Night She Disappeared* has been published all around the world, and Sugar the guinea pig sadly passed away ten days ago from an illness entirely unrelated to losing her fur. And in a perfect full-circle moment that could not have been designed, yesterday I delivered the final draft of the book I had barely started to think about this time last year.

Now you know the genesis story of the book you've just read, and I can assure you that it was every bit as surprising and unexpected as it sounds. I began my career in 1999, a former secretary writing so-called 'chick lit'. I spent a decade trying to override the negative connotations of that term (along with a hundred other excellent female writers of commercial fiction). Even headlining on stage with Paul Burston at Polari back in December 2019, with eighteen successful novels under my belt, I felt a bit of a fraud: a straight writer at an LGBTQ+ event; a commercial writer in a line-up that included an academic and a poet. So to find an email in my inbox from a male academic, expressing an interest in writing a book about my writing year, was quite a shock to the system.

I was slightly nervous before that first Zoom call with Will. Although he had made it abundantly clear during our meeting in September of the previous year that he was a proper, copper-bottomed fan of my novels, I still wasn't sure how the project was going to work. Would we gel, would we get each other? Would it feel awkward, or strange? Would I regret it? Would *he* regret it?

I also wondered about my own motivation for getting involved in such a project. I told my friend about it two weeks after the first Zoom – 'that sounds very seductive', she responded. I thought, yes, my ego is involved somewhere here and I'm not sure how I feel about that. I'm not an ego-driven person, or at least my ego does not normally require boosting. Could this be a bad thing? To open myself and my writing up to someone I barely knew from a starting point of being flattered?

But then I told myself that the bottom line was – would I want to read the book that Will Brooker was planning to write about me if it was about one of my contemporaries instead? And the answer was a resounding yes. I would want to read this book if it was about Louise Candlish or Paula Hawkins or Lucy Foley. Absolutely. And if it was about someone further from my own section of the bookshelves: Donna Tartt or J. K. Rowling or Ian McEwan? Yes, again. I would, I realised, want to read the book that Will was going to write about me if it was about *any* working writer. Writers writing books are inherently fascinating. All writers. All books. I always want to hear about a writer's daily rhythms, their publication story, their planning techniques, their crises, their triumphs, their backgrounds and their hopes for the future.

Why, I thought, should the subject of such a book *not* be me?

So, off we went – into the year, into the book. And I would say that, while every book feels different to write – and it's hard to separate the inherent differentness of each book from the differentness of this one, because I was being shadowed – having Will reading, metaphorically, over my shoulder did add a level of fun and incentive to the process. And it reminded me that, in fact, this was how I wrote my very first novel, *Ralph's Party*, back in the late 90s, with my friend Yasmin waiting in Sydney for me to email her the chapters as I wrote them. I wonder now, as I contemplate writing my twenty-first novel 'alone' again, if I will miss that extra layer of company and involvement.

And now I've read Will's book, from beginning to end, and it's odd to see myself and my work written about in the context of (primarily male) literary giants, almost as if I were a 'real' author, not just a nice woman in a jumper who writes books that lots of people seem to like. But then again, maybe it's about time, too. Maybe this has been a long time coming, not just for me, but for all the women who create the books that people want to read in their thousands upon thousands upon thousands every single year.

It was odd, also, to see myself being caricatured in the early chapters of the book as Will tried to make me into his idea of what a successful author is meant to be, squeezing and manhandling me into some sort of glamorous, aloof shape that neither I, nor any of my author friends, fit into. We all have to juggle difficult families and messy homes and elderly parents and dogs with upset stomachs with months and months spent alone in corners of our homes making up stories. We then all have to flick switches deep down inside our – generally – introverted hearts, to wake us up into the sorts of people who can talk in front of crowds and chat on live radio and meet strangers who want to share their souls with us and speak to camera for marketing campaigns as if we just tumble out of bed every morning feeling ready to do these things. Women writers in particular rarely get to prioritise their writing over their domestic responsibilities. The glamorous moments are few and far between. 'Writing' is not a persona or a lifestyle, it's something squeezed into every-day life, sometimes even relegated to the sidelines of that life. I was glad that through the process of being privy to the rhythms of my year, Will was able to see through the illusion and into the reality of a writer's life.

Another unexpected thing I've taken from my reading of Will's book is the revisiting of the deleted passages, aborted storylines and cancelled characters that only normally exist in anonymous-looking files on my computer, never looked at or thought of again. But here, in a way, they are given immortal-ity. Lucy and Rachel's meeting outside Stella's school, Lucy's trip to Cornwall to see Clemency, Marco's early-morning flit to Rachel's apartment in Camden Town; all the things that had to *not happen* in order to let the story grow into its proper shape, like pruning a bonsai. They call it *killing your babies*, but that's not right, because cutting extraneous prose never leaves you with a sense of loss, only a sense of rightness and satisfaction. But here, these malformed babies have been saved and given another sort of life. Which is strange, but also nice.

And now, to the next book. The book that came to me during the moment Will refers to halfway through the year when I had a vodka-inspired 'you-could-be-anyone' wobble about the project. And, of course, 'letting the wrong person in' forms the basis of many a thriller plot. So thank you, Will, for your company and your insight, for being my lockdown pen pal, for being so open to my interrogations and my (only very) occasional tendency to try to shape your book to my will. And thank you for being 'just Henry enough' to give me something to write about next, but not so Henry that I had to move to Chicago to get away from you. It's been an amazing experience writing my book alongside you writing your book. And by the time summer comes, they will be out in the world together like slightly strange siblings; like Lucy and Henry maybe, totally different but forever connected by their shared experiences. Like family, in other words . . .

Lisa Jewell
London, 28 January 2022

Notes

Part One

The Houses I Want to Live In

p. 4   'it was just the . .' Coates, Jon, 'Bestselling author Lisa Jewell
       on favourite photograph' *Daily Express*, 2017

The Support Act

p. 14   'walking into Ryman's . . .' Jewell, Lisa, *Watching You*, Arrow
        Books, 2016, p. 150

p. 14   'he saw something . . .' Ibid., p. 150

p. 14   'He saw a . . .' Ibid., pp. 150–1

p. 14   'the shockwaves of . . .' Ibid., p. 151

p. 15   'good and bad . . .' McEwan, Ian, *Atonement*, Vintage, 2002, p. 40

p. 15   'show separate minds . . .' Ibid., p. 40

p. 15   'Was she, Jenna . . .' Jewell, Lisa, *Watching You*, Arrow Books,
        2016, p. 201

p. 15   'She felt a . . .' Ibid., p. 201

p. 16   'she was going . . .' Camus, Albert, 'La Femme adultère', in
        Exile and the Kingdom, Penguin Books, 1986, p. 26

p. 16   'His soul swooned . . .' Joyce, James, 'The Dead', in *Dubliners*,
        Penguin Books, 1967, p. 220

p. 16   'And there followed . . .' Jewell, Lisa, *Watching You*, Arrow
        Books, 2016, pp. 133–4

p. 16   'fresh-faced and scrubbed'; 'still in her . . .'; 'and there, sta-
        tioned . . .' Ibid., p. 134

p. 17   'he saw something . . .' James, Henry, *The Ambassadors*, World's Classics, 1985, pp. 388–9

p. 17   'for a moment . . .' Jewell, Lisa, *Watching You*, Arrow Books, 2016, pp. 164–5

Rachel and Revisions

p. 26   'had been writing . . .' Jewell, Lisa, *Before I Met You*, Arrow Books, 2013, p. 295

p. 26   'the Great British . . .' Jewell, Lisa, *Vince and Joy*, Penguin Books, 2018, p. 362

p. 26   'Publishing – it's all . . .' Ibid., p. 151

p. 26   'book. Or in . . .' Jewell, Lisa, *The Family Upstairs*, Arrow Books, 2019, p. 73

p. 26   'with shoes on . . .' Jewell, Lisa, *The Making of Us,* Arrow Books, 2012, p. 119

p. 27   'Patricia Cornwell. Ruth . . .' Jewell, Lisa, *One-Hit Wonder*, Penguin Books, 2020, p. 152

p. 27   'She'd have put . . .' Ibid., p. 275

p. 27   'wasn't one of . . .' Jewell, Lisa, *Thirtynothing*, Penguin Books, 2020, p. 209

p. 27   'since I was . . .' Jewell, Lisa, *The Night She Disappeared*, Century, 2021, p. 300

p. 27   'like the last . . .' Jewell, Lisa, *After the Party*, Arrow Books, 2016, p. 45

p. 28   'see if her . . .' Jewell, Lisa, *The Night She Disappeared*, Century, 2021, p. 64

Origin Stories

p. 29   'Doomed planet. Desperate . . .' Morrison, Grant and Quitely,

Frank, *All-Star Superman*, Issue 1, DC Comics, August 2013, p. 1

p. 30 'Bestselling author recalls . . .' Coates, Jon, 'Bestselling author Lisa Jewell on favourite photograph' *Daily Express*, 2017

Author Theories

p. 37 'The Death of . . .' Barthes, Roland, 'The Death of the Author' in *Image Music Text*, Fontana Press, 1977, p. 142

p. 38 'vanilla hair and . . .' Jewell, Lisa *The Family Upstairs*, Arrow Books, 2019, p. 52

p. 38 'charged air filled . . .' Jewell, Lisa, *Watching You*, Arrow Books, 2016, p. 65

p. 38 'burning particles of his . . .' Lisa Jewell, Lisa, *Vince and Joy*, Penguin Books, 2018, p. 252

p. 38 'hadn't really worked . . .' Jewell, Lisa, *Ralph's Party*, Penguin Books, 2019, p. 11

p. 38 'can draw quite . . .' Fink, M. M., 'Q&A with Lisa Jewell', 6 June 2016, http://booksbywomen.org/qa-with-lisa-jewell/

p. 39 'was wearing a . . .' Jewell, Lisa, *After the Party*, Arrow Books, 2011, p. 367

p. 39 'tanned to an . . .' Ibid., p. 462

p. 39 'a stunning redhead . . .' Jewell, Lisa, *Thirtynothing*, Penguin Books, 2020, p. 435

p. 40 'Dido greets her . . .' Jewell, Lisa, *The Family Upstairs*, Arrow Books, 2019, pp. 106–7

p. 40 'but felt completely . . . '; 'Instead of . . .' Jewell, Lisa, *Vince and Joy*, Penguin Books, 2018, p. 198

p. 40 'the trio of . . .' Jewell, Lisa, *The House We Grew Up In*, Arrow Books, 2014, p. 419

p. 40 'wasn't a room . . .' Ibid., p. 419

p. 41   'Victorian tasselled lamps . . .' Jewell, Lisa, *A Friend of the Family*, Penguin Books, 2020, p. 205

p. 41   'an overhead light . . . '; 'a bench . . . with . . . '; 'a faded blue . . . '; 'she didn't like . . .' Jewell, Lisa, *Watching You*, Arrow Books, 2016, pp. 313–16

p. 41   'nice grey suit . . . '; 'foul baggy grey . . .' Jewell, Lisa, *Ralph's Party*, Penguin Books, 2019, p. 50

p. 41   'A black Fred . . .' Jewell, Lisa, *Vince and Joy*, Penguin Books, 2018, p. 39

p. 42   'shirts that looked . . .' Jewell, Lisa, *Then She Was Gone*, Arrow Books, 2017, pp. 402–3

p. 42   'Twins!' Ibid., p. 106

p. 42   'Women tend to . . . '; 'as easy to . . .' Jewell, Lisa, *Thirtynothing*, Penguin Books, 2020, p. 89

p. 42   'had never really . . .' Jewell, Lisa, *A Friend of the Family*, Penguin Books, 2020, p. 26

p. 43   'compared hairstyles and . . .' Jewell, Lisa, *Vince and Joy*, Penguin Books, 2018, p. 18

p. 43   'It is very . . .' Jewell, Lisa, *After the Party*, Arrow Books, 2011, p. 66

p. 43   'Essentially it's about . . . '; ' "My father, Anthony . . ." ' *Belfast Telegraph,* 18 July 2014

p. 44   'a pied-à-terre in . . .' Jewell, Lisa, *The Night She Disappeared*, Century, 2021, p. 166

p. 44   'Rich old men . . .' Ibid., pp. 216–17

p. 46   'aggressively competitive . . .' Cowley, Jason, 'How Good is Martin Amis?', 2011, https://www.jasoncowley.net/essays/martin-amis-the-information

p. 46   'more full of . . .' *A Friend of the Family* review, *Independent on Sunday*, 2003

p. 46   'appeared to have . . .' Jewell, Lisa, *Thirtynothing*, Penguin Books, 2020, p. 1

p. 46   'I awoke with . . .' Amis, Martin, *Success,* Vintage, 2004, p. 111

p. 46   'a spectacular hawk . . .' Ibid., p. 127

p. 46   'wandered towards the . . .' Jewell, Lisa, *A Friend of the Family*, Penguin Books, 2020, p. 23

p. 47   'made an extra-special . . .' Jewell, Lisa, *Thirtynothing*, Penguin Books, 2020, p. 87

p. 47   'I'll brush my . . .' Amis, Martin, *Success*, Vintage, 2004, p. 41

p. 47   'dry paving of . . .' Ibid., p. 30

p. 47   'And so then . . .' Jewell, Lisa, *The Family Upstairs*, Arrow Books, 2019, p. 414

p. 48   'I do a . . .' Amis, Martin, *Success*, Vintage, 2004, p. 33

p. 48   'There was a . . .' Jewell, Lisa, *The Family Upstairs*, Arrow Books, 2019, p. 416

p. 48   'People always want . . .' Amis, Martin, *Success*, Vintage, 2004, p. 8

Henry and His Fans

p. 51   'but there is . . .' Barthes, Roland, 'The Death of the Author' in *Image Music Text*, Fontana Press, 1977, p. 148

p. 54   'it would appear . . .' Winick, Charles, 'Tendency Systems and the Effects of a Movie Dealing with a Social Problem', reprinted in Brooker, Will and Jermyn, Deborah (eds), *The Audience Studies Reader*, Routledge, 2003, p. 47

p. 55   'suddenly he'd remember . . .' Jewell, Lisa, *A Friend of the Family*, Penguin Books, 2020, p. 34

Characters Flat and Round

p. 57   'I never will . . .' Dickens, Charles, *David Copperfield*, Chapman & Hall Ltd, 1892, p. 136

p. 57   'and there she . . .' Forster, E. M., *Aspects of the Novel*, Edward Arnold, 1974, p. 47

p. 57   'round . . . she waxes . . .' Ibid., p. 48

p. 57   'Pip and David . . .' Ibid., p. 49

p. 57   'The disc has . . .' Ibid., p. 52

p. 58   'famous for being . . .' Jewell, Lisa, *Ralph's Party*, Penguin Books, 2019, p. 272

p. 58   'the joys of . . .'; 'a look of . . .' Ibid., p. 355

p. 58   'He slammed his . . .' Ibid., p. 332

p. 59   'They both leaned . . .' Jewell, Lisa, *After the Party*, Arrow Books, 2011, p. 188

p. 59   'growing in her . . .' Jewell, Lisa, *One-Hit Wonder*, Penguin Books, 2020, p. 173

p. 59   'whichever way she . . .' Jewell, Lisa, *Vince and Joy*, Penguin Books, 2018, p. 150

p. 60   'she noticed that . . .' Ibid., p. 152

p. 60   'Joy discovered that . . .' Ibid., p. 152

p. 60   'George had a . . .' Ibid., pp. 153–4

p. 60   'I'd go so . . .' Ibid., p. 157

p. 61   'He really was . . .' Ibid., p. 158

p. 61   'a very small . . .'; 'so icy cold . . .'; 'a pair of . . .'; 'a gigantic spliff'; ' "You just keep . . ." ' Ibid., pp. 176–8

p. 62   'The flat smelled . . .' Jewell, Lisa, *Thirtynothing*, Penguin Books, 2020, p. 160

p. 62   'to say "sitting . . ." ' Jewell, Lisa, *Vince and Joy*, Penguin Books, 2018, p. 253

p. 62   'a damp flat . . .' Jewell, Lisa, *One-Hit Wonder*, Penguin Books, 2020, p. 152

p. 63   'though he saw . . .' Jewell, Lisa, *Vince and Joy*, Penguin Books, 2018, p. 253

p. 63   'If Flaubert had . . .' Davis, Lennard J., *Resisting Novels*, Methuen, 1987, p. 114

p. 63   'In essence, the . . .' Ibid., p.114

p. 64   'Very well then . . .' Whitman, Walt, 'Song of Myself, 51' in *Walt Whitman: The Complete Poems*, Penguin Books, 1986, p. 737

p. 64   'Das heisst: Ich . . .' Meyer, Conrad Ferdinand, *Huttens letzte Tage,* Berliner Ausgabe, 2015, p. 26

p. 65   'I can most definitely . . .' http://www.wordswithjam. co.uk/2017/09/

p. 66   ' "I googled you . . ." ' Jewell, Lisa, *The Night She Disappeared*, Century, 2021, p. 249

p. 67   'Not only do . . . '; 'Yes absolutely'; 'I feel sad . . .' Marsh, J. J., 'In Conversation with Lisa Jewell', 20 September 2017, http://www.wordswithjam.co.uk/2017/09/in-conversation-with-lisa-jewell.html

p. 68   'His cheeks were . . .' Jewell, Lisa, *A Friend of the Family*, Penguin Books, 2020, p. 4

p. 68   ' "You're just kidding . . ." ' Ibid., p. 283

p. 68   'Dig thought to . . .' Jewell, Lisa, *Thirtynothing*, Penguin Books, 2020, p. 258

p. 69   'Her smallness, her . . .' Jewell, Lisa, *31 Dream Street*, Penguin Books, 2019, p. 154

p. 69   'Say to yourself . . .'; 'it broke the . . .'; ' "Thank you. Thank . . ." ' Jewell, Lisa, *Invisible Girl*, Arrow Books, 2020, pp. 391–2

p. 70   'post-coital tears . . .' Amis, Martin, *Success*, Vintage, 2004, pp. 18–19

p. 71   'peeing, that strange . . .' Jewell, Lisa, *Ralph's Party*, Penguin Books, 2019, p. 146

p. 71   ' "it's a bit . . ." ' Jewell, Lisa, *31 Dream Street*, Penguin Books, 2019, p. 205

p. 71   'He favours paint-by-numbers . . .' Amis, Martin, *Success*, Vintage, 2004, pp. 20–21

p. 71   'That top . . . you . . .' Jewell, Lisa, *The Night She Disappeared*, Century, 2021, p. 69

p. 71   'quite pretty'. Ibid., p. 70

Sequels

p. 73 'always swore blind'; 'I did make . . .' 'Q&A With Author Lisa Jewell', Mumsnet, 30 May 2012, https://www.mumsnet.com/Talk/what_were_reading/1483973-Q-A-with-author-Lisa-Jewell-ANSWERS-BACK

p. 74 'had allowed her . . .' Jewell, Lisa, *After the Party*, Arrow Books, 2016, p. 33

p. 75 'over twelve years . . .' Ibid., p. 3

p. 75 'you have a . . .' Ibid., p. 7

p. 75 'Jem has begun . . .' Ibid., p. 7

Signs of the Times

p. 81 ' "Techno-bimbo?" '; 'slowly, line by . . .'; ' "They're websites". Jewell, Lisa, *One-Hit Wonder*, Penguin Books, 2020, pp. 251–2

p. 81 'tiny, state-of-the-art machine'. Jewell, Lisa, *Ralph's Party*, Penguin Books, 2019, p. 130

p. 81 'love in the . . .'; ' "I'll see what . . ." ' Jewell, Lisa, *Vince and Joy,* Penguin Books, 2018, pp. 191-2; 193

p. 82 ' "Ana! Hi! Lol." ' Jewell, Lisa, *One-Hit Wonder*, Penguin Books, 2020, p. 96

p. 82 ' "the *current* Gap . . ." ' Jewell, Lisa, *The Family Upstairs*, Arrow Books, 2019, p. 155

p. 83 'overweight Chinese teenager'. Jewell, Lisa, *The Truth About Melody Browne*, Arrow Books, 2016, p. 252

p. 83 ' "put in what . . ." '; ' "acoorut" '. Ibid., p. 253

p. 83 'an emaciated little . . .'; 'an ugly little . . .'; 'there was something . . .' Jewell, Lisa *Vince and Joy*, Penguin Books, 2018, pp. 185; 223; 493

p. 84   'Bend Dicks', Jewell, Lisa, *The Making of Us*, Arrow Books, 2012, p. 426

p. 84   'a handsome negro'. Jewell, Lisa, *Before I Met You*, Arrow Books, 2013, p. 248

p. 84   'two adorable piccaninnies . . .' Ibid., p. 479

p. 84   'I changed my . . .' 'Lisa Jewell meets Michelle McManus', *Observer*, 1 February 2004, https://www.theguardian.com/observer/omm/qanda/story/0,,1133399,00.html

p. 85   'different music for . . .' Jewell, Lisa, *Thirtynothing*, Penguin Books, 2020, p. 238

p. 85   'she did like . . .' Jewell, Lisa, *The Making of Us*, Arrow Books, 2012, p. 15

p. 85   'everything from Bowie . . .' Ibid., p. 308

p. 85   'epic . . .' Ibid., p. 407

No Plan

p. 87   'I am not . . .'; 'I start with . . .' Fink, M. M., 'Q&A with Lisa Jewell', Books by Women, 6 June 2016, http://booksbywomen.org/qa-with-lisa-jewell/

What Pares Do to Help Their Kids

p. 99   'the pretty room . . .' Jewell, Lisa, *After the Party*, Arrow Books, 2016, p. 342

p. 99   'bright as sunlight . . .' Jewell, Lisa, *Watching You*, Arrow Books, 2016, p. 442

p. 99   'there's a kind . . .' Jewell, Lisa, *The Family Upstairs*, Arrow Books, 2019, p. 45

p. 100   'dark as damsons'. Ibid., p. 11

p. 100   'boats against the . . .' Fitzgerald, F. Scott, *The Great Gatsby*, Charles Scribner's Sons, 1953, p. 121

p. 100 'Arlette felt a . . .' Jewell, Lisa, *Before I Met You*, Arrow Books, 2012, p. 192

p. 100 'Inside Maggie's head . . .' Jewell, Lisa, *The Making of Us*, Arrow Books, 2012, p. 113

The Jewelliverse

p. 103 'London, thought Ned . . .' Jewell, Lisa, *A Friend of the Family*, Penguin Books, 2020, p. 14

p. 103 'Amanda London . . . it's . . .' Ibid., p. 166

p. 103 'thought she'd find . . .' Jewell, Lisa, *Vince and Joy*, Penguin Books, 2018, p. 252

p. 104 'The centre of . . .' Jewell, Lisa, *Before I Met You*, Arrow Books, 2012, pp. 19–20

p. 104 'night-time air of . . .' Jewell, Lisa, *Ralph's Party*, Penguin Books, 2019, p. 38

p. 104 'filled to overflowing . . .' Jewell, Lisa, *The Making of Us*, Arrow Books, 2012, p. 319

p. 105 'shops give way . . .' Ibid., p. 319

p. 106 'cockney/mockney art school . . .' Jewell, Lisa, *Before I Met You*, Arrow Books, 2012, p. 140

Hearing Voices

p. 111 ' "Well, yes, I'm . . ." ' Jewell, Lisa, *The Making of Us*, Arrow Books, 2012, p. 9

p. 111 ' "It is a . . ." ' Ibid., p. 377

p. 111 ' "So . . . where you . . ." ' Jewell, Lisa, *A Friend of the Family*, Penguin Books, 2020, p. 53

p. 111 'She also knows . . .' Jewell, Lisa, *I Found You*, Arrow Books, 2017, p. 19

p. 112 'A nice house . . .' Jewell, Lisa, *A Friend of the Family*, Penguin Books, 2020, p. 8

p. 112 'tied her hair . . .' Jewell, Lisa, *The Making of Us*, Arrow Books, 2012, p. 413

p. 112 'It looked nice . . .' Jewell, Lisa, *One-Hit Wonder*, Penguin Books, 2020, p. 304

p. 112 'As the tight . . .' Jewell, Lisa, *Before I Met You*, Arrow Books, 2012, p. 61

p. 113 'How fresh, how . . .' Woolf, Virginia, *Mrs Dalloway*, Penguin Books, 1995, p. 3

p. 113 'Lily, the caretaker's . . .' Joyce, James, 'The Dead', in *Dubliners*, Penguin Books, 1967, p. 173

p. 114 'It was always . . .' Ibid., p. 173

p. 114 'heavenly'. Jewell, Lisa, *Before I Met You*, Arrow Books, 2012, p. 299

p. 115 'quickly plays a . . .' Jewell, Lisa, *The Family Upstairs*, Arrow Books, 2019, p. 85

Suspense

p. 117 'We are now . . .' Truffaut, Francois *Hitchcock/Truffaut*, Simon & Schuster 1984, p. 73

p. 118 'even the bulge . . .' Jewell, Lisa, *Before I Met You*, Arrow Books, 2012, p. 299

p. 119 'He rolls his . . .' Jewell, Lisa, *The Night She Disappeared*, Century, 2021, p. 355

p. 119 'can feel Scarlett's . . .' Ibid., p. 356

p. 119 'strangely like something . . .' Ibid p. 367

p. 119 'can feel the . . .' Ibid., p. 379

p. 120 'He releases one . . .' Ibid., p. 385

p. 121 'moist'; 'ripe'; 'pungent'; 'angry'. Jewell, Lisa, *Ralph's Party*, Penguin Books, 2019, p. 90

p. 122 'He'd silenced her . . .' Jewell, Lisa, *The Family Upstairs*, Arrow Books, 2019, p. 441

p. 122 'And I could . . .' Jewell, Lisa, *The Night She Disappeared*, Century, 2021, p. 98

p. 122 'stiffened slightly . . . touched . . .' Jewell, Lisa, *The House We Grew Up In*, Arrow Books, 2019, p. 106

Lucy

p. 126 'owns a house . . .' Jewell, Lisa, *The Family Upstairs*, Arrow Books, 2019, p. 10

p. 126 'Youth. Life. Ellie . . .' Jewell, Lisa, *Then She Was Gone*, Arrow Books, 2017, p. 3

p. 126 'towards the man . . .' Jewell, Lisa, *Invisible Girl*, Arrow Books, 2021, p. 2

Thresholds

p. 127 'just sold the . . .' Jewell, Lisa, *The Making of Us*, Arrow Books, 2012, p. 119

p. 127 'a commission that . . .' Jewell, Lisa, *Thirtynothing*, Penguin Books, 2020, p. 69

p. 127 'for a lot . . .' Jewell, Lisa, *The Making of Us*, Arrow Books, 2012, p. 38

p. 127 'as though money . . .' Ibid, p. 28

p. 127 'a stupid number . . .' Jewell, Lisa, *The Family Upstairs*, Arrow Books, 2019, p. 431

p. 128 'big wind-up'. Ibid., p. 23

p. 128 'gave the flat . . .' Ibid., p. 10

p. 128 'Libby feels her . . .' Ibid., p. 48

p. 128 'Oh my God . . .' Ibid., p. 47

p. 128 'she feels very . . .' Ibid., p. 26

p. 128 'a reminder of . . .' Jewell, Lisa, *Thirtynothing*, Penguin Books, 2020, p. 365

p. 129 'what Nadine didn't . . .' Ibid., p. 29

p. 129 'that if her . . .' Jewell, Lisa, *A Friend of the Family*, Penguin Books, 2020, p. 2

p. 129 'Eight small steps . . .' Jewell, Lisa, *The House We Grew Up In*, Arrow Books, 2019, p. 60

p. 129 'And then the . . .' Jewell, Lisa, *Then She Was Gone*, Arrow Books, 2017, p. 13

p. 129 'A moment. That's . . .' Jewell, Lisa, *After the Party*, Arrow Books, 2016, p. 457

p. 129 'it was almost . . .' Ibid., p. 170

p. 130 'literally, a showing . . .' Lodge, David, *The Art of Fiction*, Penguin Books, 1992, pp. 146–7

p. 130 'an image flashed . . .' Jewell, Lisa, *Watching You*, Arrow Books, 2019, p. 442

p. 130 'a human being . . .' Ibid., p. 150

Part Two

Capital

p. 135 'an experience that . . . '; 'Faces opened up . . .' Jewell, Lisa, *Before I Met You*, Arrow Books, 2012, p. 339

p. 138 'conventional at first . . .' Jewell, Lisa, *Then She Was Gone*, Arrow Books, 2017, p. 402

In-between Days

p. 151 'There is a . . .' Jewell, Lisa, *The Family Upstairs*, Arrow Books, 2019, p. 11

How Is It Done?

p. 166 'Freddie had zoomed . . .' Jewell, Lisa, *Watching You*, Arrow Books, 2019, p. 268

In These, Our Private Lives

p. 176 'matte, not gloss'. Jewell, Lisa, *The Night She Disappeared*, Century, 2021, p. 108

Publication Day

p. 188 'as Saturday dawns . . .' Jewell, Lisa, *The Family Upstairs*, Arrow Books, 2019, p. 77

The Bengal Lancer

p. 195 'Alice roasted beef . . .' 'I Found You by Lisa Jewell', Novel Meals, 16 October 2019, https://novelmeals.wordpress.com/2019/10/16/i-found-you-by-lisa-jewell/

p. 195 'Miniature Thai crabcakes . . .' Jewell, Lisa, *Ralph's Party*, Penguin Books, 2019, p. 308

p. 196 'Sean had prosciutto . . .' Jewell, Lisa, *A Friend of the Family*, Penguin Books, 2020, p. 154

p. 196 'a mosaic of . . . '; 'foie gras parfait . . . Ibid., p. 401

p. 196 'he started rhythmically . . .' Jewell, Lisa, *The Making of Us*, Arrow Books, 2012, pp. 348–9

p. 197 'What about restaurants?' Jewell, Lisa, *Thirtynothing*, Penguin Books, 2020, pp. 75–6

p. 200 'Jan is just . . .' Radway, Janice, *Reading the Romance*, University of North Carolina Press, 1991, p. 47

Popular

p. 206   'She listened to . . .' O'Farrell, Maggie, *The Hand That First Held Mine*, Headline Review, 2010, p. 187

p. 206   'a sense that . . .' Jewell, Lisa, *Watching You*, Arrow Books, 2016, p. 201

p. 206   'A drop of . . .' O'Farrell, Maggie, *The Hand That First Held Mine*, Headline Review, 2010, p. 290

p. 207   'Vera Claythorne, in . . .' Christie, Agatha, *And Then There Were None*, p. 3

p. 207   'Fizzing hot day!' Ibid., p. 11

p. 208   'Mr Justice Wargrave . . .' Ibid., p. 2

p. 208   'Philip Lombard said . . .' Ibid., p. 23

p. 208   'Mr Blore was . . .' Ibid., p. 32

p. 208   'Drowned . . . Found drowned . . .' Ibid., p. 28

p. 208   'flailing against the . . .' O'Farrell, Maggie, *The Hand That First Held Mine*, Headline Review, 2010, p. 314

The Reverse Out

p. 211   'tremendous amount'. Christie, Agatha, *And Then There Were None*, p. i

p. 215   'He was incredibly . . .' 'Lisa Jewell on the books that shaped her life', penguin.co.uk, 2021

House of Words

p. 230   'handsome, sensitive, mogul . . .'; 'fluffy orange sweatpants'; 'Cartwheel right over . . .' Mlynowski, Sarah and Jacobs, Farrin, *See Jane Write: A Girl's Guide to Writing Chick Lit*, Quirk Books, 2006, p. 21

Phantom Threads

p. 235   'Precision is the . . .' Miéville, China, *The Scar*, Macmillan, 2002, p. 546

Seeing France

p. 248   'is it a . . .' Lodge, David, *Thinks* . . . Penguin, 2001, p. 1

The Sense of an Ending

p. 257   'Et c'est là . . .' Alain-Fournier, *Le Grand Meaulnes*, Éditions Émile-Paul Frères, 1913, p. 14

Acknowledgements

Thank you to Selina Walker for trusting this project, to Sophie Whitehead for her tight, bright editing, and to Veronique Baxter, always-excellent agent.

Thank you to Paul Burston for the introductions and to Andy Martin for the early encouragement.

Thank you to Lisa Jewell, of course, and my family, as ever.